# DATA DRIVEN NONPROFITS

# DATA DRIVEN NONPROFITS

Steve MacLaughlin

Saltire Press

**DATA DRIVEN NONPROFITS**
by Steve MacLaughlin

Copyright © 2016 Steve MacLaughlin
Printed in the United States of America
Published by Saltire Press

**Design:**      Veronica Volborth
**Editing:**     Erin Duff
**Indexing:**   Schroeder Indexing Services, Inc.

September 2016: First Edition

ISBN-13: 9780988850712
ISBN-10: 0988850710
Library of Congress Control Number: 2016905527

# CONTENTS

# 01

# CONVERGENCE

*"History is a gallery of pictures in which there are few*
*originals and many copies."*

- ALEXIS DE TOCQUEVILLE

APRIL 5, 1905

A cool spring morning in the nation's capital brought with it nearly an inch of rain. The historical weather records for that day tell us the sun eventually made an appearance in Washington. The temperature would reach a high of 77 degrees that Wednesday, especially warm for that time of year in the District of Columbia.[1]

The front page of *The Washington Post* reported on President Roosevelt's speech in Louisville, Kentucky before the start of a vacation trip to the Southwest. There was a lead story about the newly elected mayor of Chicago and another headline regarding the arrest of a suspected terrorist in Saint Petersburg, Russia following a bombing in Warsaw just a week before.

On page two of *The Post* was a lengthy article headlined "MONEY IS BEST TALKER" that reported on a fundraising dinner held the night before.[2] The Washington Young Men's Christian Association (YMCA) had attempted to raise $300,000 for a new building for the past three years. This was no trivial amount of money in that day and age.

Featured speakers at the dinner included Charles Ward, international secretary of the YMCA and Lyman Pierce, general secretary of the Washington YMCA. These two men would go on to transform nonprofit fundraising, but first, there was the small matter of raising the remaining $80,000 for the building project. For several years now, both Ward and Pierce honed their money raising skills in places like Grand Rapids, Denver, Cedar Rapids, Omaha, and Trenton.

Charles Sumner Ward was born in Danville, Vermont in 1858 and went on to earn a degree from Dartmouth College. He was involved with the YMCA during his undergraduate days and took up a position with the organization following graduation. Ward worked his way up through the ranks of the YMCA with stints in Lexington, Kentucky; New Britain, Connecticut; and Grand Rapids, Michigan before landing the role of international secretary at the YMCA's headquarters in Chicago. He developed a reputation as a methodical planner and ran short-term fundraising drives in ways never seen before at the organization.[3]

Lyman Love Pierce was born in Stockton, New York in 1868 and would go on to attend the University of Minnesota. Like Charles Ward, Pierce was involved with the YMCA during college and accepted a position with the organization in Denver. Then it was on to Omaha, Nebraska and a later promotion to general secretary of the Cedar Rapids, Iowa YMCA. Pierce tripled the membership of the Trenton, New Jersey YMCA before being transferred in 1901 the Washington YMCA to serve as general secretary.[4]

After arriving at his new role in Washington, Pierce launched an ambitious fundraising campaign to erect a new building for the local YMCA. The campaign started out strong and a significant amount of money was raised from board members. Pierce also managed to get a major gift pledge of $50,000 from John D. Rockefeller, the world's richest man. But by 1905, the campaign had hit a wall and the YMCA's top fundraiser was sent from Chicago to Washington to help.

*The Washington Post* story was part of a focused effort to get the campaign back on track. Ward and Pierce announced that there was a May 1 deadline to raise the remaining funds for the project. They also noted that a large department store, Woodward & Lothrop, would make a corporate gift of $25,000 if the goal was met by the end of the 27-day campaign.

Behind the scenes, they hired a full-time public relations expert and paid for advertising. A campaign clock was used to show progress as the deadline loomed. There was a hurried dash to the finish with more than $15,000 raised in the remaining hours of the campaign. A follow-up story in *The Washington Post* on May 2 was headlined "VICTORY IN LAST HOUR" and the success of the fundraising effort was celebrated. What Charles Ward and Lyman Pierce did together that spring in Washington, D.C. was just the beginning.

Together they developed a simple formula for fundraising success: Time-bound campaigns launched with sizable pledges already secured from major donors and corporations that were tied to reaching the overall fundraising goal; the use of public relations and paid advertising to generate attention and awareness; and, campaign clocks and thermometers to remind the public about progress along the way.

These tactics alone would raise more than $27 million during the next decade for the YMCA. Ward worked to raise money throughout the United States. Pierce would take their formula to Australia and New Zealand, where it had equal measures of success. This is not to say that there wasn't some media scrutiny on the practices of Ward and Pierce. The occasional editorial in a local newspaper would be critical of the perceived pressure being put on members of the community. Still, the success of these fundraising campaigns continued and could not be ignored.

During the next 20 years, Ward and Pierce would set in motion momentous change in the art of fundraising. They would iterate, perfect, and repeat their success in campaign after campaign. Both men would eventually leave the YMCA to take on fundraising campaigns on behalf of other nonprofits before reuniting in 1917. Together once again, they would raise a staggering $123 million for the American Red Cross in eight days. A year later, a similar Red Cross campaign would raise $181 million for the World War I relief effort.[5]

Consider for a moment that between that first campaign in 1905 and 1923, Ward and Pierce would help nonprofit organizations around the world raise more than $350 million. They did capital campaigns, pledge drives, membership programs, and annual funds. They did cause marketing before it was called cause marketing. They did crowdfunding in 1913 before it was called crowdfunding. They brought along apprentices like Carlton Ketchum and Arnaud Marts, who would go on to further develop the art of fundraising. Ward and Pierce created most of what we recognize today as nonprofit fundraising.

And they did all of this without modern technology. No donor databases or websites. No marketing automation or lock boxes. No wealth screening or electronic funds transfer. No real-time dashboards or spreadsheets. We do not live in that world anymore. Ward and Pierce used the most advanced technology of their day, but more than 100 years later, the same cannot be said for the majority of nonprofits.

## JULY 20, 1969

A journey of more than 238,900 miles from the Earth to the Moon came to a dramatic conclusion as the *Eagle* landed on the Sea of Tranquility. Neil Armstrong and Buzz Aldrin had about 25 seconds of fuel left when they touched down on the surface. The crew of the Apollo Lunar Module also had to contend with an overloaded computer than needed every bit of its primitive software to touch down safely.

The Apollo Guidance Computer was a marvel of technology at the time but is an ancient relic by today's standards. It weighed in at 70 pounds, had 64 kilobytes of memory, and each unit cost more than $150,000—not to mention the team of specialized MIT engineers, led by Margaret Heafield Hamilton, that developed the delicate software. Only a few were ever made and today the one on board the *Eagle* rests in some unknown impact site on the Moon.

Compare that to today's latest technological wunderkind: The Apple Watch weighs less than four ounces, has 512,000 kilobytes of memory, and costs a little more than $299. It can run countless applications developed by people all over the world for a variety of purposes—and it tells time too. It is a mass-produced item and several million units will one day rest in a landfill somewhere.

The rate of technological change since the first Moon landing is almost blinding. Computers that once took up entire rooms have been reduced to wearable fashion accessories. Processing power that was once limited to only large companies or had to be reserved at a university is now a few clicks away in the cloud. Storage space that used to be extremely cost prohibitive is now given away free or as an extremely cheap option for the everyday consumer.

Not long after the Moon landings, the growth in computing capabilities would begin to shape the nonprofit sector. Universities began to give access to their research computing facilities to fundraising and alumni associations. Nonprofits began using databases to manage growing direct mail programs during the 1970s. The personal computer revolution of the 1980s finally brought hands-on access to software that nonprofits could use, but only after an unlikely convergence of events.

In 1979, Anthony Bakker moved to New York City from the United Kingdom for a job with Manufacturers Hanover Trust. Bakker learned computer programming while studying physics in college and quickly grew bored with his job at the bank. In 1981, the Nightingale-Bamford School in NYC posted a want ad in *The New York Times* looking for a computerized billing system. Bakker won the contract and developed the software program during his nights and weekends. Before long, Bakker had other schools interested in the software and set up shop in a one-room office above a storefront in Long Island. The company's name was Blackbaud. Today, Blackbaud is the largest provider of software and services to the nonprofit sector with more than 35,000 customers in 60 countries.[6] And that first customer, the Nightingale-Bamford School, is still a customer nearly four decades later.

Nearly 50 years after that "one small step" on the surface of the Moon, the nonprofit sector is a significant consumer of technology that helps drive organizations' missions. From fundraising to communications to program management and grants administration, websites, direct mail lists, membership cards, scholarship programs, clean water projects, and just about every facet of the modern nonprofit could not function without the aid of technology. Just looking at the fundraising side of the nonprofit sector reveals an abundance of technology options. Fundraising consultant Robert Weiner has identified more than 60 donor management systems currently in use.[7] All of them come with different capabilities and price ranges for nonprofits to choose from.

Technology is no longer a limiting factor for nonprofits. We also know that simply having the technology is not enough. The mere possession of Microsoft Word® does not guarantee a best-selling novel. Likewise, having a powerful email marketing tool does not mean supporters will respond to the content. The emergence of mainstream computer use also led to the age of "Big Data" we find ourselves living in today. The convergence of technology and data brings the opportunity to transform how nonprofits drive change in the world. But first, the data has to be big enough to be worth using.

## OCTOBER 23, 1997

It is the fourth day of the eighth annual conference on visualization held by the Institute of Electrical and Electronics Engineers (IEEE) Computer Society. Attendees make their way into the Crescent B room at the Sheraton Crescent Hotel in Phoenix, Arizona. The scene resembles just about every conference that you have ever been to: people networking in the hallway; and, a few late nights of socializing. Except at this conference, something with far-reaching consequences was about to happen.

The 10:15 a.m. session was about to begin as condensation slowly built on the pitchers of water scattered across the room. Two researchers from NASA's Ames Research Center in California were about to present their latest report titled "Application-Controlled Demand Paging for Out-of-Core Visualization." Both Michael Cox and David Ellsworth have been pushing the limits of all that post-Apollo supercomputing to visualize Computational Fluid Dynamics (CFD). In short, CFD involves analyzing how liquids and gasses interact on everything from an airplane to the Space Shuttle or a probe landing on Mars.

CFD requires a lot of supercomputing horsepower to process large amounts of data, not to mention rendering graphics so that researchers can see what's happening. At the time, Cox and Ellsworth were running into problems with datasets larger than 100 gigabytes. The size of the data was becoming too large for even the most expensive graphics workstations to handle. The machines did not have enough memory to even load all that data in the first place. This is how Cox and Ellsworth described the problem:[8]

> "Visualization provides an interesting challenge for computer systems: data sets are generally quite large, taxing the capacities of main memory, local disk, and even remote disk. We call this the problem of *big data*."

Michael Cox and David Ellsworth were the first to use the term Big Data in a modern context. In a few short pages, they identified the challenges of data storage, dealing with structured and unstructured data, loading and memory management, and the need to make it easier for end users to leverage all this data. Fast-forward nearly 20 years and the term Big Data has become commonplace, even if its real meaning is not fully comprehended. The technical issues that Cox and Ellsworth described in that Phoenix hotel conference room are still the core problems that Big Data tools help us solve today.

Big Data is a term describing the storage and analysis of complex sets of data to extract value regardless of the size of the data set. Data is both captured and stored in such massive volumes. Modern tools are required to perform analysis. Answering important questions from all this data requires new skills, as well. This is not the stuff of complex spreadsheets and pivot tables. The technology and data available to companies and nonprofits now allow us to solve the problems Cox and Ellsworth first described in 1997.

This convergence of technology and data allows for insights beyond what was previously thought possible. It is how Walmart knows to stock up their stores with Strawberry Pop-Tarts® when a storm is approaching[9] and how Facebook knows that people really have just three and a half degrees of separation.[10] The ability of companies to collect, manage, and analyze data is driving growth and innovation in just about every sector of the commercial world. Big Data is not just a buzzword for these companies; it is a way to transform how they meet the needs of customers and improve their effectiveness in entirely new ways.

Most nonprofit organizations are still at the beginning of the beginning when it comes to the use of data to accelerate their decision-making and growth. For most of the past 20 years, the use of data by staff at nonprofit organizations has moved at a slow pace. A generous estimate suggests that any form of advanced analytics is used at only 3% of the nonprofit organizations in the United States. Harnessing the insights from data to drive decisions has the potential to transform the amount of change nonprofits can make in the world.

We live in a world of convergence. The rapidly accelerating capabilities of technology are merging with the escalating volume of data to converge with the work done by nonprofits. But for all the frenetic growth in technology and data, the yearly increases in charitable giving seem to be stuck in slow motion.

## JUNE 14, 2016

For 60 years, *Giving USA* has reported on charitable giving trends in the United States. It is considered the gold standard for trends in charitable giving for individual, foundation, bequest, and corporate giving. On June 14, 2016, *Giving USA* reported that overall charitable giving in the United States grew by 4.1% in 2015 compared to the prior year.[11]

Over the years, *Giving USA* has also charted changes in giving to different types of organizations. Of the estimated $373.25 billion given to nonprofits during 2015, about 32% went to religious organizations followed by 15% to education, 12% to human services, and 11% to foundations. These groups account for 70% of all charitable giving in the United States. Nonprofits serving the arts, health, environment, international affairs, public and society benefit, and animal welfare sectors make up the remaining 30%. Charitable giving from individuals represents 71% of the total followed by 16% from foundations, 8% from bequests, and 5% from corporations.

Since the 1970s, charitable giving as a percentage of Gross Domestic Product in the United States has hovered around 2%. To put that in perspective, the agriculture, forestry, fishing, and hunting industry represents 1.1% of GDP, mining is 1.7%, and administrative and waste management services is 3.1%.[12] Sitting somewhere in the middle is charitable giving, putting it between a rock and a waste place.

# INDUSTRY AS A PERCENTAGE OF US GDP

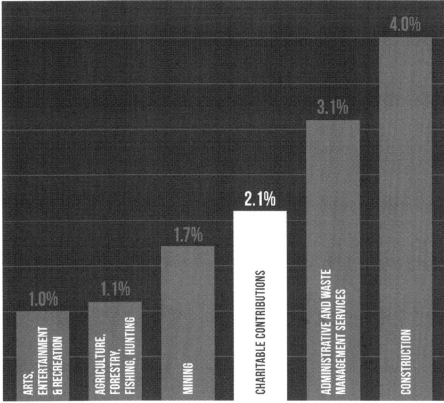

Source: U.S. Bureau of Economic Analysis

Perhaps more troubling than the GDP trend line is the data on individual donors over the past 40 years. The percentage of disposable income given to charity has been stuck at about 2% since the mid-1970s. Compare that with about 3% of average annual household spending on apparel and services and 5% spent on entertainment in the United States.[13] Both giving as a percentage of GDP and donations from disposable income have essentially been flat for 40 years while the number of nonprofits and the missions they serve have continued to grow.

The nonprofit sector has grown significantly during the past two decades. Since 1996, the total number of registered nonprofit organizations has grown from 1,085,296 to 1,571,056 in 2016. Since 2011, 354,980 nonprofit organizations have had their status automatically revoked by the U.S. Internal Revenue Service.[14] The IRS approved 86,915 new charities in 2015, double the rate from a couple of years prior.[15] At the same time, other organizations are merging, closing, and oscillating. This is the circle of organizational life that both the corporate world and nonprofit sector cannot escape. Despite this cycle of creation, cultivation, and churn in the number of nonprofit organizations, the amount of private support is growing at a relatively slow pace. Giving in the U.S. has been 2% of GDP and 2% of disposable personal income for 40 years.

Something is broken in the nonprofit sector and donors are the canary in the coal mine. The number of new and existing donors has been in decline for more than 10 years now. "Donor numbers have generally been on a slow decline since the U.S. Gulf Coast hurricanes of Q3 2005," according to the "donorCentrics Index of Direct Marketing Fundraising," published by Target Analytics, a division of Blackbaud. This report analyzes direct marketing giving from 71 organizations, including more than 34 million donors and more than 78 million gifts totaling over $2.7 billion in revenue.[16] Direct mail is the dominant revenue source for most organizations, but web, telemarketing, canvassing, and other gifts considered to be direct marketing are also included in the analysis. Unfortunately, the decline in donors is not the only problem.

The first year retention rate for new donors is a slim 29%. That means roughly seven out of 10 new donors do not give again to the organization the next year. Few are brought back once they stop giving. Reactivation rates for lapsed donors one to five years after the first gift are only 8.4%. Imagine running a small business or a restaurant where only three out of 10 of your first customers ever returned. That is simply not a sustainable model for a business or a nonprofit. We have stretched the canvas in the art of fundraising to the breaking point.

29%

FIRST YEAR DONOR RETENTION

*Source: Target Analytics, a division of Blackbaud*

The good news is that the multi-year retention rate for donors is 61%. When nonprofits keep their donors for more than one year, the economics dramatically change. When they engage supporters, steward relationships, communicate impact, and focus on donor loyalty, their efforts show up in the results. This is a bright spot amongst the many negative trends. As a sector, we do need to see that things can get better with the right people, process, data, and technology.

The reason for so much focus on fundraising performance compared to other aspects of the sector boils down to one simple point: No money. No mission.

The merits of programs and outcomes and the real change that the non-profit sector is driving in our world can be argued and discussed. The role of volunteers and board members and staff should not be overlooked either. There is no mission without infrastructure, engagement with the community, and people delivering needed services. But the element most needed to make the social good ecosystem habitable and sustainable is funding. Money is not the only substance needed in the soil of the nonprofit sector, but there aren't signs of life without it. Just like on Earth, the atmosphere is made up of only 20% oxygen, but you're not reading this book without it.[17] For this reason, this book will primarily focus on fundraising as the critical element needed to drive growth in nonprofit organizations.

Combined with grants and program revenue, fundraising drives the growth and success of the nonprofit sector. That brings us back to where our story began: Charles Ward and Lyman Pierce created a revolution in fundraising beginning in the early 1900s. Just about any nonprofit today utilizes recognizable elements of what Ward and Pierce pioneered more than a century ago. Nonprofits are also using a good amount of technology for both fundraising and mission delivery. But the use of data to drive decision-making, linking the art and science of fundraising, is not as prevalent as it needs to be.

Convergence is all around us – that gradual collision of the analog world being consumed by modern capabilities. The traditional "dollar in the gift basket" is being replaced by the digital donation. Money raised by hand is shifting to fingertips on a mobile phone. Technology that was once limited to technocrats or institutions with deep pockets is now available to the masses. The vital skills needed to utilize technology are less about writing lines of obscure code and more about the ability to embrace and adapt to constant change. Data that was once lost as exhaust is now feeding an engine for growth. Data scientists are in high demand, and the need for data literacy will only continue to grow. Our ability to cope with the sheer scale of data relies on new tools and approaches that detect signals amongst all the noise.

Would any of us who are deeply committed to the nonprofit sector claim that change is happening there at a similar pace? Are we seeing the same kinds of disruption and innovation that the convergence of technology and data has brought to the commercial world? Or, are some nonprofits still trying to wring out the last remaining benefits of "best practices" created more than 100 years ago? The macro trends in giving and what we know is happening with donors all indicate a turning point.

Perhaps we think that Big Data is just for companies such as Google, Facebook, Amazon, and Walmart. Much like some believe only the largest nonprofits can invest in better data, analytics, testing, and donor stewardship. Nothing could be further from the truth. Sometimes we just need to be shown where the future is happening today to give us the courage and curiosity to take our own first steps.

The use of data to drive decision-making is not data science fiction — it's today's reality for a wide range of organizations. John Deere uses sensor data on equipment that allows farmers to make better decisions and minimize downtime. Fitbit has sold more than 20 million wearable devices and is driving growth in people who are better informed about their health. Transport for London is using data to understand the travel patterns of commuters and anticipate the needs of a city approaching 10 million people. The analytics that drive Netflix began with measuring four simple data points: customer ID, movie ID, rating, and date watched. The Royal Bank of Scotland is investing $145 million to use analytics to restore a more personal level of service to banking. Disney introduced the MagicBand at its parks in 2014 and it is transforming the customer experience for people of all ages.[18] A study by McKinsey & Company estimates that data and analytics can help reduce between $300 billion and $450 billion in healthcare spending.[19]

The future is data driven, and companies and governments both know it. Now is the time for nonprofit sector leaders to embrace the possibilities of what data can do. Data driven nonprofits accelerate change in the world when staff use data to influence strategy and inform decisions that produce value and impact. In order to make change happen, we need to create more value and data is the raw material that does just that. When nonprofits focus on converting data into information and insights, value is created.

The value from data helps to reduce operating costs. For example, using data to focus on the right donors at the right time using the right channels of engagement. The value from data helps increase effectiveness. Analytics and predictive models based on good data produce better results compared to the absence of data. The value from data makes and measures real impact in the world. Measuring the mission of the organization allows improvement in programs and services.

Some might suggest that being data driven takes the human element out of a nonprofit, but nothing could be further from the truth. Throwing more people at the challenges faced by nonprofit organizations is a broken model.

That approach does not scale. The art and science of any nonprofit activity is enhanced, not inhibited, by the use of data. We need to give nonprofit professionals the modern skills, capabilities, and tools to create more value.

When data is leveraged properly, it creates scale and increases the effectiveness of the entire organization. Without data, decisions are left to tribal knowledge or worse, the whims of the Highest Paid Person's Opinion (HiPPO). Consider these scenarios at any nonprofit of any size: Take two major gift officers. Give one of them data insights about their prospects and don't give that information to the other. Take two online marketing managers and give one data about their email performance and one none of it. Take two program staff and provide only one of them with metrics about the health of the programs. Who is more likely to get better results? This is the value of being data driven.

Let me go further and suggest that being a donor-centric nonprofit is impossible without the use of data. Being a multichannel nonprofit is impossible without the use of data. Being a transparent and accountable nonprofit is impossible without the use of data. Being a modern nonprofit in the 21st century is impossible without the use of data. You can bet for damn sure that if Charles Ward and Lyman Pierce were alive today, they would be using data to drive decisions.

Do not be overwhelmed by the deluge of data. Instead, focus on converting it into information, insights, and value. Do not be deceived by the hype about Big Data. The strategies, goals, and actions that you focus on are more important than the technology behind them. Throughout this book, we will explore how nonprofits can become more data driven. This is a journey, not a sprint, to the future of the charitable sector. There will be challenges along the way, but there are many nonprofits and experts that have helped pave the way. Let's get started!

# 02

# DELUGE

*"We are drowning in information but starved
for knowledge."*

- JOHN NAISBITT

## 90 PERCENT

We are told that 90% of all the data in the world has been generated in the last two years.[20] Since that statistic was first cited, the amount of data in our world and our lives has grown tremendously. We are awash in data whether it's from the reports we monitor, the alerts on social media, or the wearable devices that monitor our every step. What data doesn't drown us certainly can leave us hanging out to dry. This is the age of Big Data and there are no signs of the deluge slowing down.

The digital world has brought with it tidal waves of data. Every minute on the Internet, Facebook users "like" more than 4.1 million posts and share 3.3 million pieces of content.[21] On YouTube, over 138,889 hours of video are watched. Twitter users tweet 347,000 times every 60 seconds and over 1 million videos are viewed on Vine. 4.1 million searches are performed on Google and 10 million ads are displayed on websites.

The analog and digital worlds collide during the span of 60 seconds. Nearly 700 passengers take an Uber ride while 51,000 Apple users download other disruptive apps. Wikipedia serves up 438,801 page views as an obsolete encyclopedia set sits idly on the shelf. Amazon.com gets more than 4,310 unique visitors and earns $143,304 in revenue every minute of the day.[22] Over 3.2 billion people now consume and create data on the Internet.[23] That's a pretty staggering figure until you compare it to the fact that 2.5 billion people on that same planet still do not have access to adequate sanitation.[24]

## T.B.U.

Yes, the data is big. Yes, the change it brings is profound. But these statistics are mostly T.B.U. — True But Useless. They are used over and over again in the media, at conferences, and during nearly every sales pitch. The original point of reciting some of these daunting digits over and over again is unclear. Are we supposed to be entertained, overwhelmed, scared, or a combination of each?

What we can say with some certainty is that most of these numbers have little to do with driving real change in the world. When Snapchat is gone, many of the inherent problems in society will still remain. There is no correlation between pins on Pinterest and planned gift likelihood. Netflix streaming video trends have little bearing on the success of a clean water program. A surge in BuzzFeed traffic is unlikely to get those lapsed donor reports delivered any more quickly.

Nonprofit organizations already experience their own deluge of data on a daily basis: The stream of opens, clicks, and conversions from this morning's email campaign. Updating volunteer information for this weekend's event. Reviewing the mid-level donor portfolio based on the latest predictive model. Preparing to give an update on program delivery at the next board meeting. Staff meetings to coordinate the next advocacy campaign and the social media posts that must be scheduled. Batching up the day's donations from both online and offline transactions. Completing the latest outcomes evaluation for an important grant. Checking a dashboard on a mobile device to see how the peer-to-peer fundraising event is performing today.

Just about any discussion of Big Data includes a mention of the four Vs: Volume, Variety, Velocity, and Veracity. Volume refers to the amount of data.

Variety refers to the different types of data. Velocity refers to the speed of the data being generated. Veracity refers to the accuracy of the data.

Even if they've never looked at it that way, nonprofits deal with the four Vs all the time. Organizations collect and manage an enormous volume of data. This data comes in a wide variety of types including biographical, transactional, and machine-generated. The velocity of nonprofit data continues to increases as digital channels like social media produce a continuous stream of information. The veracity of a nonprofit's data is extremely important to analysis and informed decision-making.

But there is another V that is often overlooked in these discussions — Value. A common definition of the word "value" is the importance, worth, or usefulness of something. A good starting point for nonprofits to become more data driven is to focus on the value that can be obtained from their data assets. Collecting a variety of data at high velocity and maintaining veracity is wasted effort if there is not any value in it. Nonprofits can avoid "analysis paralysis" by first focusing on what is important and understanding what is not. It's not about the volume of the data – it's about the value.

NUMERACY

Understanding how nonprofits have been using (or not using) data over the past hundred years is important. A historical perspective provides context and helps explain why data has been undervalued in the nonprofit sector. The problem often contains the solution, which is why it is necessary to explore how we got here as an industry and what we can do to use data more effectively.

Roger Craver is a veteran fundraiser with over 55 years of experience in the nonprofit sector. He got his start in higher education capital campaigns during the 1960s, helped build a new generation of direct marketing-driven advocacy organizations in the 1970s, like Common Cause, Greenpeace, Amnesty International, The National Organization for Women, Environmental Defense Fund, and many other citizen action social change organizations. He spent the '80s and '90s fundraising for the Democratic Party in the United States before switching to focus on online and digital channels for the past 20 years. Today, Craver is the editor of *The Agitator,* a daily digital newsletter and blog that focuses on driving change in the nonprofit sector, and the founder of two other ventures, Donor Voice and Donor Trends, which focus on donor research and experience.

"For all intents and purposes, organized fundraising the way we know it today began in the late 1920s and began to hit its stride in the Depression when a number of today's major gift or capital gift companies – Marts and Lundy, John Price Jones, and Ketchum – were started to manage campaigns run for colleges, universities, and social service organizations," says Craver. This was the evolution of the profession after Charles Ward and Lyman Pierce pioneered campaign fundraising in the early 1900s. Many of these early professionals, including Arnaud Marts and Carlton Ketchum, worked with Ward and Pierce before venturing off to start their own consulting firms.

"These were the principal organized fundraising efforts up until the late 1960s. They were not data driven. The information about donors was maintained physically on three-by-five cards. Communications was done by postal mail and phone. There was not much direct mail those days either. There wasn't database fundraising the way we think of it today. In fact, the management of donor records was largely limited to some giving history and name and address and, in the case of colleges and universities, class year," says Craver.

High-tech fundraising in the 1960s involved the use of a machine called the Addressograph. It was first patented in 1896 by Joseph Smith Duncan of Sioux City, Iowa and used metal plates to stamp addresses on envelopes. The process of mailing donors was literally a foot-pedal-driven process using trays of metal plates and the Addressograph. It wasn't until the late 1960s that huge mainframe computers were used to maintain alumni records for the first time. "It's no coincidence that the first organizations to use this new technology were the colleges and universities because it was the college and universities that had access to mainframe computers for research purposes," says Craver.

This is the origin story of database administrators and why for decades they, instead of the fundraisers, have controlled the data and systems. "They are the ones that had the technology and controlled it because it was part of the university's ongoing information services. Up until the early '70s, there really was no effective economical use of computer technology for fundraising data or, frankly, marketing data of any type," he says. The information technology departments controlled data processing across the entire organization and were unlikely to turn that responsibility over to a bunch of fundraisers. Especially since it wasn't until the 1980s that everyday staff members began using computers as part of their job. The personal computer revolution may have begun during the '80s, but it was not an overnight transformation.

Craver notes, "Until the early to mid-1990s there was no practical, applied use of data the way we know it. What ruled instead of sophisticated analytics, and largely still does, is the tradition of so much tribal wisdom and myth that continues to infect our craft today." These myths-as-best-practices ruled everything from capital campaigns to mailing programs to membership renewals. As other commercial industries began to adopt technology and analytics, the nonprofit sector stayed, for the most part, firmly tied to techniques that were crafted over a century ago.

"All of this trade was very 'art'-driven. It was not empirical, nor data oriented. This is the tradition that has, by and large, maintained itself across the nonprofit sector to this day. There still isn't the use of empirical data to inform decisions on the part of most nonprofits," says Craver. He adds that analytics, as we know it today, "is a product of the last two decades and mainly the last decade. It is still foreign to most nonprofits and it is an empirical science that has yet to work its way into the mainstream."

With technology now widely available and the use of data significantly increasing in importance all around us, what might be holding the nonprofit sector back? Craver strongly asserts that "the nonprofit industry by and large is innumerate, meaning they do not understand numbers, which is somewhat ironic since they deal with money and figures." He adds, "Ours is an innumerate profession and it doesn't guide itself by metrics in many ways that are meaningful, nor does it really compile and analyze information the way it needs to." He believes both the skill set and the mindset of many nonprofit professionals hold organizations back. "The added irony is that the current technology gives these organization an immense capacity to do analysis, but they don't do it. And that's a function of mindset, not a function of whether it can be done or not. There just is not a premium placed on most of these organizations to do analytics," adds Craver.

The cure for innumeracy is not just skills and training. This goes beyond simple math and measurement know-how. As Craver points out, "not knowing what data is significant to begin with and then not understanding how to apply it is the biggest problem that we face." It bears noting that all of the data can't be important. Nonprofits have to mine a lot of rock to get to the actual gold. Then there is more work to take action on the valuable information.

"The challenge is to make certain that people understand what is important. To separate what is important from what is not important. That's where I distinguish between what I call 'vanity metrics' and 'value metrics,' and vanity metrics are things that provide measurement of something you're not going to do anything about it. You can't do anything about, for example, the number of friends, the number of likes, the number of followers, the number of unique visitors," says Craver. Vanity metrics might look good for a moment in the mirror, but they are here today and gone tomorrow.

Craver says, "Almost all that stuff is worthless but it's treated as though it's somehow important data as opposed to looking at things like retention rates or lifetime value: key metrics which you can really act on and guide things on." He suggests that the nonprofit sector needs to do a better job of educating people on the value of different types of metrics. Organizations should focus on what is valuable and ignore the vanity metrics.

The short-term nature of so many fundraising campaigns, especially in direct mail, perpetuates the problem of not focusing on value metrics. Craver says that the most useful numbers are the "longer-term metrics like lifetime value and retention rates because there you can really steer the organization toward doing better. Unless the organizations use the right type of metrics, they are never going to get out of the no-growth plateau they're in."

This brings us back to a question that has already been posed earlier in the book: Is individual giving relatively flat because more people won't donate or because nonprofits are using more modern methods to grow fundraising?

Craver responds that the reason is not that "people won't give, it's because organizations settle for far too little and don't take the time of putting in the skill and investment to grow. You look at the metrics that an apparently flat organization or a no-growth organization uses and you'll find most of them are short-term, campaign-focused metrics."

Having the right data and metrics is essential to growth and success. Otherwise, we are back to talking about true but useless statistics that do not move the needle. "If it is not driven by the proper metrics then it's not likely to get done. What you measure is what you do and what you measure matters. It matters in terms of where you're going to spend money. If you're measuring things by likes or page views and open rates and that sort of thing, then you're going to concentrate on SEO and all kinds of stuff, whereas if you're really measuring things on lifetime value or on retention or on donor loyalty, the things that are predictive of the future, then you are in much better shape to grow an organization," says Craver.

Take myths about fundraising, combine them with vanity metrics, and all you need is a strategy concocted in a spreadsheet to send you heading in the wrong direction. Craver says he often wishes two things were never invented in fundraising, the word processing program and Excel, because they "make it far too easy simply to copy over one year to the next or one message to another and not to do the initial thinking to start from zero." He adds, "The result is an awful lot of strategy by spreadsheet in the nonprofit sector. That's very dangerous in the sense that it prevents growth because it blocks thinking outside the box or outside of last year's plan."

Just having access to modern technology does not mean that it is used in the right ways. Craver says, "Many organizations still use technology as an electronic filing cabinet. They don't use the power of that software to do what they could with it, and that's because they don't understand what can be done with it. This is rather sad because the fundamental part of doing most of today's fundraising is data-based." The volume and variety of information inside a typical nonprofit can be completely overwhelming, and yet that flood of data contains the solutions to many of the problems organizations face.

Data and modern technology can help to solve many of these issues, but they are still just tools. Having Microsoft Word® does not guarantee that you will write the next great novel. Hand me a Stradivarius violin and you won't hear anything that could be called music. "The fact is you can do things with technology that you never were able to do 30 years ago or 10 years ago. People are just not asking the right questions using the right data," says Craver. Copy and paste is not the answer. For all the claims that fundraising is an art, there are an awful lot of cover bands just playing someone else's tunes over and over again.

Does that mean we're trapped in this downward spiral? While Craver can sound like a curmudgeon at times, his years of experience point to when we might expect a tipping point in the nonprofit sector. "Historically, the way this has happened is when one organization or one group of organizations sees others doing so much better than they are. Then they tend to adopt and change and do it fairly quickly," he says. Craver points to the acceptance of direct mail by a majority of nonprofits in the 1970s after decades of shunning it. "There was absolutely no belief that direct mail could be used to raise significant money. The saying in those days by the major gift firms was 'You can't get milk from a cow by sending it a letter.' That was the favorite put-down of direct mail. You have to work with the beast and touch it and talk to it," says Craver.

All that changed in the summer of 1970 when Common Cause was launched. The organization went from 0 to 500,000 dues-paying members in a year thanks to the use of direct mail. "Once the herd saw that one of the animals was eating better, they all followed. That's been the history of a herd mentality for change in this sector. Someone suddenly breaks through and does really well and the others get interested in it and follow. Change almost always comes from organizations that are forced to do something different because they have no alternative," explains Craver.

Today, we find ourselves in a similar situation with the adoption of more data driven practices by nonprofits. Yes, you'll hear people say that the art of fundraising can't be replaced with robots and analytics. "You can't get milk from a cow by using predictive modeling," say the skeptics. These are the same people who said no one would ever give money on the Internet. 20 years later, online giving in the United States alone is over $20 billion. There is an old saying that if you keep your head buried in the sand, then all you ever do is get kicked in the ass.

At the beginning of this chapter, I said that most of the metrics around social media and technology are true but useless. The vanity metrics are useless, but what they tell us about consumer behavior is important. Remember that consumer behavior is donor behavior. In 2015, 68% of adult Americans had a smartphone.[25] That jumped to 83% for those aged 30 to 49 and 87% of those living in households earning $75,000 or more annually. This trend helps to explain why 14% of online donations in 2015 were made on a mobile device.[26] That is consumer behavior turning into donor behavior.

"Going forward, we'll see that adaptation is going to be faster because the technology is so inexpensive. It was still expensive in the old days to do this because you had to rent computer time, you had to put the card decks in the trunk of your car, and go around and find what mainframes were available to run the data," says Craver. Now organizations have modern technology and the power of the cloud. The data and systems are no longer controlled by just the IT department. "These older folks in the direct response industry are very slow to change. They've grown up on a business model that's based largely on volume. You get paid by the number of records you process, you get paid by the number of pieces you print, you get paid by the amount of printing you can mark up. All the incentives are geared toward a very successful 1970 and are not geared toward a very successful 2020," he says.

And 2020 is not too far away. We're closer to it than 2010 at this point in time. A successful nonprofit in 2020 will focus a lot more on the value of data than the volume of donors. Craver says, "Volume doesn't matter as much anymore, it's value. It's no longer who has the biggest database, it's who has the most valuable database. There is no equivalency between size and value. Yet the metrics like percentage of response and average gift were all used to run that old volume model." Craver says organizations should now focus on how their "database's lifetime value is increasing year over year. The consultants and the staff should be rewarded for how much increase and lifetime value there is, not how much they are mailing or how many new members they got."

Once we get past feeling overwhelmed by the deluge of data and start using it to measure the right things for the right outcomes, real change begins. Today, there are a growing number of nonprofit organizations that have made the transformation to being data driven. The growth of the philanthropic community is heading towards a tipping point where being data driven is no longer optional. Numeracy is the new normal for nonprofits.

# 03

# TREASURE

*"Data is a precious thing and will last longer than
the systems themselves."*

- TIM BERNERS-LEE

## HIDDEN

"The Purloined Letter," a well-known detective short story by Edgar Allan Poe, first appeared in 1844. The story begins with a visit by Monsieur G—, the Prefect of the Paris police, to discuss a new case with the amateur detective C. Auguste Dupin. A very important letter is alleged to have been stolen from the royal apartments. The police have searched the entire building, room by room, along with every cabinet, cushion, tabletop, bed post, and even the "moss between the bricks" on the grounds of the houses. But they have been unable to find the valuable letter. The Paris police are "a good deal puzzled because the affair is so simple," to which Dupin cleverly replies, "Perhaps it is the very simplicity of the thing which puts you at fault."[27]

A month later, the Prefect returns to find Dupin with the mystery still unsolved. Monsieur G— offers 50,000 francs to anyone who can help him solve the case. "In that case," replies Dupin, opening a drawer and producing a checkbook, "you may as well fill me up a check for the amount mentioned.

When you have signed it, I will hand you the letter." The story goes, noting that "the Prefect appeared absolutely thunderstricken. For some minutes he remained speechless and motionless…then, apparently in some measure, he seized a pen, and after several pauses and vacant stares, finally filled up and signed a check for 50,000 francs, and handed it across the table to Dupin." Dupin then pulls out the purloined letter and handed it to the Prefect, who quickly rushes out the door. As it turns out, the valuable letter was "full in the view of every visitor" and completely overlooked by everyone looking for it, except Dupin.

Any discussion about nonprofit data reminds me of Poe's story because so many organizations have a very valuable asset left out in plain sight. Nonprofit data is often overlooked and undervalued at the organization. In reality, the data that nonprofits have about their constituents, volunteers, supporters, advocates, programs, and donors is the most valuable asset they possess. And yet so many nonprofits don't maximize the hidden treasure sitting before their very eyes.

I have heard horror stories more gruesome than those Poe might have penned about nonprofits purging valuable data. Nonprofits both large and small have been guilty of doing this. In some cases, years of data have been thrown away to save money or because the data has been poorly maintained over time. These nonprofits may avoid paying the short-term price, but they do not count the long-term cost.

Data is the building block for analytics, whether that is a simple report or an advanced predictive model. It all begins with the quality of the data. If you start out with bad data, then it only gets worse from there, never better. Perhaps because we often call it "data hygiene," people tune out. Visions of sitting at the dentist or other less-than-desirable situations may come to mind. That is why I prefer to call it "Data Health," because that name implies it is not only good for you but also necessary.

Like any good public health marketing program, the case for improved data health needs to start with just how much bad data is costing nonprofit organizations. Target Analytics recently analyzed the data health of thousands of nonprofit organizations. The goal of the analysis was to see how the best performing nonprofits compare to the average or even worst organizations when it comes to data health.

For starters, Target Analytics looked at the data health of one of the most basic building blocks of data: address information. The analysis ran millions of records through a data health screening process to look for outdated addresses, invalid addresses, and deceased supporters. Outdated addresses happen when people move, and nonprofits have not regularly kept this information updated. Invalid addresses occur when bad data, like an address not standardized or wrong postal codes, is present in the system. Deceased supporters are, well, people no longer living, but that has not stopped nonprofits from attempting to send them mail.

*Source: Target Analytics, a division of Blackbaud*

The combination of these three data elements results in unmailable addresses. In the best performing nonprofits, about 6% of their database file is unmailable. In average nonprofits, that number jumps to 26% and, in the worst performing organizations, 67% of their file is unmailable. We aren't talking about more exotic forms of data here. This is fundamental information that drives a lot of engagement and communication with donors. A conservative estimate is that all this bad address data results in $21.8 million in wasted mailing costs across nonprofit organizations. That is either a big lost opportunity or a massive amount of wasted money, depending on how you look at it.

These fundamental data health issues also exist with other important types of nonprofit data. Imagine that we're living in a digital age and email communication is an important way for nonprofits to communicate with supporters. (No need to imagine this — it's reality.) Now, whether you believe it was Ray Tomlinson who invented email in 1971 or Shiva Ayyadurai in 1978, the reality is that email has been widely used by the general public for decades. This suggests that nonprofit organizations should have a very low percentage of missing email addresses in their house files.

Target Analytics found that the average nonprofit was missing email addresses for 74% of their constituents. The worst are missing 96% of their email addresses. For the best nonprofits, 43% of their email addresses are missing. We aren't even getting into whether or not the email addresses nonprofits do have are still valid or active. And having email addresses is not dependent on age either. A common excuse about anything digital is that nonprofits have older donors that may not be using the Internet. Let's stop using that excuse, especially since the average nonprofit is missing 70% of the ages of their constituents too. How would most organizations know if this was true or not if they are missing age data on most constituents?

You might be wondering why something as simple as address data and email data can have a big impact on the performance of your nonprofit. First, if you're unable to capture, maintain, and manage the basic elements of data, then you'll never get to the more valuable information. Address, deceased status, phone, age, and email address information are the ABCs and 123s of data health. Nonprofits then need to layer in additional biographic, demographic, and descriptive data about constituents. This is extremely difficult to do if even the basic data elements aren't collected or correct.

*Source: Target Analytics, a division of Blackbaud*

Second, most of these data elements can be managed or acquired through a variety of sources. It's not as if having correct address data is overly complicated or impossible to obtain. In the United States, the National Change of Address (NCOA) service allows nonprofits to get updates from over 160 million permanent change of address records. Canada has its own version of NCOA too. In the United Kingdom, the Postcode Address File is maintained by the Royal Mail to provide accurate address data that is constantly updated.

Most countries also have address validation data this is both available and affordable. The same is true for deceased data, including the Social Security Death Index (SSDI) in the United States.

Nonprofits need to stay on top of managing the quality of their data. Keep in mind that in the United States, about 12% of the population moves every year.[28] Performing address data clean-up at least four times a year is not just a good idea; it also helps nonprofits continue to receive postal discounts in the United States. The death rate in the U.S. is 821 deaths per 100,000 people, but that climbs to 4,461 per 100,000 for people 65 and older.[29] This is especially important because the average age of a donor in the U.S. is about 65 years old. Marking constituents as deceased helps to avoid wasted direct mail costs and can be used as part of a planned giving program.

The third reason why even basic data is so important to nonprofits is that it forms the basis for using advanced analytics. The first advanced use of data is often called descriptive analytics. It allows a nonprofit to know what happened with a very specific group of constituents. This is why data like address, age, income, and other variables is so important to have and be updated regularly. Descriptive analytics is a very good tool for grouping known constituents into segments for marketing or engagement activities. If you have ever broken up a mailing into separate groups based on different criteria, then you have used descriptive analytics. Descriptive analytics can be very useful, but keep in mind that it only tells you about the constituents in that particular data set.

To understand what might happen in your data, then you need to use predictive modeling. Predictive modeling takes an organization's data and combines it with external data to help predict what might happen in the future. That external data may consist of things like income, real estate holdings, private company ownership, stock transactions, being on the board of a nonprofit, and donations made to other nonprofit organizations. Be warned that predictive modeling requires some data science skills to get right. This is not something done with duct tape and a spreadsheet.

Predictive modeling helps to identify constituents in the data that have a higher likelihood to engage, donate, lapse, or renew their support. It is also used to predict the likelihood that someone is a good prospect for a major, planned, or principal gift.[30] For example, let's say that you want to know who is most likely to make a donation of $1,000 to $10,000 to your nonprofit. Descriptive analytics can tell you who has previously made a donation of that size, but it can't predict who else might. For that, you need a predictive model that scores donors based on their likelihood to do something. A predictive model uses a combination of existing data and additional external data to identify the independent and dependent variables in the model. The independent variable is the "cause" variable (what is to be expected) and the dependent variable is the "effect" variable (what is to be explained). Predictive models use data science and statistical know-how to determine the best performing cause of the desired effect.

Advanced analytics can also be used to determine how much a nonprofit should ask a donor to give. Yes, predictive modeling can be a powerful way to determine the recommended next ask amount for a donor. Target Analytics' research across thousands of nonprofit organizations reveals that a lot of money is being left on the table. The average nonprofit is missing out on $3,781,461 in untapped giving potential. That is a combination of under-asking with both annual gifts and major gifts. The analysis revealed that an average upgrade capacity of $52 was possible for annual donors and a potential lift $1,197 existed for major donors.

Source: Target Analytics, a division of Blackbaud

The ability to recommend the next ask amount for a donor is an example of how external data can help make more data driven decisions. Many non-profits base their ask amounts only on their data. This illustrates a blind spot for nonprofits: while they may know how much someone donates to them, they don't know how much that same donor gives to other charities. In the United States, people who give to charity tend to support multiple organizations each year. How many nonprofits they give to does vary by age and other factors, but it can range from four to eight or more charities per year. Companies like Target Analytics have built up unique data sources on charitable giving that can be used as part of ask amount recommendations.

For example, a donor to your nonprofit has been giving $150 every year for many years now. A best practice is to try and move that donor up to a higher amount over time. This is a good idea, in part because donors tend to get stuck on a giving amount and become difficult to move upward after too long. While they may have the capacity to give more, these donors have been trained to only give a certain amount and moving them to a higher gift level can be challenging. A predictive model is able to look at not only your donor data but also external charitable giving data to recommend an optimal ask amount. That $150 donor may be giving more to other nonprofits or they may have data characteristics that suggest a higher capacity and affinity to make a larger donation.

These are just some examples of how data can be used to reveal hidden treasure. Throughout the rest of this book, there will be other examples of how data can be used to make more informed decisions. Nonprofit organizations of all shapes and sizes have the potential to unlock the hidden treasure in their data. Uncovering and utilizing your organization's vast data assets is one of the first steps to becoming a more data driven nonprofit.

# 04

# DRIVEN

*"If we have data, let's look at data. If all we have are*
*opinions, let's go with mine."*

- JIM BARKSDALE

## PARADOX

When you have something valuable, the more you have of it, the richer you become. If you have more time or talent or treasure, then those valuable things increase your overall value. The same is not true for many nonprofits and their data. This is what I call the Nonprofit Data Paradox: the more you have of something valuable, the less valuable it becomes.

Data should be a valuable asset that enriches nonprofits and helps them grow. Instead, many get overwhelmed by the flood of data, fail to maintain it, or choose to ignore it all together. The constituent records are spread across multiple systems. The analytics tool is connected to the website, but no one is paying attention to what is happening. The mailings go out, the undeliverable mail comes back in. Donors, members, alumni, activists, volunteers, and any other group the nonprofit engages with are kept apart in their data cages. Decisions are made solely based on opinions without data having its say. The data piles up and up. Oceans of data in silos. Gathered up in the digital attic for storage. Left to endure the elements in the file cabinet farmhouse. The more you have, the less valuable it becomes.

But we are not prisoners to this paradox. Nonprofit organizations can break free. We can not only unlock the hidden potential in the data but also drive more results that help make change in the world. All we need is a vision for the future, a path to get there, and the willingness to take the first steps in the journey to becoming data driven nonprofits.

VISION

Data driven nonprofits accelerate change in the world by using data to influence strategy and inform decisions that produce value and impact. The strategy of a nonprofit is influenced by data and acts as a compass to confirm that the organization is heading in the right direction. The decisions made at a nonprofit are all informed by data as opposed to just mere opinion. Value and impact are created by transforming data into information and insights.

# DATA DRIVEN NONPROFITS

Data driven nonprofits accelerate change in the world by using data to influence strategy and inform decisions that produce value and impact.

The first step to becoming a data driven nonprofit is understanding that every byte yearns to become wisdom. The modern discipline of knowledge management began with the idea that organizations must acquire, share, and effectively use information. The data and the organizations mature over time as the data is turned into insights.

Russell Ackoff popularized our modern notion of how data matures. Ackoff was an accomplished management consultant and former professor of management science at the Wharton School of the University of Pennsylvania. This is important because Ackoff's focus was not on the technical underpinnings of data, but instead on the practical use of it by humans. To drive his point home, Ackoff would note that "on average, 40% of the human mind consists of data, 30% information, 20% knowledge, 10% understanding, and virtually no wisdom."[31]

Even Ackoff's slightly cynical view on data use has matured over time to form the basis for modern information management. The Data-Information-Knowledge-Wisdom hierarchy is often represented as a pyramid and used across a wide variety of industries to put data use into context. The same evolution in the use of data happens in nonprofit organizations across the globe. They are harnessing the power of data to create measurable value in their organizations.

Being a data driven nonprofit does not remove the need for the human element. At the end of the day, people are making the decisions based on the information that they have. No one is suggesting that we turn over critical decisions to robots or the Big Data wizard in the cloud. Instead, the use of data by nonprofit professionals to enhance the work they are doing has the biggest opportunity to create more growth and change.

By itself, data is just a raw material and needs refinement. Nonprofits should avoid collecting data just for the sake of it. Data only matters if it drives action. Otherwise, it can be just a distraction. Data is the glue that holds people, process, and technology together. It is the common undercurrent that gives insights into what is really happening.

Data driven decisions help to provide direction to nonprofit leaders. We often hear of the desire to have a complete view of constituent engagement and activities. But a 360-degree view without direction just leaves you running around in circles. The future of the nonprofit sector is one in which passionate professionals are armed with data insights to maximize their performance in critical areas. In the future, there are more donor-centric organizations because they made the choice to leverage data to build relationships at scale. Nonprofits are more accountable and transparent in the future thanks to the use of data and metrics. This is an exciting time to work in the nonprofit sector and the opportunities in front of organizations are immensely valuable.

It must also be acknowledged that this journey to the future will not be an easy one for some organizations. Everyone likes change, but not everyone likes changing. Being data driven will push people outside their comfort zone and beyond the confines of their current experiences. This is as much about personal growth and development as it is about what happens to the nonprofit. There is no growth without change. There is no change without bringing people along on the journey. All the data in the world does not replace the importance of the human element.

## PATH

The journey to becoming a data driven nonprofit is not an unknown path. For decades, companies, governments, and nonprofit organizations have matured in their use of data and analytics to improve performance. The emergence of data analysis, business intelligence, and Big Data has unlocked the barriers to getting more value out of data. Over time, the resources needed to extract this value from the data have become not only commonplace but also more affordable.

Over the years, a data maturity scale for the nonprofit sector has emerged. This scale is a way to measure how nonprofits are using data and understand the types of value that can be obtained. It covers everything from a baseline level of the use of data in its raw form all the way up to prescriptive analytics to drive decision-making. While nearly all nonprofits use data and reports, a transition to more advanced analytics needs to happen eventually. As nonprofits mature along the scale, they move from decisions made in hindsight to more data informed decisions with foresight.

The beginning of the path to being a data driven nonprofit starts with the collection of raw data and proactive cleaning of that data. Collecting and managing the data answers the question: Did it happen? That also implies that if you don't have the data, it did not happen. Many nonprofits train their staff members to know that if data for a particular activity is not collected in a system, it cannot be used or measured for performance purposes. Having healthy data is tables stakes for the world we live in. This is because data health is the baseline requirement for all other analytics that help data driven nonprofits. In an earlier chapter, we reviewed the importance of data health along with the key building blocks for collecting data, managing it, and keeping it clean. Every step up in the nonprofit data maturity scale depends on healthy data practices and processes.

The next step on the path to data driven enlightenment is the use of descriptive analytics. Descriptive analytics answers the question: What happened? Nonprofits use data in descriptive analytics to make decisions about what happened with a fundraising appeal, an email campaign, or a recent event. Descriptive analytics takes form in standard reports and ad-hoc reports that are commonplace in just about every nonprofit. This also includes all those custom reports created for people who always seem to need just one more column added to a report in order to unlock the mysteries of the universe. Descriptive analytics like age, income, geography, and actions are used to segment constituents into distinct groups. If you have ever written a query or asked for a list of constituents, then you've used descriptive analytics. The major shortcoming of descriptive analytics is that it only tells you what happened in the past. Driving using the rearview mirror might be useful for a few feet, but it is not recommended for long distances. Descriptive analytics is used to understand things in hindsight but is not useful to see what is happening right now or what might happen in the future.

Diagnostic analytics is the next step up on the nonprofit data maturity scale and its use has grown tremendously over the past decade. With it, nonprofits can begin to see data being turned into information and knowledge. The ability to see a cause and effect relationship allows nonprofits to understand why something happened. Today, the most common uses of diagnostic analytics are dashboards and alerts across the systems being used. Dashboards surface a distilled set of information to users rather than overwhelming them with all the raw data. Think about the dashboard of your car and the bite-sized pieces of information it displays to keep you informed. Speed, direction, and fuel consumption are all displayed in an easy to consume manner. A "Check Oil" alert is displayed rather than the exact amount of oil detected in the reservoir by a sensor in the engine. The same is true for dashboards and alerts that are commonplace among most nonprofit organizations. How is that email campaign performing? How close are we to the goal on event registrations? How many major gift prospect visits have been made this month versus the planned goal? But be careful not to overdo it with dashboards or alerts. Only put information on them if you actually intend to take action if something changes. Diagnostic analytics gives nonprofits insights into what is happening across the organization and enables it to make decisions based on information. That convergence of small bits of information, decision-making, and insight might seem trivial, but it helps build muscle tone for bigger data driven decisions. The presence and use of diagnostic analytics is a key sign that a nonprofit organization is maturing in its use of data. It helps set the stage for bigger opportunities.

Level three nonprofits utilize predictive analytics to take what they know about the past and present to help predict the future. Reports only tell a non-profit what happened in the past, alerts tell them what is happening right now, and predictive analytics tells them the likelihood of something happening in the future. This level of maturity involves the use of statistical analysis and predictive modeling, which require a step up in skillset and data know-how. Statistical analysis is an effective way to help forecast what will happen in the future to help make better decisions. If you wanted to set a goal for an end-of-year fundraising appeal, then would you just take last year's number and add 10%, or would you use forecasting? That is not a trick question. In prior chapters, we discussed at length the ways that predictive analytics can be used at a nonprofit organization. The key concept to understand is that predicting the likelihood of something can be a powerful way for nonprofits of any size to create more value. Predictive modeling removes the guesswork from prioritizing the best opportunities and allows a nonprofit to focus more time on the right prospects or donors. At this level, we see nonprofits building in-house expertise and using the help of external partners. Throughout the rest of the book, you will get firsthand examples from nonprofits using predictive analytics. The most successful organizations tend to purchase external data and modeling services and leverage their internal team of data analysts to improve their foresight.

The top level in the nonprofit data maturity scale involves the use of prescriptive analytics. Here we see organizations focus on using all their data assets to support decision-making and optimize their performance. Prescriptive analytics suggests the optimum decision for a situation given all the underlying data. Nonprofit staff still make the final decision, but they are informed by descriptive, diagnostic, and predictive analytics in that process. For example, in traditional predictive modeling, a donor might be given an annual gift likelihood score on a scale from zero to 1000. A trained prospect researcher might understand the difference between a 705 and an 862, but other fundraisers may not. Prescriptive analytics might suggest not only that this constituent is an ideal annual fund donor, but also recommend an ask amount. At this level, organizations also use analytics for performance management. Understanding the appropriate number of visits to a major gift prospect or the conversion rate needed to reach a goal can all influence decision-making. Although less than 1% of nonprofits make use of prescriptive analytics today, it holds a tremendous amount of promise for the future of the nonprofit sector.

## FIRST STEPS

The first steps in any journey are critical to the success of the endeavor. Skeptics await the first signs of failure and the anxious members of the group need to see signs of success early on. This is why the first steps to becoming a more data driven nonprofit need to be measured and specific. Building a culture of data use is about evolving people's attitudes, behaviors, and habits.

As the nonprofit data maturity scale suggests, everything begins with quality data. This must be one of the first steps your nonprofit takes. Data analysts commonly spend 80% of their time cleaning and managing data before any major analysis is done. Some like to use the cliché "garbage in and garbage out" to describe the flow of data. I reject this mindset and favor a No Garbage Rule that states: We collect data that is actionable, clean data that is valuable, and recycle information that is meaningful, but we don't keep garbage data. Keeping your data healthy is essential to determining what is trash and what is treasure.

Establishing a regimented and rigorous data health program is an important first step. If your organization has done a relatively good job of maintaining data health over time, then this is going to be a quick win. If your organization has ignored the health of your data, then there is going to be some short-term pain followed by long-term gain. A fundamental part of any data health program is to focus on implementing regular data check-ups and building habits that contribute to better data quality, like running address updates and validation against the constituent data at least four times a year. Deduplicating the data on a regular basis as well as after significant imports helps increase overall quality and reduces costs. Appending additional demographic and descriptive data such as age, phone number, email address, and other information on an annual basis is recommended. The best performing nonprofits have more extensive data health processes in place, but those have been built up over time. They took similar first steps at one point in time to get where they are now. During the first few weeks and months, building the right habits around data health that form the basis of long-term value creation is the top priority.

The other important first step is to start eliminating rogue sets of data throughout the organization. That spreadsheet with event attendees sitting on someone's computer and not in a centralized system. The homegrown pivot tables that maroon data on an island of mystery. Every nonprofit should have an amnesty program that rewards staff for turning in their secret stash of data. The good news is that the presence of these disparate data sets shows that people view information as an important part of their job. The bad news is that, for a multitude of reasons, they aren't having their needs met and have gone rogue. A sign of progress in your data driven evolution will come when people willingly use common systems and data as opposed to making it up as they go. Ultimately, data is democratized across the organization where people have access to it so it can be used to help them solve real problems.

Another early step to becoming more data driven is to find a project for the organization that involves answering an important question. Having all this data doesn't mean much if you're not doing something valuable with it. The goal here is to have a real-life test drive of data informed decision-making by a team of people at the organization. Do not pick an area that is too big or complex to start with. Likewise, don't choose a question that can be answered in an afternoon. This project needs to involve multiple people across the organization working together as a team. No points will be awarded for heroic individuals that go off and get the answers on their own. That's not the point of the exercise. You are trying to build habits and behaviors for the entire organization, not just one person. Time box the first project to 30 days and set the expectation that the team will be expected to present a set of decisions based on data at the end of the project.

The meeting where the team presents its findings and recommendations is another big first step in becoming data driven. Meetings are one of the biggest opportunities for nonprofits to become more data driven—and over time actually spend less time in meetings. At an organization that is data driven, the first part of a meeting should be spent reviewing the data as a group and answering questions. Do not fall into the trap of sending out the presentation slides in advance and assuming that everyone will read it. Instead, build good habits by giving people the opportunity to ask questions if they don't understand something or need help analyzing the information.

If you focus on using more data in meetings for 90 days, then I can almost guarantee that changes in attitudes, behaviors, and habits will happen in a positive way. The skills needed to analyze data are important, but we should be careful not to overlook the importance of how information is communicated. Does the team working on the data informed decisions review the findings before the meeting to practice their presentation? Are charts clearly labeled and easy to understand? Is there supporting commentary and not just facts thrown onto a page? The use of data is as much about the people working with it and the problems they are solving as it is about the technology involved.

Notice that the review of specific technologies and tools is left out of this discussion. That's intentional. Strategy comes before technology in the dictionary and so too it should in your planning. Far too many people jump to technology as the answer before they have even heard the question.

The focus should be on what problems you are trying to solve and what questions you want the data to help answer. Does it matter to a fundraiser that Sqoop is used to move terabytes of data into a four-node Hadoop cluster where MapReduce sorts and summarizes values so that Hive can produce a data warehouse for analysis? No, it does not.

From personal experience, I can tell you that the tools used to perform sophisticated analysis on Big Data are a changing landscape. As new problems emerge that need to be solved, so too will new tools. Three years ago, Apache Spark had not even been created yet. Today it has grown in popularity for solving the challenges of processing stream data. A solid strategy helps guide technology decisions and it accounts for tools and systems to be changed over time.

Over the past few years at Blackbaud, we've used a variety of technologies to manage and extract value from hundreds of terabytes of data. We began by implementing Hadoop, an open-source software framework for storing Big Data in a distributed fashion on large clusters of commodity hardware. From there, we layered in tools like MapReduce, Apache Hive, Cloudera Impala, Amazon Redshift, and other solutions.

In each case, we made a technology decision based on strategy and the problems we wanted to solve. It goes without saying that we also used data to inform that decision-making process. When you are processing tens of millions of records a day, understanding the volume and velocity of the data is extremely important. KPIs and dashboards help us see what is happening, which is always an input to the decision-making process.

The needs of our customers and business users also were part of the technology decision-making process. Target Analytics uses SAS for advanced analytics and predictive modeling development. SAS is not only the preferred tool by our data scientists but also considered the best solution on the market today. Whatever decision we made about our Big Data infrastructure needed to support SAS. We were able to find that through informed decision-making.

As it turns out, one of the co-founders of SAS, John Sall, has been very active in the nonprofit sector. His pioneering work in statistical modeling and visualization is matched by his passion for global conservation and environmental issues. Sall serves on the World Wildlife Fund board and the Smithsonian Institution's National Museum of Natural History advisory board and is also a former board member of The Nature Conservancy. Sall is a former trustee of North Carolina State University, where he studied graduate-level statistics.

Today, Sall is a co-founder and executive vice president at SAS where he leads the company's JMP business division. He notes that "the value of statistics is realized when it is translated, taught and delivered with accessible computing environments to the scientists and analysts who use it."[32] Sall's depth of experience with data, statistics, and the role they can play at a nonprofit gives him a unique perspective on what is happening right now. "It wasn't a surprise that the use of data has grown with the growth in the storage of data. It has been surprising that it is seen as a computer science versus a statistics discipline," says Sall. He also believes that with great data comes great responsibility to manage expectations. "It can be a little over-hyped and people have very high expectations. When they have Big Data they expect miracles and they aren't going to get miracles," he says.

Over the years, Sall has seen firsthand how the use of data has had an important impact on these organizations. "The use of data has grown popular with nonprofits in the same way it has with for-profit business. It is a way to help improve fundraising and other aspects of your operations," says Sall. The technology is important, but there are other factors influencing the productive use of data at a nonprofit. "A culture of experimentation is critical to the nonprofit mission. It is important to try out different approaches in the way you do your appeals with the web, email, or direct mail," he says.

Sall has seen the use of analytics evolve since he co-founded SAS with Jim Goodnight and two others in 1976. As the use of computers became more commonplace during the '80s and '90s, it meant that data also become more accessible. "In the 1990s, Six Sigma woke people up to take a look around to see what they could improve. It motivated them to try new things. It was a change in attitude that led to a change in methods. People need to stay awake, start experimenting, and see what works. The metrics allow you to see what works," says Sall.

It is also helpful to get his perspective as a board member for many years in the nonprofit sector. "In nonprofit board meetings, I see a lot of summary information that tries to bring to the front what really matters. I want to see what is mission-related, what advances the organization, and performance measures that use the best possible visualization to go with the data," says Sall. This is helpful insight and advice as data driven nonprofits need to have data informed boards to be successful.

One concern expressed by some nonprofit leaders is the challenges they face in measuring the effectiveness of their fundraising or programs. It is certainly true that not everything that counts can be counted. "People ask, 'Does this program really work? Does it deliver the things we really want?' Sometimes those are hard questions. It's not always easy to measure effectiveness," says Sall. He acknowledges that the mission of some organizations can be hard to measure or that incremental changes may not be as visible when viewed in isolation. "A lot of the organizations that I'm engaged with work on hard-to-measure problems, like climate change. It's easy to measure carbon dioxide, but hard to measure the impact of any one action on carbon dioxide. Every action is a small drop in the bucket. You might be effective and not able to see it. It's difficult, but in a lot of cases it's still possible," he says.

Nonprofits of all sizes and missions face challenging work. There are situations that cause frustration and questioning decisions. But we know that data can be a valuable tool in understanding the impact of this work. It is possible to have a vision for the future and being more data driven can be a positive force for change. Understanding where your nonprofit organization is today on the path to becoming data driven and the first steps to take is invaluable. Understanding the barriers nonprofits face on this journey is also important. Pretending that they don't exist does not make them go away any faster. Instead, the right skills, behaviors, attitudes, and habits can help nonprofits overcome challenges and create measurable value.

# 05

# MAGIC

*"Any sufficiently advanced technology is*
*indistinguishable from magic."*

- ARTHUR C. CLARKE

## PRESTO

To the uninitiated, the use of more advanced forms of analytics can appear to be either magic or witchcraft. Some nonprofit professionals look on with astonishment as predictive analytics perform feats of magic that appear to conjure insights from out of the unknown. Others have a more skeptical view, as if the dark arts of witchcraft were being used by charlatans in an attempt to fool fundraisers.

Over the years, I've seen very experienced nonprofit staff members express reactions to analytics ranging from "How did you do that?" to "How do you really know that will happen?" when presented with the results of predictive modeling. The perspective that analytics is a form of magic is at least closer to acceptance than a view that the data cannot be trusted. Those with the most skepticism about analytics are often people who have developed their own elixirs for donor segmentation, subject lines, or major gift cultivation. As if tribal knowledge should carry the same weight as rigorous testing.

There is a mistaken belief that this is a battle of art versus science for the survival of the nonprofit sector. That's pure rubbish. The debate over whether fundraising is an art or a science is a false choice. The reality is that successful nonprofits need both art and science. Unfortunately, there is not a magic wand we can wave that will make this transformation simple and painless. But we do have people, process, technology, and data to make it happen.

The corporate world is several years ahead of the nonprofit sector in its adoption of data and predictive analytics. Behind all the hype of Big Data, there are a lot of amazing things going on. An entire new career option has been created in the past few years: the data scientist. Even Hal Varian, the chief economist at Google, is quoted as saying, "The sexy job in the next 10 years will be statisticians. People think I'm joking, but who would've guessed that computer engineers would've been the sexy job of the 1990s?"[33] These data scientists bring to the table not only bring highly sought after skills but also a natural curiosity to solve problems. Later in this book, you'll hear from some of them on how they are driving real change in the nonprofit sector.

Data and data scientist are just one part of the change equation. If we want to find solutions to make nonprofits more data driven, then we need to first understand the problems that have prevented many of them from being more mature in the first place. When I decided to write a book about how nonprofits could better leverage data, there was a short list of people in the nonprofit sector that I considered true experts on the subject. At the top of the list was Chuck Longfield.

For more than 35 years, Longfield has been a pioneer in helping nonprofits effectively use technology and information to improve their fundraising performance. Longfield is widely known as the founder of Target Software Inc. and Target Analysis Group, Inc., which were both acquired by Blackbaud in 2007. Since then, Longfield has served as Blackbaud's chief scientist and has continued to drive innovative approaches to the use of data in the nonprofit sector.

The nonprofit sector has also recognized his expertise, insights, and contributions to the industry. Longfield was honored by *FundRaising Success* in 2007 with a lifetime achievement award for his contributions to the nonprofit sector and he was given the Direct Marketing Association's Max Hart Nonprofit Achievement Award in 2012.

Longfield has also turned his professional commitment to philanthropy into personal action through board service with the WGBH Educational Foundation, Mount Auburn Hospital, Lesley University, and other nonprofit organizations. Beyond the accolades and his years of experience, Longfield has always been willing to share his time to help others better understand the importance of data in the nonprofit sector.

What follows are excerpts from several transcribed conversations I had with Longfield on a range of topics. During the research work for this book, there were a number of burning questions that I wanted to try to answer. One of them was that if we know the use of data can significantly improve the performance of nonprofit organizations, then why aren't there more data driven nonprofits? Longfield begins his answer by noting, "Before I actually get to the specific question about data, let me talk about something that is probably the biggest impediment from taking advantage of this data. That impediment is the way most nonprofits take advantage of their data through segmentation and systems which enable that through queries."

Nearly every nonprofit of every shape and size wants to query their data to put constituents into actionable segments for mailing, phoning, emailing, prospecting, and other key engagement activities. "It's very common for a nonprofit to say, 'I want to send a letter to everybody who gave between $10 and $1,000 in the last three years.' That is a very standard renewal segmentation. In other words, I don't want to send it to the people over $1,000 because those people are going to receive a first class letter, and I don't want to do it to the people below $10 because they didn't give us enough money. And I don't want to go back more than three years because the response rate is too low on long lapsed donors and I'd be wasting my money. That's the segment that I'm looking at," explains Longfield.

This context is very important to understanding how nonprofits use data as part of their daily routine. Longfield goes on to say, "The reason that I bring this up and why it's important to explain is that when you have two variables like that, segmentation is really easy. Most nonprofits can even deal with a third variable, like the number of gifts. But if I were to introduce three more variables, like gender, income, and age, then the world becomes way too complex."

The complexity quickly escalates and becomes overwhelming for most people. "In fact, one way of thinking of segmentation is that if have three variables and each variable has three breaks, then you have 27 segments (3 x 3 x 3). If you introduce three more variables, then very quickly the possible number of segments goes into the thousands or the millions," he says.

If you were trying to do the calculations in your head, then imagine trying to do the actual segmentation work manually or through brute force. "Nobody's going to be able to type the query or write the memo that says to the database administrator, 'I want to take the people who are male, who came to the website twice, who called the call center, who gave between $50 and $100, and on and on and on. I want to send them this letter and I want to ask them for this amount of money through this channel,'" says Longfield.

This leads to nonprofits using only very basic segmentations that are not robust enough to produce better results. This helps to explain why Recency, Frequency, and Monetary (RFM) segmentation has been widely adopted by fundraisers. You can hold these three variables in your mind at the same time, but adding another 10 or 20 is impossible. The art can't scale to keep up with the science.

Longfield notes, "RFM dominates because I can visualize what I'm doing. By the way, RFM are three awesome variables because they also have continuity, so they don't jump around. Amounts go from $0 to $10, $11 to $20, $20 to whatever. The other great thing is that the variables are directional: $10 is better than $5, $25 is better than $10, $100 is better than $25, and on up. If I gave a year ago, that's better than giving my last gift two years ago, better than giving my last gift three years ago and on. Two gifts are better than one gift, but three are better than two."

Both continuity and directionality are two great characteristics to have in a data set. Longfield adds that they're also "completely continuous from zero to infinity." He says, "I can chop them up into segments. In terms of where the value is, each group increases in value. It's not like the $100 people are worse than the $50 supporters."

This all helps to explain why RFM was borrowed from the world of direct marketing and applied to nonprofit fundraising with great fanfare. "RFM has ruled for decades. I can write the memo. I can visualize the world. I can create value and know this segment is better than that segment and if I have to cut some segment out because I don't have the money to send all that mail or make that many phone calls or whatever, I know where to cut. I cut at the lower dollar amounts or the fewer gifts," he says.

You might be wondering what the catch is, so here you have it: "That's RFM, but people have immense amounts of data in their systems and they have had it for decades. They know whether the person volunteers or gives through multiple channels. They know whether the person has opened an email or called the call center. Yet, the tool through which all this data must be funneled to create value can't handle it," explains Longfield.

I've come to call this problem the Nonprofit Data Paradox: the more you have of something valuable, the less valuable it becomes. Data is one of the most valuable assets that a nonprofit has because of its potential to drive revenue, programs, and change in the world. And yet its value dramatically drops for many nonprofits as the volume, variety, and velocity of data increases. Something that should exponentially increase in value actually decreases at a very precipitous rate. Staff members can't do (or aren't equipped to do) more than the most basic segmentations. But not all hope is lost. If you look hard enough, then you often find that the problem itself contains the solution.

Longfield's 35 years of experience in the nonprofit sector help to reveal a solution to this problem. "What do nonprofits need? They need predictive models. They need something that says what the correlation is of each of these variables to the thing that they're trying to predict or generate," he says. Correlations are important because they show a predictive relationship between variables in the data. It's not random chance or mere coincidence that causes someone to take action, give a gift, participate, and be a vocal supporter of a nonprofit. These things are knowable and predictable.

Longfield says, "If I'm trying to do the ask string and I want someone to give more money, it would be nice to know how wealthy they are, but I also need to know how that was correlated. If men give more money than women, then I need to know how much more, because I need to know how that's correlated to the ask string and on and on: giving over the Internet, using my credit card, any number of things. If I simply wanted to set the ask string that was going to be used based on your last gift of $100 and I want to say $100, $200, $300, and if you're wealthy maybe I want to use $110, $220, and $330."

The variables and the correlations can also differ at nonprofit organizations in other parts of the sector. "If you were in the university market, there are three great variables: were you on financial aid and you feel indebted to the university? Did you play varsity sports? Is your family a legacy? That is, are your children at the university or did your parents go there? Every one of those things would maybe bump up that ask string just a little bit, and make me a little more aggressive in my fundraising or mail you one more time than the people who didn't have these characteristics. But I can't do that with segmentation. Nobody could write the query. Nobody could write the memo," says Longfield.

If the first major barrier to being more data driven is the lack of the use of predictive models, then the second obstacle comes back to not having the right incentives in place to capture key data in the first place. This can become a costly spiral as the lack of the right data prevents better predictive analytics, which means resources to get better data never get funded. The key step is for nonprofit organizations to both incentivize people to get the right data and then actually do something with it.

Longfield has done a lot of research into the hidden value inside data that is often ignored by nonprofits. "A variable I've highlighted is that if somebody calls the customer service desk and they say, "You guys are the best. I love you guys." I say that in an email, I say that in a text message, I say that over the phone, but I actually say it to you, that you guys are the best," he explains. "If you were the call center or the person reading those emails and you're supposed to get through 1,000 of them today or the phone is going to be all backed up and ringing and people are on hold, if you're not incentivized to put that data into the system, what you'd probably try to do is get off the phone call. Or you read the email and you don't reply or you don't put it in the system. That staff person doesn't do the kinds of things that would help pass that information along because they don't get any benefit from recording it. Doing that just makes the amount of time that you're spending in these interactions longer and you're probably incentivized to not have the phone ring very much or for people being put on hold for very long wait times," says Longfield.

As you might imagine, that piece of information is highly unlikely to either get recorded or passed along to the right person if someone is not incentivized to do so. "The person who would benefit might be a major gift officer who now knows that a wealthy person really loves you, and that's the person I should be spending time stewarding. How does the major gift department incentivize the customer service desk to capture the information that might be valuable to them?" asks Longfield.

A great example of this is the relationship between direct mail donors and planned gift donors. As it turns out, a significant source of planned gift prospects are individuals that have been giving by direct mail for many years. We have all heard stories of someone giving a large bequest to a nonprofit in their will out of nowhere. The reality is that the bequest did not come out of nowhere. The plural of anecdote is not data.[34] Most good predictive models would have identified that individual with a high likelihood to make a planned gift. Which brings us back to the right incentives and actions. If you cut back on direct mail for certain prospects or supporters, there could be a downstream negative impact on planned gift donors.

Longfield tells a story in which "a large national nonprofit had a direct marketing person whose direct mail was being cut back because acquisition wasn't doing as well." He continues, "If you were judging direct mail on simply the amount of money in that silo, so, I spent a certain amount of money ($200) to find a new donor and, over the next five years, that new donor gave $300, then I just spent $200 to generate a net of $100. Somebody might say at some point, 'That ROI isn't worth it,' but if one out of every 1,000 people give planned gifts that average $25,000, then you would say, 'I would do more acquisition, not just because of the money that's in the direct mail silo, but because of the money that's also being generated in planned giving.'"

In an ideal world, the organization would strategically choose to invest more in the short-term to get the better long-term results. Unfortunately, the siloed nature of nonprofits means that groups often need to be incentivized to do the right thing. In this example, the planned giving department actually paid the direct marketing department to keep mailing to donors that at first glance might look like a poor investment.

For some, the potential value of doing things the right way is not enough to drive behavior. The fear of losing can often be more motivating than the prospect of gaining something. Economists and psychologists call this phenomenon "loss aversion." Several research studies suggest that losses are twice as powerful as gains. With that in mind, Longfield has identified some tangible examples of how not having the right data leads to lost opportunities. For example, what is the cost to a nonprofit when they misspell someone's name? As it turns out, donors are 10% less likely to make a donation to a nonprofit when their name is misspelled. Those donors with misspelled names that continue to give to the nonprofit decrease their gift by up to 12%. A typo costs as much as 20% of the revenue from those donors. Now ask yourself, whose job is it at a nonprofit to prevent typos?

The other opportunity cost is spending time with prospective donors when the investment really does not make sense. As we discussed before with direct marketing, these programs make decisions like this all the time. They understand the hard costs of pursuing relatively small donations where there is not the potential for a return on investment. They pivot and choose to spend their time and money when there are better opportunities. Longfield says, "In major giving, they tend not to do that very well. They don't have the volume of records to do that mathematically, nor are they really inclined to think that way. Some organizations have gotten better at creating milestones and evaluations around the likelihood that this person is going to give a gift in this fiscal year, what's the expected amount of money, and then rewarding major gift officers for getting better at that. Smaller organizations tend not to do that enough."

At smaller and even mid-sized nonprofits, there is a fear of writing off someone who might have big gift potential. This is a great example of loss aversion influencing behavior. Part of this comes from a flawed understanding of statistics and the notion that everything has a 50/50 chance of happening. "If that is your view of statistics, then every solicitation is either going to get me a big gift or not get me a big gift. Whereas if I really understand that this person has only a one in 100 chance and the amount of gift that I'm expecting is $10,000, then I simply do that multiplication," Longfield explains. "1/100th of $10,000 is $100, so this person's expected value to me is $100. Is that worth me having another dinner with them? No, it isn't. Whereas, someone else, if they're a one out of 10 chance of happening this year and they're a $1,000,000, then they obviously are a better ROI. Some organizations do that calculation on a regular basis," he adds. One of the things predictive analytics do is to help identify the likelihood of a donor being in the one-out-of-a-hundred group or the one-out-of-ten group.

This is where we really shift from fundraising as an art form to the science that helps drive better decision-making. Longfield has had a front row seat for this shift in the nonprofit sector over the last three decades. As with many debates that tried to choose one way or another, in reality, it's a false choice. Fundraising is not art or science — the best organizations recognize that it is art and science. Longfield says, "I think the challenge is that fundraising doesn't have the rigor in professional education. There really isn't an educational program when you compare it to, for example, a doctor going through the rigors that they go through. People who tend to get attracted to the fundraising profession aren't science or math kind of people to begin with." He goes on to note, "I think the people that get attracted to fundraising are very caring people who tend more to be, and I'm generalizing here, in the liberal arts, humanities, and they enjoy more the crafting of the letter or throwing an awesome event, et cetera, and that's all the art. When the science comes in, it's just a mismatch of skills."

Over the past few years, many of Longfield's presentations at nonprofit events across the sector have drawn other comparisons between the fields of medicine and fundraising. "As an industry, we either need to educate these people to be better at the science or--and none of these are mutually exclusive--build more of the science into the tools. Medicine does that a lot. When you're in a hospital bed there are five things that are typically monitored constantly, like your temperature, your heart rate, oxygen level, et cetera. It turns out that if you feed those five variables into a computer model, that leverages information about the correlation to catastrophic things that could be happening to you. You can actually predict heart attacks and other bad events hours before they happen. That's what's happening now. All that data is not necessarily going to the physician or nurse anymore. It's going to the predictive model that is saying to them, 'By the way, this guy's going to have a heart attack in about an hour,'" explains Longfield.

Longfield gives an example of how this exact same approach should be applied by fundraising professionals. "For a long time, on the direct marketing side, people have tried to build models that predict that somebody is going to stop giving to you so you can actually do something before they stop giving," he says. "Somebody who used to give you $100 dollars gave you $50 instead; that's an early warning sign. If somebody gave you $100 in December every year but this year didn't give it in December, or gave you an additional gift and now didn't give you the additional gift, or any number of things like that, then you could do something about it if the system said to you, 'By the way, this guy has a high risk of leaving you,' just like, 'This guy has a high risk of a heart attack,'" says Longfield.

Just like in the medical profession, there is a certain degree of specialization that happens in nonprofit organizations. Oftentimes, the fundraising profession expects people who are really only skilled in a specialty, like annual giving or major giving, to be general practitioners across a variety of giving programs. "I now have looked at enough organizations' entire fundraising program in detail to say with a fair amount of data that most organizations, almost irrelevant to size, are usually pretty good at one or two things and not good at the others. In other words, nobody is uniformly good, nor is anybody usually uniformly bad," says Longfield.

This tends to happen because nonprofit organizations have scarce resources, there is a lot of churn in staff, and people bring a certain skill set or bias to an organization. Longfield explains, "If I came from a university and I was a major gift officer and now I'm running your organization's fundraising department, then we're going to be good at major gift fundraising, but we're not going to be that good at direct marketing. Maybe we'll be good at matching gifts because we did that at my university too. On the other hand, if I came from an organization that just had a direct mail list and we used to mail to that list and people sent in gifts, maybe I stink at major gift fundraising."

The long-term problem that this creates is a lack of innovation or diversification in revenue channels for a nonprofit organization. If 80% of your revenue is tied to direct mail or major giving or any one source of revenue, that creates a tremendous amount of risk and exposure for the organization. Just as we need to reject the art versus science debate, we also need to have a sense of urgency to diversify fundraising.

Longfield has identified several reasons why this does not happen at most nonprofit organizations. The first issue is that most nonprofits do not understand the financial opportunity of doing a better job at a particular activity. He cites an example from a public broadcasting station that has gone from single digits to now 40% of their donors being monthly sustainers. "They saw that if they did better at sustainers, then they had a big opportunity and there wasn't anything else that they could do that would generate that kind of money. Matching gifts wasn't enough, fixing duplicated donors wasn't either, but sustainers was a big enough opportunity," he says.

In the absence of knowing what opportunity exists, there is no incentive or willingness to go after it. The opportunity is invisible to the organization, so they just say that sustainers or matching gifts or whatever would not work at their organization. "That's pretty much what people said. 'It doesn't work, so that's not an opportunity.' On the other hand, I could simply have a bias. I don't like major gift fundraising. I don't like doing it. You're going to ask me, as the development director, to go meet with these people and ask them for gifts. I simply don't like doing it, so I'm not doing it. But when you actually show it on a report and say, 'It's a $2 million opportunity,' then it makes it a little more tangible," says Longfield.

The second reason that nonprofits do not diversify their fundraising programs is they don't know the business practices that allow them to maximize an identified opportunity. "You say I should be doing 3% in matching gifts and I'm doing 1/10 of 1%. I already put on my reply device that if you work for a matching company, please send it in, so what else do you want me to do? It's not clear to them that there are five other things that you could be doing and they're all easy and if you did the five of them, you'd be at 3%, not at 1/10 of 1%," says Longfield. They don't know the best practices like contacting every matching gift donor from last year and reminded them to match their gift again this year. "I don't know what the business practices are, so I can't judge whether I have the capability of doing it or whether the cost of doing it is actually worth the revenue that I could gain," he says.

The third issue of why nonprofits don't reduce risk and diversify their giving programs is that there is not a willingness to invest. Longfield says, "Nonprofits make poor financial decisions simply because they don't have the money. It's just extraordinary how unbusinesslike that is." He went back to his example in public broadcasting to prove the point. David Preston was the membership director at Twin Cities Public Broadcasting. His magic trick was going from single digits to 40% of the donor base becoming sustainers. To do that he first used analytics to size the opportunity of growing his sustainer donors, but then he ran into a problem that stops most nonprofits.[35] "When David Preston saw that he could do a better job converting single gift donors to sustainers, but he couldn't afford to go get them because, if you go get them, you lose about half of their revenue in the first year," explains Longfield. "What David did, which was very creative, is he went to the CFO and he asked for a loan, a half million-dollar loan. He got the loan and said he'd pay it back in a couple of years. Then he went and got the sustainers. That is way too businesslike for the average nonprofit. Nobody would trust a fundraiser with a half million-dollar loan to go do something like that, and most fundraisers wouldn't even want to go take the risk," he says.

An opportunity clearly remains for the nonprofit sector and the companies that serve it to help create more scale. We already see this today with tele-marketing, direct mail, and other key functions that are done at scale for lower cost to nonprofits. With the exception of a few organizations, most would not invest to run their own mail house or telemarketing operation. But where is the high scale and lower cost option for matching gifts or sustainers? Could there be a way to engage more mid-level donors if collaboration or economies of scale were created? Admittedly, there are more questions than answers on how to solve the investment problem in the nonprofit sector. Perhaps a good place to start is that the status quo is not sustainable and we need to be open to different approaches throughout the nonprofit sector.

The last challenge that prevents the nonprofit sector from improving its results is the shadow belief that everyone's donors are different. I've stopped counting the number of times someone has told me, "Steve, you just don't understand, but our donors are different, and fill-in-the-blank would never work here." Nonprofits might be able to make the case that their organizations are all unique, but the common denominator among each of them is the human donors. Even from a DNA perspective, humans are 99.9% the same.[36] Decades of data and research reveal common patterns of behavior among donors. And it's not just the signals in the data that are the same, but the actual donors themselves.

With over three decades of nonprofit data analysis behind him, Longfield's most recent research serves as a wake-up call for the nonprofit sector. "My newest research is just how few donors there really are in the country. All that money is mostly being given by a relatively small pool of people," he says. "The donor pool is actually smaller than people think because people think the donor pool is all of the households in the country, so 140 million households, but it really isn't. The donors are really in 70 million households. Of that 70 million households, about 10 million households are responsible for most of the money. We're down to something like 10 million or 20 million people," says Longfield.

You may have heard of the Pareto Principle and how 80% of the effects come from 20% of the causes. Its namesake is Vilfredo Federico Damaso Pareto, an Italian philosopher, engineer, sociologist, and economist. In 1896, Pareto published research that showed that 80% of the land in Italy was owned by 20% of the population.[37] The Pareto Principle's 80–20 distribution also shows up in biology, economics, and a host of other areas. But in fundraising, the law of the vital few is more severe. Longfield's recent analysis of over $18 billion in charitable giving found that 82% of gifts come from only 10% of donors. "Those people are responsible for most of the giving in the country and those people are fairly generous," he explains. "What's even worse is that while you may have donors from other segments outside those 10 million or

20 million people, those other donors give you less money. If I said, 'How many of your donors are in this 10% sweet spot?' it might be 60% of your donors. If I said, 'How much of your money comes from donors in that sweet spot?' it's not 60%, it's 70 or 80% of your money," says Longfield.

The donorCentrics Index of Direct Marketing Fundraising Performance shows that since 2010, there has been a 12% decrease in donors and a 17% drop in new donors to nonprofits.[38] The only thing that has produced revenue growth is better donor retention from some organizations and increased generosity by a smaller pool of donors. The growing emergence of the sweet spot is hiding somewhere in all that data. This all points back to the need to use both art and science to improve fundraising. Longfield says, "You're way more dependent on this universe of donors. There are lots of people on the outside of this sweet spot that dabble. They give one gift to a cancer organization and they give one gift to an animal charity, but they're not the bulk of donations in this country. So if you're going to focus on anybody, it's those 10 million people and they are getting asked by everybody, so you better get better at what you're doing." Getting better is not going to come from more tactics or clever tricks. It's going to come from artful application of data science to fundraising.

Over the next decade, there will be a widening divide between data driven nonprofits and those that remain anchored to their tribal knowledge tactics. Supporters will begin to gravitate to those nonprofits where donor engagement, cultivation, and stewardship happen through the art and science of fundraising. Longfield has his own predictions for the coming future of the nonprofit sector: "It's going to continue to get more competitive. It's going to continue to get more technical. People are going to need greater scale and capacity to be able to compete. The nonprofits at the low end are going to continue to struggle." In terms of offering some hope, he says, "If a few organizations can learn to collaborate and create virtual scale better through collaboration, they'd be better off."

That is sound advice from someone who has probably done more data analysis on the nonprofit sector than anyone else in the past three decades. His concern for the nonprofit sector goes beyond his professional interests. It's personal, too. Many people don't know that Longfield once taught math to middle and high school students before starting the Target companies. That background is evident in the work of the Longfield Family Foundation to increase the number of high-performing schools in Boston. He doesn't just talk about the importance of data, he's also investing his own time and money to make real change in the world. He is as genuine as he is wise, and I consider myself very fortunate to have had the opportunity to work with him over the years.

# 06

# PYRITE

*"Supernovas are where gold forms; the only place.*
*All gold comes from supernovas."*

- ALAN MOORE

## FOOL'S GOLD

One of them is rare. One of them is a common mineral. One is extremely valuable. One is practically worthless. One is only made in the supernova of a star. One naturally occurs in rock formations. The only thing they have in common is how they look on the surface. And for that reason, they are easily mistaken for one another.

Gold is both a rare and valuable metal. A single ounce is worth more than $1,000. Gold does not rust or tarnish and it can't be counterfeited. Gold is portable, divisible, durable, consistent, and very convenient. All the gold that has ever been discovered would only fill two Olympic-sized swimming pools. Pyrite, on the other hand, is not rare at all and is worth very little. Pyrite has a yellow color but exposure to the elements can make it turn red, purple, orange, or blue. But people are often confused by the outward appearance of pyrite and mistake it for gold. Pyrite is often called "fool's gold" because of its deceptive appearance.

The easiest way to distinguish gold from pyrite is a by doing a streak test. When gold is scraped against a piece of unglazed white porcelain it will always leave a yellow streak. Pyrite leaves a green or black streak. The worlds of data and statistics also have their own tests to ascertain their validity. Whether you are a nonprofit professional, a service provider to the nonprofit sector, or a member of the media that covers the industry, you need to have a certain level of data literacy. We don't even need to get into the discussion of a p-value or analysis of variation (ANOVA) to understand the difference between good statistics and bad ones.

Once released into the wild, statistics have a tendency to take on a life of their own. It's much like the telephone game that we played as children: One person whispers something to someone, who whispers it to another person, and on it goes around the room. Then the last person shouts out what they heard and it's completely different from the original message. Laughter and general merriment ensue. This is a less amusing game when a statistic gets distorted far afield from its original meaning or intent.

A frequently cited statistic in the nonprofit sector is that 95% of Americans give to charity. A search of the Internet and social media finds all manner of variations on the statistic:[39]

- "95.4% of households donate to charities"
- "The majority of American households, 95.4%, donate to charities"
- "Each year, approximately 95.4% of households give to charity"
- "95.4% of households give to charity"
- "While it's estimated that 2/3 of people in the U.S. give to charity every year, that adds up to an impressive 95.4% of households that give to charity"
- "95.4% of Americans participate at some level of charitable giving"
- "According to the latest statistics from the National Philanthropic Trust, a whopping 95.4% of all U.S. households give to charity"

There's just one problem with this statistic — it's not true. Wait! What? Yes, this statistic is repeated time and time again and, like the telephone game, it no longer resembles the original message. Even the source of the statistic appears to be a mystery.

While I was working on this book, the author, strategist, and media expert Brian Reich tweeted, "I take issue with Blackbaud's data (for example, their ridiculous claim that 95% of people give)." We exchanged tweets and I let him know that Blackbaud wasn't the source of that stat. But I made a vow to actually dig into this wayward data point and explain its true origins.

My detective work began by tracing down when the statistic began being used and what source it was attributed to. Many media reports said that it came from the National Philanthropic Trust. Further searching led me to find that the National Philanthropic Trust cited a study by Bank of America and Indiana University. Alas, I found a copy of "The 2014 Bank of America Study of High Net Worth Philanthropy conducted by the Center on Philanthropy at Indiana University" online. But even this report points to an earlier study and notes, "Almost all (98.4%) high net worth households gave to charity in 2013, an increase from the 95.4% that gave in 2011."[40] The mystery of the disputed statistic continued.

More statistical sleuthing was required to find the 2012 version of the same report that was based on 2011 data. The 2012 report notes that "the vast majority (95.4%) of high net worth households continued to give to charity in 2011. Although the findings show a 3 percentage point decline in the rate of giving by these households from 2009." The 95.4% statistic is not only not the latest version from 2014, but the number also appears to have changed between the 2009, 2011, and 2013 data sets.

Aha! So the mystery has finally been solved. We now know that the 95.4% statistic is from a 2012 report based on 2011 data. But that's not the biggest problem with this statistic. Saying that "95.4% of Americans give to charity" is not what the report actually says. In fact, the study actually reports that 95.4% of high net worth households gave to charity in 2011 based on a survey sent to "20,000 high net worth donors in America's wealthiest neighborhoods."[41] The 12-page survey was only completed by 996 of the 20,000 high net worth donors it was sent to. After excluding those donors not considered to be high net worth, the final sample size for this survey was 701 households.

Oh, and "high net worth households" were defined as "only households with incomes greater than $200,000 and/or net worth more than

$1,000,000 — excluding the monetary value of their home." The average net worth of households that responded to the survey was $10.7 million. In case you're wondering, the U.S. Bureau of the Census estimates that there about 124 million households in the country and the University of Michigan's Panel Study of Income Dynamics (PSID) noted that median household income in the U.S. was $56,335 in 2013.[42] Not exactly the typical American household.

After all this data detective work, the real statistic should be: 95.4% of high net worth households in the United States claim to have donated to at least one charity in 2011 based on a survey of 701 households with an average net worth of $10.7 million. But perhaps that's just too long for a headline or a tweet. Instead, the telephone game turns it into something very different — fool's gold.

## VANITY METRICS

The Internet has brought with it an explosion in the amount of content and cat videos in recent years. One popular content trick is what is called a "listicle," which is simply a list or ranking of things used as the main element of a story. This format has spawned the "Top 5 Things Nonprofits Can Learn from Game of Thrones" or the "Top 25 Nonprofit Blogs" and "450 Email Subject Lines From End of Year Fundraising." I will take full responsibility for that last one.[43]

Some of these lists can be helpful, but you always need to read the fine print to see what data is being used. Let's take the article "2015's Most and Least Charitable States" from WalletHub as an example.[44] These kinds of lists are a marketer's dream because they get headlines like "Utah 'Most Generous State,' Analysis Finds" from both national and local media.[45] This article, in particular, got a lot of attention on social media and a fair amount of shares too.

At the very end of the article, WalletHub explains that their methodology "analyzed each of the 50 states across eight key metrics. Each metric was given a value between zero and 100, wherein 100 is the best value for that metric and zero is the worst." Those eight metrics and their weighting were:

- Volunteer Rate: Full Weight (~10.53 Points)
- Percentage of Adjusted Gross Income Donated: Double Weight (~21.05 Points)
- Percentage of the Population Who Claim to Have Donated Time: Full Weight (~10.53 Points)
- People Who Donated Money to Charity (percentage of taxpayers who donated money to charity and percentage of the population who claim to have donated money): Full Weight (~10.53 Points)
- Growth in Charitable Giving (2012 vs. 2006): Half Weight (~5.26 Points)
- Number of Public Charities per 10,000 Residents: Full Weight (~10.53 Points)
- Community Service Requirement for High School Graduation: Full Weight (~10.53 Points)
- Number of Volunteering Hours per Capita: Double Weight (~21.05 Points)

WalletHub also explained where the data came from: "Data used to create these rankings were obtained from the U.S. Census Bureau, the Corporation for National & Community Service, Education Commission of the States (ECS), the National Center for Charitable Statistics, the Internal Revenue Service, The Chronicle of Philanthropy, and Gallup."

On the surface, this list and the methodology look to be well done and somewhat legitimate. But a closer look starts to show some holes in the analysis that the typical reader might not be aware of. For starters, the weighting of the data has a strong bias towards volunteering. When all the volunteering-related activity is added up, it represents 53% of the total score.

Only two of the weighted values look at amount donated, "Percentage of Adjusted Gross Income Donated" and "People Who Donated Money to Charity," and they only account for 32% of the total score. Except neither of these measurements can show the total dollar amount given to nonprofits by residents of each state. The remaining 15% of the score comes from "Growth in Charitable Giving" and "Number of Public Charities per 10,000

Residents," which suggests that having more charities in your state means that you're more generous. And did I mention that the article also says that "95.4% of households donate to charities" — which we now know is a red flag.

Yes, I understand that people donate their time, talent, and treasure. Not all giving is financial in nature. The article does note that being charitable is more than just donating money. Unfortunately, these types of statistics are essentially vanity metrics. They sound good and might make residents of one state feel better, but it's not really clear what we are supposed to do with this information.

CHARTJUNK

Infographics have been all the rage in recent years. When done well they can help turn complex data into more digestible nuggets of visual information. Unfortunately, a byproduct of infographic-mania is that some combine data from a lot of different sources. This often results in comparing apples to oranges and confusing the intended audience.

Network for Good, a Certified B Corporation software company, has published statistics about online giving for many years now. In 2016, they published an infographic called "2015 Year in Review: The Digital Giving Index" on their website.[46] The first section on the infographic, called "The Growth of Online Donations," showed that online giving grew 9% in 2015 and overall giving grew 2% in the same year. They cited Blackbaud's Charitable Giving Report for those statistics. I recognized the stats right away as I've authored that report for many years now.

Right next to those statistics is a chart labeled "Donation Totals Since Inception." Is this chart showing the growth of all online giving? Has only just over $1.4 billion been given online since 2001? How does that compare to the amount of overall charitable giving? You have to read the fine print to know that the answers are: 1) No. 2) No. 3) It doesn't.

As it turns out, the chart is a cumulative total of online donations processed only by Network for Good since 2001. This chart is counting and not measuring, and the difference is very important. It does not show a year-over-year comparison, but instead just a running count over many years. The two charts shown at the top of the infographic are from completely different sets of data.

Are all these statistics true? Yes, this really is a count of donation data from Network for Good. Are these statistics accurate? Yes, but only when approached as independent data sets and with context. When we combine these without context, we are mixing apples with oranges. The sample sizes in the two data sets are also dramatically different: The data set cited from Blackbaud is from $18.2 billion in overall giving and $2.2 billion in online giving from 2015. The Network for Good data set used is only $242 million in online donations from 2015.[47]

You might be wondering if perhaps this is just a tempest in a teapot. Does it really matter? Yes, it absolutely matters because nonprofit organizations, the media, and the general public are influenced by these sound bite statistics. Nonprofit leaders and their boards also draw conclusions and make decisions based on data that is published. These pieces of data are used, shared, repeated, and, before long, they are accepted as a representation of reality.

In another example, data was picked up by the media and published online with the title "Online Giving Through Network for Good Exceeds $215 Million in the Past Year," which again is counting and not measuring.[48] How much more online giving was that than the prior year? Is that for the same nonprofits or does it include new nonprofits? Are some nonprofits doing better than others? Which ones, on a year-over-year basis? There are a lot of important questions that counting can't answer.

As a nonprofit decision-maker, I can make better decisions with the help of measuring. Value is found in knowing how much more or how much less online giving is growing, particularly for organizations like mine as it relates to performance year-over-year. An apples-to-apples comparison of the same organizations over the same exact period of time allows a nonprofit to take the data and measure their own results relative to the industry trends.

This same article references additional data from Network for Good with the following statements made:

- "Donors who gave from 55 and 59 times a year donated a median of $3,328 over the year, more than any other group."
- "Human Services groups received far more donations than any other cause."
- "California donors, who gave more than any other state, contributed $10,358,687 to Human Services groups and $40,699,487 to all causes combined."

Are all of these statements true based on the data set analyzed? Yes. But as a decision-maker, I might conclude from these statements that we should become a human services nonprofit in California and focus on donors that give between 55 and 59 times a year. On further inspection of the data, we might want to rethink that idea.

If you dig deeper into the donors who made the most gifts, you'll discover that there were only 43 donors that gave 55 to 59 times. The median amount given per donor is skewed by the fact there are so few of these donors. Compare that with the 985,707 donors that gave between one and four online gifts. While interesting to see, highlighting the median yearly giving per donor is not as actionable a statistic. What is the direction or decision that a nonprofit should make based on this data?

When you look at the giving by type of nonprofits, the human services organizations appear to be getting the most donations. Keep in mind that only 12% of all charitable giving in the United States goes to human services nonprofits. Because the data is not weighted it could lead to a small number of large nonprofits skewing the data. Otherwise this would be a surprising phenomenon in online giving that should be getting more attention.

Looking at giving by geography or state is a common way to present data. When data says that Californian donors gave more online than any other state, does that mean that donors in California are more generous? No. California is not more generous, it's just more populous. Without normalizing the data, California will almost always appear larger by comparison to other states. Normalizing data is the process of adjusting values on different scales to a more common scale. A more precise use of the data would be to report online giving on a per capita basis to make it a more normative representation of what is really happening in each state. This simple change would allow for a more effective comparison between large states like California and smaller ones like Delaware.

As a sector, we need to up our game when it comes to the use of statistics in published content. We need to stop counting when we should be measuring. We need to use standard practices in the analysis of data. We need to be more aware as information consumers about what the data is telling us and what it is not. This requires a higher level of data literacy from nonprofit professionals, the companies that serve them, and the media that covers the sector.

## DATA LITERACY
Data literacy is one of the most valuable skills that you can have today and as you move into the future. A data literate person possesses the skills to gather, analyze, and communicate information to support decision-making. The communication of information includes speaking, writing, and visualization. If you are reading this book, then you already have general literacy, the skill that allows us to derive information from the written word.

Literacy was a core part of the curriculum you were taught as a child. But most of us have had no formal education to make us data literate. This helps explain why data literacy is a challenge in the public, private, and nonprofit sector. One study estimates that "by 2018, the United States alone could face a shortage of 140,000 to 190,000 people with deep analytical skills as well as 1.5 million managers and analysts with the know-how to use the analysis of big data to make effective decisions."[49]

The good news is that elementary schools across the United States and several other countries are now making data literacy part of the curriculum for children. The topic of data literacy is also getting a lot of attention from researchers and higher education professionals. This would suggest that future nonprofit professionals will come into the sector with better data skills, but also higher expectations about the use of data in the decision-making process. Unfortunately, the nonprofit sector can't wait for Generation Z to graduate and join the workforce. We are going to have to put time and resources into improving our own data literacy and sharpening these skills across our organizations.

Among the dearth of scholarly research, there is a simple definition for us to work with: "Data literacy involves understanding what data mean, including how to read graphs and charts appropriately, draw correct conclusions from data, and recognize when data are being used in misleading or inappropriate ways."[50] Notice that this definition does not get into the technology involved or the data science skills required to develop things like predictive models. Instead, the key to data literacy is being able to use the information to make decisions. This also requires us to be able to recognize when the data we are being shown might be misleading or used in an inappropriate way.

A good place to start is how we consume and interpret external data from industry reports, infographics, and news articles. Here are some recommendations for improving your ability to analyze and get value from these types of external information:

**Always read the methodology:** Understanding if the data came from a survey, econometric model, self-reported data, or actual transactional data is very important. How did they analyze the data and what level of statistical rigor went into creating the findings? Surveys and self-reported data are especially problematic because they tend to be full of selection bias in the results. For example, online surveys are not a representative sample of the whole population and tend to overstate trends. For example, an online survey about the use of social media is likely to have a higher percentage of respondents saying positive things about social media. Self-reported information often has recall and response bias, especially when you ask people to rate how well they are doing in a particular area. For example, asking people if they did better or worse in their fundraising performance last year tends to overstate actual giving trends based on data. If there is no published methodology, then you probably need to question how the researchers came to their conclusions.

**Always find the sample size:** Knowing how much real data or how many responses make up the findings of the survey is critical. Is the sample size of 701 households out of 124 million total households significant? Are we measuring $242 million in online giving or $2.2 billion? Sample size makes a difference. Things quickly drift into discussions of confidence internals and whether the findings are statistically significant. Sample size is also very important when showing growth rates. If you read about a claim of an 86% growth rate, but they never disclose the sample size, alarm bells should be going off. Would you rather have 86% growth on $2 million or 2% growth on $86 million? This is not a trick question.

**Always be willing to learn:** There are a lot of great resources available to improve data literacy. First on the required reading list is Darrell Huff's classic book *How to Lie with Statistics* from 1954. The book is still available in print and explains in simple terms why sample size is important, how chart chopping trickery is done, and lots of other statistical chicaneries. *Naked Statistics: Stripping the Dread from the Data* is another great read from Charles Wheelan. The best-selling author states that "the book has been designed to introduce the statistical concepts with the most relevant to everyday life," and it certainly delivers.[51] These two books alone offer a wealth of insights without being completely overwhelming.

For visual learners, there is *The Cartoon Guide to Statistics* by Larry Gonick and Woollcott Smith. This books throws you into the deep end of the probability pool but does so with helpful cartoon illustrations. Then move on to Edward Tufte's books *The Visual Display of Quantitative Information, Envisioning Information, Visual Explanations: Images and Quantities, Evidence and Narrative*, and *Beautiful Evidence*. Tufte also still teaches a one-day course that includes all four of his books. There are other great resources but start with these ones first.

Tufte's work, in particular, has changed how many people use and consume information. Elaborate visual displays of data are exactly what Tufte describes in his 1983 book, *The Visual Display of Quantitative Information*, as chartjunk:[52]

> *"The interior decoration of graphics generates a lot of ink that does not tell the viewer anything new. The purpose of decoration varies — to make the graphic appear more scientific and precise, to enliven the display, to give the designer an opportunity to exercise artistic skills. Regardless of its cause, it is all non-data-ink or redundant data-ink, and it is often chartjunk."*

Tufte's famous essay, "PowerPoint is Evil," notes that "the standard PowerPoint presentation elevates format over content, betraying an attitude of commercialism that turns everything into a sales pitch."[53] Almost all of us have seen chartjunk or been a witness to the evils of PowerPoint presentations, which is why how we use information inside our organizations is an important part of being more data literate. This is a broad topic with a lot of research covering many areas, but let's start with how data is used in meetings.

One of the places where data is used on a daily basis to make decisions is in meetings. If we can improve how data is presented and consumed in meetings, then there's hope it will start to permeate other parts of the organization. A lot of time could be spent on how to use charts and graphs in meetings. Topics like why pie charts are often misused, how tables can be overwhelming, and why the bullet graph is probably one of the best and most underused ways to display information. Search the Internet for "how to find the right chart type for your numeric data" and you'll find a helpful chart chooser diagram.[54]

Instead, if there is one thing that you can do to improve the use of data in meetings, it is this: storytelling. Know the story that you want to tell with the data and be able to tell it. Good data has even better stories. As data visualization expert Stephen Few puts it, "Numbers have an important story to tell. They rely on you to give them a clear and convincing voice."[55] While Big Data is a new concept, storytelling has been with us for thousands of years. Humans are wired to respond to stories in a way that raw data can't replicate. Pairing the narrative of the story with the visuals of the data creates a powerful combination. Do not fall into the trap of believing that the data should speak for itself.

Finally, a good measure of common sense needs to be applied to the presentation of data, whether it is inside or outside the organization. Understand the context of the data being presented. Know your audience and anticipate in advance the common questions they might have about the data. Be your own skeptic and look for holes in the story. Practice and socialize your data story before any important meeting. Speak softly, be passionate, and bring data. Learn to know the difference between fool's gold and the real thing.

# 07

# CULTURE

*"Culture eats strategy for breakfast."*

- PETER DRUCKER

## MINDSET

We have explored how data contains hidden treasure that can be unlocked by nonprofit organizations. We understand some of the historical and day-to-day challenges that nonprofits face when trying to become more data driven. We understand that being data driven is a journey and that nonprofits can measure their progress along the way. We understand the role that technology plays in helping nonprofits make more meaningful change in the world. We understand that being more data literate is an important skill that can help use understand fact from fiction.

## T.B.N.E.

All of these statements are T.B.N.E. — True But Not Enough. You need the right data, but that's not enough. You need the right skills, but that's not enough. You need good processes, but that's not enough. You need the technology, but that's not enough. The extra ingredient that nonprofits need to be more data driven is the right organizational culture. The right culture accelerates the use of data and the wrong one will resist change at every step.

During my research for this book, I spoke with a significant number of people across a wide range of nonprofit organizations and those that serve them. While everyone noted the importance of the right skills, processes, and technology to extract the most value out of the data, they also made clear what an important role culture plays in being data driven. You can follow a checklist of instructions, but without the right culture, the results will be mixed at best.

Yes, culture is often used as a buzzword these days. This includes a lot of talk about building the right culture or making changes in people's behaviors over time. In short, culture is the operating system for an organization that contains the instinctive habits and emotional responses that determine how things are done. We can talk about the importance of data, but the real test is when people feel emotionally energized to do the right things when no one is looking. It is not sufficient for leadership to say that the organization needs to be more data driven. Adding a bullet point to a presentation or putting a few signs up are not enough.

Exploring the importance of culture with someone who has seen first-hand the difference it makes in nonprofits of all shapes and sizes is worthwhile. Beth Kanter is a master trainer, best-selling author, speaker, blogger, and she has over 35 years of hands-on experience in the nonprofit sector. Over more than three decades, she has taught thousands of nonprofits how to incorporate technology to get better results. You might not expect someone who flunked math and once feared measurement to have co-authored the best-selling book *Measuring the Networked Nonprofit*, but Kanter has become a recognized expert on how nonprofit organizations use data and measurement to improve results.

"We have the human side and we have the technical side of measurement. They are kind of yin-and-yang. You need to have them perfectly balanced to really to reap the benefits of continuous improvement," Kanter explains. "On the technical side, you have data hygiene, identifying outcomes, statistics, results-based outcomes; all what I call the hard skills. Then the human side has to do with getting consensus on your outcomes and actually using your data to make improvements," she says. "Those two skills are really important and a lot of times people just see the one side of measurement —we need the tools, we need the metrics, and go get the data," she adds. But in reality, nonprofits also need to make sense of the data, not just collect it. The hard skills also need to be balanced by the soft skills, like curiosity, to truly systematize the use of data in the organization.

Kanter has seen first-hand the emergence of meaningful discussion about data in the nonprofit sector in recent years. "There's been a lot of discussion about the continuous use of measurement, data for continuous improvement, and outcome-based measurement More people in the field are moving towards that as a practice and there's been a shift from collecting the meaningless data to the 'What is it that we are really focusing on? What are we trying to achieve, and what is the evidence that is telling us we are on that road and how to improve?" she says. Data and measurement can be used as both a compass and guardrails for a nonprofit.

What separates a nonprofit that uses data well from those that don't is not merely the technology or technical skills. "I first thought using data was all going to be really straightforward. It's just a technical skill: Here is the step-by-step, and then just do it. But it's not just a technical skill. There is a cultural aspect to it and there is a leadership piece of it too," says Kanter. The more she explored what was happening with measurement, the more she could see what an important role culture plays in the success of a nonprofit. "I call it a culture of curiosity and a culture of continuous improvement. You have to have a high tolerance for things that are imperfect," she says.

Using data to understand what is working also allows you to better understand what is not working. Whether a nonprofit sees that as a learning moment or an opportunity to spread blame often comes down to organizational culture. Kanter notes that "the data isn't there to tell you that you're doing a great job or to give you reinforcement. You're there to get objective evidence about whether you're on track or not."

The term culture is often overused, so understanding exactly what we are talking about here is important. "If you break down the components of culture you have Purpose: connects daily work to the vision. Values: beliefs about what's most important. Behaviors: actions that are guided by values. Recognition: applauds those who bring the values to life. Rituals: repeated behaviors that establish a community and Cues: reminders that keep people in touch with purpose," explains Kanter. The culture of a data driven nonprofit incorporates all of these elements.

Kanter also believes that these cultural elements build a mindset in people that makes a big difference in being more data driven. "People that have growth mindsets also tend to have data informed mindsets," she says. Kanter references some of the research work done by Carol Dweck, a psychology professor at Stanford University. Dweck's research has found significant differences in performance between people that have a growth mindset versus those that have a fixed mindset. The core of Dweck's findings is that people with a fixed mindset believe their basic qualities, like their intelligence or talent, are simply fixed traits. They spend their time documenting their intelligence or talent instead of developing them. On the other hand, people with a growth mindset believe that their most basic abilities can be developed through dedication and hard work; brains and talent are just the starting point.[56]

"Growth mindset people in a nonprofit are driven by this intrinsic motivation of making things better. Data informed nonprofits understand that there are three possible reactions to failure: you just deny it, you blame other people, or you blame yourself," explains Kanter. "Those with a growth mindset understand what it feels like to fail and if they know what the reaction is, then they know how to manage that and manage their team around it. And they successfully embedded that mindset into the culture. If you want to be data informed you also have to have growth mindsets," she says.

A certain culture and mindset are necessary to believe that getting better is more important than just being good. Nonprofit organizations that want to become more data driven need to have or adopt certain cultural behaviors, responses, and habits in order to be successful. This explains why you can have all the right process, skills, and technology, but not be any more data driven than the day before. Culture is the key ingredient to being more data driven.

FORMULA

Culture is not set in stone, but it does not change overnight. Instead, it is an evolving organism that can change over time with the right behaviors, emotional responses, and reinforced habits. Changes in leadership, strategic priorities, and recognition of the right behaviors all help with culture change. As leaders, nonprofit professionals also have to provide emotional support to staff while the change is happening. Some will move at a quick pace while others will need to gradually transition over time. Change is almost always an evolution, not a revolution.

The first step is acknowledging that the culture you have is what it is. You may be risk averse. You may be all art and no science. You may be data rich, but analytics poor. You may be using data, but know there is still more to be done. That's fine. Accept it. Embrace it. Then understand that over time the culture of your nonprofit organization can adapt and change to become more data driven.

There is no one-size-fits-all when it comes to organizational culture. Instead, there are multiple culture types that create the right environment for data driven nonprofits to take shape and grow. There are at least seven different major culture types of successful data driven nonprofits:

**Culture of Champions:** There is support from the organization's leadership and motivational members of the staff that embrace being data driven.

**Culture of Testing:** There is a belief that measurable improvements can be made through iteration and testing throughout the organization.

**Culture of Change:** There is a natural curiosity to try new things and take calculated risks to adapt to changing conditions in the nonprofit sector.

**Culture of Sharing:** There is a willingness to share data and collaborate to achieve better results and a disdain for creating or maintaining data silos.

**Culture of Growth:** There is a focus on continuous improvement where success is measurable and visible across all levels of the organization.

**Culture of Agile:** There is empowerment of people to interact and collaborate that allows them to adapt and respond to a changing environment.

**Culture of Data:** There is a high value placed on data and it is a fundamental driving force to support and validate decisions at the nonprofit.

Over the next seven chapters of the book, we'll explore these types from the perspective of nonprofits that have these kinds of cultures. You may find yourself noticing aspects of what these nonprofits do that fit with your own organization. And there will be moments when you recognize that one nonprofit's culture is not at all like yours. That's fine. Accept it. Embrace it. But know that being data driven is possible and that these nonprofits provide valuable insights into the culture that it takes to get there.

It is important to note that these culture types do not necessarily have a linear progression. One culture type is not always a prerequisite for another. For example, an organization may not have a culture of sharing, but they do have a culture of testing that allows them to become more data driven. Your nonprofit can start anywhere and go everywhere in its cultural evolution.

These culture types are also not mutually exclusive. Some nonprofits have multiple culture traits, but there usually is a dominant culture type that has made them more data driven over time. You may have champions in the organization, but it's really a culture of growth that is the most important driver of behavior, responses, and habits. The important thing is that you recognize how your organization's own culture can evolve to have some of the traits of other data driven nonprofits.

Recognizing the importance of culture as part of any change is an important first step. From there you can continue the journey of adopting a more data driven culture at your organization. Here are the ABCs of data driven culture adoption:

**Acknowledge the Current Culture:** You are unlikely to have a lot of success changing mindsets by throwing the current culture under the bus. First, acknowledge the strengths of the current culture and how they are a building block for where the organization wants to go. Put away the laundry list of aspirational culture traits and begin with what you have today. You can't suddenly change culture, but you can evolve it over time. Focus on the bright spots that exist and discuss what one step forward would mean for the organization.

**Baby Step Behaviors:** You need to pick prevalent behaviors in the current culture and selectively pick a few to move forward. Focus on behavior changes that are observable, actionable, repeatable, and measurable. Do not attempt to move the entire organization all at once. Start by engaging staff members that are known to be early adopters; that person who always has the latest gadget or someone who volunteers to try something new can help beta test these behavior changes. Mix in others who are well-networked within the organization. When other people see them changing, there will be a ripple effect across the organization. You also need to include at least one person with a reputation for resistance to change. Involve them in the process and support them in making just a few important behavior changes. Support them and acknowledge the changes they are making to others. When behaviors change, mindsets will follow.

**Culture Aligns with Strategy:** You will have a lot more success if the culture of the organization is aligned with the strategy. Proclaiming that the organization needs to be more innovative or must achieve certain goals is a recipe for disaster if the culture is not a fit. A culture of testing will fit with a strategy to improve results through more experimentation. A culture of growth will align with a strategy that emphasizes measurable improvements as part of program and individual evaluations. A great framing question for matching culture to strategy is: What if it was all about _____? Insert the outcome that you want to achieve to the cultural behaviors, emotional responses, and habits that need to be developed. What if it was all about improving data health? What do you do at your organization to reinforce that behavior? What if it was all about using Key Performance Indicators (KPIs) to measure the critical parts of the nonprofit's performance? What would you stop doing, starting doing, and how would you know that it's working? Be sure to monitor and manage this transition over time.

Understanding the importance of culture also means understanding the formula for change in any kind of organization. The roots of the equation can be traced back to David Gleicher, who Richard Beckhard and Reuben Harris reference in their breakthrough research on organizational change.[57] Their research was later simplified by Kathleen Dannemiller and Robert Jacobs to this version:[58]

$$C = (D \times V \times F) > R$$

Change (C) will occur when sufficient Dissatisfaction (D) with the current system exists, when there is clear a Vision (V) of what is possible, when there are First (F) steps towards that vision, and the product of these three factors is greater than the Resistance (R) to change. If any of the three factors are missing, then the resistance to change will never be overcome. You might have high dissatisfaction with the current state, but if there is not a vision for the future or first steps towards it, then you are unlikely to succeed. There may be a vision for the future all printed up on posters, but if the first steps have not been taken, then the resistance will keep things the same.

Culture will indeed eat strategy for breakfast, goals for lunch, and tactics for dinner. But culture can be a powerful force for change in a nonprofit organization. In the following chapters, we will explore first-hand how several organizations of different sizes, causes, and locations have become data driven nonprofits. Their stories can not only inform your perspective but hopefully inspire you too. It helps to know that others have made the same journey that you are on now.

# 08

# CHAMPION

*"For the first time ever, everyone in the organization – not just the boss – is expected to lead."*

- SETH GODIN

## OUTSIDE

A common theme in just about anything ever written or presented about change and organizational culture is the importance of leadership. It has become almost cliché to say that any major initiative or program must begin with top-down leadership setting the goals, standards, and expectations for staff.

We hear phrases like "leadership buy-in" and "executive project sponsors" recited like ingredients for baking a cake. Mix one-quarter cup of enriched senior managers, a tablespoon of tiger team extract, one highly refined project charter, and then bake for six months in a dedicated team space. In reality, senior leaders saying that the organization should be doing something doesn't make it so. The support of the organization's leaders is absolutely necessary, but experience shows that this alone is not enough to drive real and lasting change.

Leadership comes from many places and is not always found in the corner office. Yes, for some organizations a top-down approach is required to set expectations and make the tough decisions. But leadership can also come from the bottom up or expand from the work of mid-level managers. Sometimes it also takes brand new leadership from outside the nonprofit to put the right people, process, and technology in place for things to succeed. That is exactly what happened at Memorial Sloan Kettering Cancer Center (MSK) back in 2002.

MSK was formed as a new corporate entity in 1960 to coordinate and guide the overall policy for Memorial Hospital, originally founded in 1884, and the Sloan Kettering Institute, established in 1945 by philanthropist Alfred P. Sloan and inventor Charles F. Kettering.[59] The main hospital building on New York City's Upper East Side is built on land donated by John D. Rockefeller.[60] In 1980, these entities were unified into a single institution, with a single president and CEO. According to US News & World Report, MSK has ranked as one of the top two hospitals for cancer care in the country for more than 25 years.[61]

That brings us to 2002, when Dick Naum and Anne McSweeney, two very successful fundraisers at Columbia University, were brought into MSK to take the organization's development programs to a new level. McSweeney brought with her a focus on transformational major and principal gifts. Naum had broad experience with running programs and operations that always had a quantitative focus. Their skill sets not only complemented one another, but the two fundraisers also had support from the MSK board.

Over time, they both recruited other experienced staff members to help implement a variety of changes in the fundraising organization. In 2006, Kate Chamberlin came to MSK from Columbia University, where she had worked with both Naum and McSweeney. Today, Chamberlin is the director of analytics and process in the office of development at MSK.

"I remember my first days in the office in 2006, when I thought, 'I don't quite know what to do with myself.' Dick's guidance to me was that Memorial Sloan Kettering has a 40-year-old direct marketing program that has been building the constituency to support cancer research nationwide over many years," says Chamberlin. "His goal was to really build a comprehensive development operation. Often fundraising operations are either mass market-focused or they are individual relationship-focused. They're not both. But that's what we're building here."

This high volume or high touch challenge is faced by many nonprofits. Organizations with a high volume but low touch approach to fundraising have struggled for decades to build successful high touch programs. A nonprofit with lots of donors giving smaller amounts looks on with envy at another organization with fewer donors giving much larger amounts. And I know from experience that nonprofits with a focus on fewer numbers of larger donors wish that they had those large donor files that other organizations have. The grass is always greener on the other side, unless it's artificial turf.

Nonprofits don't fail to successfully grow either their high touch or high volume fundraising programs because donors prefer one over the other. Too many organizations fall for the tyranny of the "or" when they should focus on the possibilities of the "and" in their fundraising programs. Organizations often make another critical mistake in trying to shift from one extreme to the other without a natural transition. MSK's different approach can serve as a good example for other nonprofits.

MSK already had a well-established direct marketing program in place that engaged hundreds of thousands of people every year. McSweeney brought with her the know-how to build a successful principal gift program. Naum understood that building a bridge between the two programs that could handle the volume and use data to identify the right mid-level, major, and principal gift donors was the key to success.

Chamberlin believes that the success MSK has had since the new team was brought in is the result of the right things coming together at the right time. "The right leadership, the right culture, and the right people. Dick really saw the potential and his insight was that Memorial Sloan Kettering had this database of millions of people from across the country who are passionate about our mission, but we were not using that resource to its full potential," she says. Chamberlin was empowered to build a team along with the right mix of process and technology to maximize the organization's opportunities.

Chamberlin notes, "We're certainly trying to maintain the mass market focus, the branding, and the acquisition through engagement of millions of people across the country in our mission. At the same time, we are raising big gifts for the Center's strategic priorities." She adds that "as much as we like to think we're on the cutting edge and doing brand new things, it's important to remember that direct mail has been applying analytics to their approach to fundraising for many years. They analyze whether something worked or whether it didn't." The team at MSK believed that the right mix of data, process, and analysis could be applied to a high-volume set of constituents to identify the right prospects for larger gifts.

Statistically speaking, she knew that the database should be full of prospects. While every nonprofit may claim to be different, the common denominator is that their donors are all humans. And humans behave in ways that can be analyzed to create predictable patterns. From there, Chamberlin says the problems they needed to solve were clear: "Can we find them? Can we identify them? Can we get the right prospects into a more personalized stream of stewardship and cultivation, and find the right projects to inspire multimillion-dollar gifts?"

In a way, they simply decided to embrace the sheer volume and variety of data that could be analyzed. "We're going further, looking at mid-level giving, event giving, peer-to-peer fundraising, and all the various ways people are engaging with us. We're trying to figure out how to work with every population in as personalized a way as possible to engage them in our mission, recognizing that we can't have a principal gift-level deep personal relationship with each one of millions of people," says Chamberlin. "Our marketing and events efforts bring roughly 250,000 new people into our programs each year. For some institutions, that's the size of their entire database. We need to be able to evaluate and verify the information in an entirely new way to make that flow as effective as possible," she says.

The analytics team at MSK focuses on identifying potential major and principal gift prospects from across millions of potential donors. These prospects may come from the traditional high-volume direct mail pool of existing donors as well the additional marketing and event programs that the institution runs. A sophisticated model has been developed and every single potential prospect is assigned a giving capacity score. Every week, the entire data set is re-scored and the top 250 prospects are reviewed by an analyst on the team. Chamberlin's team also refines their models over time as they learn more about what variables in the data produce better results. Using this high volume prospect identification process, the team at MSK can verify more qualified prospects in a year than they previously could in 10 years using the old process.

Over the years, the team has grown to seven staff members focused on analysis projects, prospect identification, forecasting, process improvement, and "anything they can dream up to use their data and technology to inform strategy and decision making." Chamberlin and the team have been able to build repeatable processes, but they are always looking for ways to innovate. "As an analytics group, we have traditionally spent most of our time looking at things from a donor-centric, outside-looking-in sort of approach, hoping to be able to accurately predict the best ways to engage with any given donor at any given time," she says. "If we're looking through the eyes of a donor, what can we learn? What myths are not true? What people can we identify who would be better served by one program or another program?"

One of the biggest potential pitfalls in data analysis is to let past experience or assumptions bias conclusions. "We try very hard not to judge the data variables ahead of time. Each variable is just a stream of information in the database, for whatever it might or might not be worth. It's important to look at the quality of the data. Is there some actual information there? Do we know how it was collected? Is that information relatively widely distributed among the population we're interested in? Sometimes the existence of a variable could lead us astray," notes Chamberlin.

One example is using the total number of notes or contacts with a constituent to draw a conclusion about that person. "Those two bits of data, showing we interacted with someone, could lead us to conclude that the fact we interacted with someone makes them more likely to give. But then we could conclude we should focus only on people we've already talked to, creating a self-perpetuating cycle, and no new prospects. Of course, in the context of a different project goal, these might be very useful variables; this is where the judgment of the analyst comes in, and thoughtful project design," she says.

Finding those opportunities in the data is an ever-evolving process at MSK. "We're all human beings, and as such, we're all storytellers. And our brains are always searching for patterns. But we can't process the amount of data a computer can, so we sometimes come to conclusions that aren't really supported by the full data set," says Chamberlin. This is the curse of knowledge problem that generates lots of opinions about donor behavior without any statistical proof.

"We often start with the anecdotal ideas people have, because they are closest to the donor, day to day. We certainly don't want to dismiss those observations. But then we look at the data and try to see whether those stories have legs or not," she says. This is where data and analytics can help to debunk myths that have become tribal knowledge over time. Chamberlin says, "After talking to a few people, we might come to the conclusion that tribute donors don't have major gift potential. Or event donors don't have major gift potential. But in our database, it is certainly not the case that event donors never make major gifts." She goes on to note that "if we just decided that nobody who ever gave to an event was philanthropic or interested in making a major gift to Memorial Sloan Kettering, that would be a major mistake."

Every nonprofit of every size has resource constraints. If you only have so much time, money, or resources, then reducing the number of mistakes is absolutely critical. One could even argue that smaller nonprofits have less margin for error than very large organizations. If a nonprofit that raises $80 million a year misses out on a $50,000 donation, then it's not the end of the world. If a nonprofit raising $800,000 makes the same mistake, then the consequences are exponentially higher. No matter the size of the nonprofit, champions for the use of data driven decision-making can play a significant role in the success of the organization.

Being a champion of using data also means looking for opportunities to put data to good use across the organization. Having a culture of champions creates an environment in which people are willing to help those outside their own department. The lines on the organization chart start to become invisible and the phrase "It's not my problem" is rarely uttered.

Chamberlin says, "We were realizing that with a lot of our analytics products, the models and other things we were coming up with, people were doing their best to implement them using existing processes. But if we could help them to streamline how things were being implemented, including how data is being collected and how model scores are being applied, we could actually enable the operation to make better use of data."

We have all seen how a well-intentioned process created years or months ago can actually overcomplicate things down the road. The process might not have changed, but the goals, staff, and technology around it always change over time. Chamberlin has seen this challenge firsthand and notes that "there is rarely time to go back and take a process apart, and build it right with the newest technology and the newest resources."

That is why the analytics team has someone on their team dedicated to process improvement. Their role is to help streamline existing processes across the organization. Over time, the team has learned that removing excuses for why data can't be better leveraged is extremely beneficial for everyone. "We recognized that fundraising is very speed-oriented, very high energy. It's a tactical, on-the-ground kind of business. And when we can find new opportunities to apply data in the operation it makes everyone's lives a little nicer," says Chamberlin. Collaboration beats confrontation. Sharing beats silos. Every time.

Perhaps another secret to building a more data driven culture is that, at its heart, MSK is a scientific institution. There was a natural culture fit to bring more science to the art of fundraising. The long history with direct mail also provided an environment where analysis was valued. Nonprofit organizations with a traditional focus on direct mail are no strangers to testing and data analysis. They not only test to improve results, but also to reduce costs and be more efficient. When you are sending hundreds of thousands or even millions of pieces of mail every year, the price for getting it wrong goes well beyond postage.

This scientific DNA already present in the organization has certainly helped Chamberlin's analytics team be more successful. But the team's goal, unlike planning the costs associated with the next direct mail campaign, is to use data to provide better insights into predicting results for the long term. Chamberlin says, "As an organization, we're more focused on using data to evaluate what broad strategies we want to follow with a particular population going forward than we are necessarily in measuring day-to-day. This might sound crazy to some extent, but I think it's actually healthy, because what's happening right this second can't really be changed rapidly, except in a few narrow cases. So we can end up fretting over something very short term rather than strategically investing for the long term."

Moving beyond the day-to-day analysis work has allowed MSK to use analytics for more forecasting. "Our primary use of forecasting throughout the year is to inform leadership's conversations with finance and the board. We forecast to establish whether we are on track to reach the goals we have set, or if we need to communicate that things may not go as planned," says Chamberlin. In this case, data is used to look ahead and understand what might happen next. She adds, "This has been a particularly hot topic in the context of the various economic upheavals of the last 10 years. It can make for some interesting conversations. Statistical forecasting is saying, 'Provided the past patterns are a good prediction for the future, here's what the prediction would be.' Forecasting gives us a useful new tool, and an additional bit of feedback to inform those conversations. But it's not a crystal ball."

Beyond forecasting, data has also been useful for MSK in terms of gathering important, long-term strategic information about donors. And just like testing a direct mail solicitation, using data to understand what doesn't work can be as important as confirming what does. Chamberlin notes, "We've done some very successful controlled experiments in our leadership annual giving program, collecting data on the impact of contacting prospects. Sometimes it's funny to describe, because when you get down to it, we proved that when you contact people, they give more. This is not in any way shocking."

Instead, the surprise was what happened in a different test using data. "We did these experiments in early 2008 in California. I'm not sure there was a worse time in recent memory to be raising money in California. Of course, when you compared results to the previous year, giving went down. A lot. Giving for the control group went down 74%," she says. "But thank goodness for the control group. Giving for the treatment group went down roughly 30%. This would look like a huge failure without the context of the control. Instead, we were able to actually demonstrate that we raised more money than we would have had we not contacted the treatment group. And we could estimate how much that was. So instead of an abject failure, a 30% decrease was actually a measurable success," explains Chamberlin.

Here again, we see the important role champions of data can play in a nonprofit. "I love the California example, because it would be so tempting to, based on year-over-year results, declare the project a disaster, blame the fundraisers, blame the program, come to the conclusion that there was something fundamentally wrong with the whole program. But it was truly a success," says Chamberlin.

Using both test and control groups with major gift fundraising prospects gets a lot of resistance from many nonprofits. They are afraid to experiment and the Fear of Missing Out (FOMO) on a gift can actually hurt their ability to improve fundraising results. "The key is the control group. But it's a brave act to select some good prospects and say, 'Okay, we're declaring these people a control and we're not going to do anything special with them,'" says Chamberlin. It takes patience and time to see the results play out. "You really need a year, and preferably two, to get the information you're looking for. Once we felt we had learned what we had set out to learn, we released the control group and those prospects are now available for assignment to annual giving portfolios," she adds.

In a world of real-time data and constant focus on the here-and-now, it's hard to have patience. Chamberlin knows this struggle all too well. "It would be so nice to get a long-term sense of how things work, but we want our answers right now. You've got to have patience. I think it is an interesting challenge for analytics broadly written. We can't just say, 'Don't worry, everything will be fine, just believe,' and ask people to accept they are not going to know whether they've achieved anything for years," she says. "On the other hand, to really get good results over the long run, you have to choose a strategy, run with it, and run with it for a good long time. Even better, also plan up front how you're going to measure your results at the end, so you're sure to be collecting the right data."

This might lead you to believe that the analytics team at MSK doesn't understand the real need for answers quickly. Nothing could be further from the truth. "We're trying to think about it in terms of surfacing the right piece of information to the right person at the right time so they can really use it on behalf of the institution," says Chamberlin. She adds, "You can say the same goes for donors. Can we give them the right information at the time they're looking for it, the right opportunities to support us in the way they wish to? Can we give them what they are looking for in terms of a relationship with MSK and a contribution to the mission to end cancer at the moment they are looking for it?"

The mission is never lost amid the data. Chamberlin and her team clearly understand the important work MSK is doing and they are trying to be champions in a race against the clock. "The timelier we can be, the nimbler we can be at every level of the operation, and the more donor-focused we really are. It amounts to having the right pieces of data at the right moment with the right person who can act to build that human relationship with our donors and gather the support the rest of the institution needs to cure cancer," says Chamberlin.

The decision by MSK's leadership to get a second opinion in 2002 and bring in experts from the outside has proven to be a wise one. Since 2003, MSK has raised nearly $3.5 billion as part of its first major capital campaign since the 1980s. Along the way, they have built a culture of champions that use data to improve the art of fundraising. Their leadership believes that you can have both a market focus and an emphasis on individual relationships.

Spread across a series of buildings in Manhattan's Upper East Side are the fundraising professionals at Memorial Sloan Kettering Cancer Center. High above the city streets there is a small team of data champions bridging the gap between an established direct mail operation and a transformational gift program on the rise. Thanks to investments in people, process, and technology these data champions are getting remarkable results.

INSIDE

Let's take a journey from the mean streets of Manhattan to the badlands of South Dakota. In 1804, Lewis and Clark camped near the mouth of Vermillion River on their way to explore the West. Over time, the city of Vermillion would grow and become the home of the University of South Dakota, founded by the Dakota Territorial Legislature in 1862 — nearly 37 years before South Dakota would become a state. The state's oldest public university has over 10,000 undergraduate and postgraduate students who are enrolled along with the state's only medical and law schools.

Margaret Williams is the director of prospect research at the University of South Dakota Foundation. She has been in this role at the foundation since 1999 and was presented with the 2015 Professional of the Year Award from the Association of Professional Researchers for Advancement (APRA), the premier international organization for professionals who specialize in prospect development in the areas of prospect identification and research, data analytics, and relationship management.[62]

Under Williams' leadership, the foundation developed its first prospect management system, which aided in the successful completion of the university's largest campaign at that time. When that campaign ended in 2007, the USD Foundation raised $137 million, surpassing its original goal of just $60 million.

Today, the University of South Dakota is in the public phase of a $250 million campaign. In three and one-half years they have already reached the $200 million mark. The use of data has so far been vital to the success of the latest campaign, set to finish in 2017. It doesn't hurt that they have someone like Williams on their side.

You might think that someone with her level of experience and esteem among prospect research peers would be a trained mathematician, but you would be wrong. Williams' undergraduate degree is in psychology and she later completed a master's degree in blind rehabilitation training. She remarks that the handful of required statistics courses trained her to think ahead of time about the questions she will want to answer at the end of an experiment. "That's pretty much what prospect research programs are – experiments," she says.

Williams' science background gave her the right skills and mindset to build a prospect management program that is respected by her peers. "From the start, I knew which actions and donor results had to be recorded so that when it was time to evaluate how the predictive modeling data helped my moves management and prospect management programs, I could easily measure what was bringing in money and what was not," she says.

Williams notes, "Back in the old days before we really had access to big data and truly predictive modeling, all we really had was demographic data and demographic statistics." This led to the use of "ZIP code-based wealth indicators like average home values and average age values," she adds. The challenge with only using this data is that while it can help with basic segmentation, it also can lead to false positives.

"With ZIP codes you can have a little shack behind the million-dollar house and that shack will have the same ZIP code," says Williams. She mentions that "seeing the wrong people – the people who can't make major gifts or a principal gift – can cause a lot of frustration in the minds of both leadership and major gift officers." She adds that danger is they might "equate the false positives with data in general not being useful and not worth buying and using."

Over time, nonprofit organizations like the USD Foundation began using more specific data. This combination of data and predictive analytics opens up a lot of new possibilities. Williams likes to use two different kinds of analytics: prescriptive and predictive. "One kind prescribes an action for you to take and if you take that action then you will probably reach your goal. This type of modeling tends to help a foundation rank order the people we already know. People in your database who come to events and answer the phone when the calling center calls belong to the alumni association, etc." In short, prescriptive analytics can help an organization prioritize and group known supporters based on their interaction data.

Williams explains that predictive analytics is all about using data to "find the people in your database who you don't know but you should know." She says, "With this sort of data modeling, a prospect researcher can recommend to the gift officers, 'Hey, this person would be a good discovery visit. They look a lot like our current principal gift prospects,' and you can find the next diamond in the rough for the gift officers to go see." Predictive analytics can help a nonprofit to identify look-alikes that might otherwise remain hidden in their data.

To those unfamiliar with the concepts, both prescriptive and predictive analytics can seem like magic or witchcraft. Making the most of the data depends on how much trust and support you have. "As the years have gone by, I've worked for four different foundation presidents. I have watched leadership go from 'That stuff doesn't work' when talking about modeling to literally 'We will be data driven,'" says Williams. She adds, "They let go of their old baggage as the new predictive modeling began to lead to success after success. Now leadership is starting to throw their weight behind those of us in research."

Leadership must not only have a level of trust in the data, but they also need to reinforce to gift officers how important it is to take advantage of prescriptive and predictive analytics. Williams notes, "The new thing we're experiencing across prospect research is that our leadership is starting to understand and have faith in the data that we have been working with all these years, and they are willing to spend the money to send the gift officer to see someone we don't know yet."

The other reason why leaders across the nonprofit landscape have been embracing predictive analytics is the realization that the low-hanging fruit is no longer enough to meet ambitious fundraising goals. "Everybody is doing these fantastic campaigns with dollar goals never attempted before. I don't care if you're an Ivy League school with a giant database of donors or a school like us with a modest size database. We all are faced with that gap at the top of the campaign pyramid where we don't have enough people we know," says Williams.

"To get to our campaign goal, we need to go see people that we don't know, and we have to do it strategically so that we don't spend money seeing the wrong people. We need to spend money seeing the right people," Williams says. She is careful to note, "You can't just buy data, stick it in the computer, sit back, and think it's going to do the work for you. You'll have to sell it to your major gift officers." This means reporting the success that is happening because of the use of data to the teams on a regular basis. "I have a hit rate with one of my data models that's 59%. A lot of the success of this particular data model is matching the prospects with the gift officers. You aren't going to get 59% hit rates if the gift officers don't trust you and the data," says Williams.

Building this trust required the support of leadership, but the need to grow the staff also resulted in some unlikely champions for making data driven decisions. "We knew in order to make the visits, to see enough people, to close enough gifts in a five-year campaign for $250 million, it's just simple arithmetic to say we need more feet on the ground," says Williams. To ramp up for the campaign, the foundation doubled its number of gift officers. Williams notes, "We hired a couple of gift officers who had never done fundraising before but they wanted to try. They were young graduates of the university, they loved people, and they had that thing that some people are born with that when you sit down with them, you find yourself leaning forward. They pull you in."

Another thing these new gift officers did not have was the curse of knowledge. "These new gift officers also came to the profession without any bias against following data because researchers like me hadn't ever accidentally sent them to the wrong prospects because of false positives in the old demographic data days." The early success of these new gift officers got the attention of more seasoned staff. "If you can get somebody out there and taking the chance, seeing the people that the data says are the right people, then once they close a couple of gifts, it makes everybody back up and say, 'Hey, it works. I want to try that too!' because nothing succeeds like success," she says.

Williams recalls one new gift officer that didn't immediately dismiss a potential major gift prospect just because no one had ever visited them in person. Instead, he noticed that the prospect had a history of answering calls from the student-led call center. Williams pointed out to him, "Somebody as wealthy as this person does not need to pick up his phone and talk to one of our callers, but he does. It's a 'Yes' signal. It means he likes us. Without blinking, the gift officer would get on a plane and go see him."

Not every champion has to have a big title or a corner office to influence the culture of your organization. At the USD Foundation, some of the most influential champions were new gift officers that only knew how to make data driven decisions. The tendency to use gut instinct to rule out a potential prospect or to prioritize a major donor list differently didn't happen. Instead, they used the predictive analytics provided by Williams' team to help them focus on the right donors. This allowed them to save their relationship-building skills for when it could really count.

On the flip side, the foundation also brought in some more experienced gift officers, but most of them had never worked with prescriptive or predictive models before. Many seasoned gift officers carry a degree of cynicism when it comes to data modeling. "They have sat in too many living rooms of 'highly scored' prospects who in reality were not in the position to give a major gift," notes Williams. "Data modeling may have come a long way since those days, but not the opinions of the seasoned gift officers who haven't used it," she adds.

Could these newer gift officers be champions to change the attitudes of their more experienced colleagues? To test this theory, Williams started using a new principal gift model to identify prospects that had the capacity, affinity, and probability to make a six- or seven-figure donation. She recalls, "One of the younger gift officers, having no reason not to trust the data (in spite of the fact that most of these prospects had fairly anemic giving histories), just went to see them and ask them for the amounts recommended by the model. Better yet, he closed these asks at or near the amounts!"

During a staff meeting when the success of the new fundraising professionals was shared, the more experienced gift officers started asking for some of these high performing prospects too. Williams says, "I pointed out that they had some of those 'good prospects' as well, but with the exception that the prospects I recommended to them had better giving histories. All they had to do was trust the data and start adjusting their ask amounts to the amounts recommended by the modeling."

As the veteran gift officers began closing rather significant gifts, they also became internal champions for the use of data. Williams recalls, "Once they enjoyed a couple of successful principal gift asks based on the modeling, they all rallied to our president's way of using and trusting data." Over a period of time, the combination of the support from leadership and the role that unlikely champions played in the organization helped to create a more data driven culture. Support for the use of data across the organization also led to a willingness to invest more in data driven insights.

Williams makes sure that she tracks the hits and misses with predictive models to show the return on investment to senior leaders and gift officers. "It's really a lot easier to buy another model when you can say, 'The $15,000 that we spent three years ago with Target Analytics has produced $58.8 million to date.' I can report that number because I took the time to track it," she says. She adds, "I'm very lucky that I'm allowed to buy a lot of data. I know plenty of people in my seat at other universities and foundations who don't have the budget that I have, but I think part of it is because they took a chance allowing me to buy one modeling service and I took the time to report on a monthly basis how much of the money raised was predicted by that model."

At this point, you may be wondering if nonprofits could hire anyone off the street, give them plenty of predictive model data, and sit back and watch the gifts roll in. Maybe even go a step further and develop sentient fundraising robots that have no need for sleep or adulation from their peers. In a word: no. Data and analytics are not a substitute for the unique skills that nonprofit professionals bring to the table.

Williams acknowledges that "it is the gift officer's ability to listen to the donor and hear what the donor cares about" that cannot be replaced by data. Instead, the use of data helps them focus on the right opportunities. "The data models just help you see the prospects they were invented to find. If it takes the same amount of time and money for a foundation to raise a small gift or a large gift, then wouldn't you prefer to raise the large gift?" she adds.

You may also be wondering if this change in culture has resulted in better fundraising results at the USD Foundation. The statistics Williams shares about the early success of the current capital campaign shed light on the difference the right use of principal gift modeling can have on an institution: "When I look at my principal giving data and my principal gift people, we have sat in 158 households. 93 of those households have given us $58.8 million. At the major gift level, we've had to sit in 567 households for 201 donors to give us $17.2 million."

Neither art nor science of fundraising alone makes these major fundraising campaigns successful; the combination of artful fundraisers equipped with data science does. Data acts as a GPS to direct fundraisers to the right people, but it can't build relationships and help donors understand the transformational impact of their gifts. The support of senior leadership is obviously important, but that alone is not enough for organizations to become more data driven. Sometimes it takes a few unlikely champions to show others the importance of being data driven.

# 09

# CHANGE

*"Do real and permanent good in this world."*

- ANDREW CARNEGIE

## ST ANDREW

Having champions in all levels of the organization is important to becoming a more data driven nonprofit. For some organizations, that simply isn't enough to get them past internal resistance. The work of a few champions can be held back by a resistance to change in the nonprofit. But some organizations have developed a culture of change that has allowed them to evolve over time. All the compelling data doesn't offer much value if there is not the willingness to act on it and make decisions that change the course of the nonprofit.

On the east coast of Scotland, where the River Eden meets the North Sea, lies a town where people have lived as far back as 5000 BC. The first religious settlement here dates back to 390 AD. Over the centuries, this place has been known as Mucrois, Cennrígmonaid, Cill Rìmhinn, Kilrule, and today we know it as St Andrews. Legend has it that a Greek monk known as Saint Regulus brought a few relics of Saint Andrew the Apostle to the "ends of the earth" for safekeeping. In the fourth century, that meant a journey to the edge of the Kingdom of Fife, in what is now the eastern coast of Scotland.

Steve MacLaughlin

Over the 1,600 years since that first settlement, St Andrews has seen a lot of change. The landscape of St Andrews is at once timeless and constantly changing. Perhaps it's the ebb and flow of the North Sea against the rocks in the harbor. It could also be the wind and rain that nurture the plants and test people's patience, especially over at the "home of golf," the Royal and Ancient Golf Club of St Andrews.

Among the relics and the ruins in the town by the sea is the University of St Andrews. Founded in 1410, it is the third-oldest university in the English-speaking world, following Oxford and Cambridge. It was here in 1978 that Dr. Colin Thompson, a highly respected research chemist at the university, started a nonprofit to support much-needed funding for cancer research. It turns out that a lot of change is happening in this place where it seems as if time stands still.

Jack Cumming is the digital marketing manager at Worldwide Cancer Research, located in St Andrews. I met Cumming years ago at a not-for-profit conference in London. At the time, the world of social media was just beginning to get a lot of attention in the nonprofit sector. Everyone had stopped using Friendster, MySpace was still king, and something called Second Life was about to experience explosive growth.

Cumming told me how his nonprofit was raising money through virtual events on Second Life, an online virtual world that at its peak had people spending tens of millions of hours per month interacting with each other. This seemed completely crazy at the time, but it was clear that Cumming and the staff at Worldwide Cancer Research were on to something before just about everyone else.

When I went looking for nonprofit organizations that knew how to embrace change, the first person that I reached out to was Cumming. Over the years, he's seen firsthand many changes to both the traditional and digital fundraising landscape. "I came here in 2003 to head up our online offering, which at that point was a very bad website and not much else. In the two or three years prior to me coming, they'd had about two donations online," says Cumming. Fast forward over a decade and Worldwide Cancer Research has a mature online, social media, email marketing, and peer-to-peer fundraising program in place.

"I suppose we've always been early adopters," says Cumming. The root of this early adopter behavior was the man who hired Cumming as employee number 13 in 2003, Retired Lieutenant Colonel Derek Napier. He was a former British Army officer who led and grew the nonprofit from an annual revenue of £1 million ($1.45 million) to £18 million ($26.10 million) with a handful of staff.[63] "I suppose risk taking was probably in his bones, but not crazy risk taking," says Cumming. "His conviction was that new things had to be tried to see if they would work. If you just kept doing what you were doing, then the charity would stay with its million pounds and that would be it," he adds. This encouragement to take calculated risks helped to build a culture that was comfortable with change. Cumming says, "I think that culture was instilled in the people that were here and that has been carried on, even though he retired almost 10 years ago."

The willingness to let the small team experiment with the earliest forms of social media allowed the organization to learn a lot of valuable lessons. "Second Life was interesting for about three or four years from a fundraising perspective because there were a lot of people on there who spent so much time in it because it is pretty immersive," he says. Worldwide Cancer Research would hold virtual fundraising events in which avatars chatted back and forth with one another. "The fundraising used to be quite successful. I think some of them felt it was almost a way of justifying the fact that they're sitting in there for five hours a night," says Cumming. The organization had more learning experiences than earning experiences on Second Life, but that prepared them for the age of Facebook and Twitter in many ways.

Those early days in social media taught Cumming the importance of being responsive to people and seeing it as a way to build relationships. "We've made it a point that we answer every single post or message we get on Facebook or Twitter. It's that kind of attitude, I suppose, that we think even if none of these people that speak to us on Twitter or Facebook ever give us a donation, we've made some progress and they understand what we do," he says.

Responding to everything posted on social media is not easy, but Worldwide Cancer Research believes it makes a difference. Cumming explains, "You look at charities that have got a million followers, and you think it's so much bigger than us. Yet, when somebody posts on their wall, they're often ignoring them. Somebody asked that question there and then somebody else asked a question and somebody else. They may have answered the fourth guy but they haven't answered the three before them. If I were those people, I'd be looking at it going, 'All right, you're plain ignoring me.'"

Those avatars in Second Life taught the organization that it shouldn't ignore people, even when the interaction is just 140 characters. "People on Twitter might say, 'Hey, I'm doing this event for Worldwide Cancer Research.' Then we can retweet it to thousands more people. That gives them encouragement because most people don't think that there's anybody listening. Most people are surprised when you get into a conversation with them," says Cumming.

We are closing in on 20 years since traditional peer-to-peer fundraising made the shift to engage donors and participants online. The walks, runs, and ride events moved from paper-based pledge forms to online fundraising platforms. Worldwide Cancer Research has seen a significant increase in online peer-to-peer fundraising as well. "One of the things that's changed is twenty years ago, if somebody was taking part in an event like the London Marathon, then it was just purely a sponsorship. They would just speak to a friend and say, 'Sponsor me 10 bucks a mile,' or something like that," says Cumming. "Now, what's happening is we'll get in contact with these people and say, 'Well, you know, you're not doing this event for six months yet. Why don't you have a night where you get all your friends around?' Suddenly they've raised all that money months before the event, and they're still going to get sponsored by other people," he says. Not only are event participants able to use better tools for engaging people, but nonprofits like Worldwide Cancer Research can also help coach them on how to be better fundraisers.

"I ran one marathon in my life back in 1983. All I could do was speak to my friends in person and say, 'I'm doing this marathon. Will you sponsor me?' Nowadays, if you set up your fundraising page and you share that out on Facebook and all the rest of it, you've got far greater reach to do stuff. Before you know it, you've hit your target," explains Cumming. These tools allow participants to engage with people, have a conversation, and help them be better fundraisers on behalf of a cause they care about. For some people, training to run a marathon is a lot more palatable than training to be an independent fundraiser. "It can be daunting. If somebody said to me, 'Go and raise £3,000,' I'd be like, 'Oh, I don't know if I know enough people.' If you can learn how to put on an event, then people are happy to buy raffle tickets, or donate prizes, or whatever," he says.

Experimenting with social media. Moving people to online fundraising events. Coaching supporters to be better fundraisers. Improving email communication. You might be wondering why Worldwide Cancer Research has made these changes such a priority. It all comes back to the fact that donors are changing and nonprofit organizations need to respond to this change too. As it turns out, the organization has been changing everything about its engagement and fundraising programs, not just the digital channels.

"When we started up 35 years ago, remember it was 100% direct mail and that's all that there was. We've still got a big chunk of our income that comes through direct mail. That supportive base is very, very aging at this point in time and decreasing," says Cumming. The organization knew that it needed to change with the times and experiment with other giving channels. "From an external perspective, we're always looking at the available data that comes through to see what's the state of the sector. Is it getting bigger? Is it getting smaller? Then we're looking at other organizations in the sector. Is there anything they're doing that we aren't doing?" he says.

The data told them that direct mail donors were in decline across the nonprofit sector. They needed to diversify into new fundraising programs to continue to be successful. Worldwide Cancer Research began using face-to-face fundraising in the late 1990s as a replacement strategy for direct mail giving. Face-to-face, also sometimes referred to as canvassing, is done through street and door-to-door fundraising in many parts of the world. "We could see that change coming both in the market and through our own internal numbers years ago. We knew direct mail was going to decline. The face-to-face program here was built as a replacement for direct mail. We know that face-to-face will decline too. It was partly out of that that we thought we needed to move online. It's unlikely to replace all of this stuff but it could certainly run alongside it," says Cumming.

Worldwide Cancer Research accepts that change is part of the cycle of nonprofit life. They look at consumer and nonprofit sector data to help make decisions around other fundraising channels to try. "We like to think that we're very data driven," Cumming says. Over the years, they have used data to make decisions about which fundraising channels to invest in and what the potential return looks like. "One of the things we look at and continue to see is that the break-even point is getting further and further away, once you look at the opportunity cost and other things," says Cumming. "If this is going to take three to five years to break even, then what else could we be doing with that money? Maybe that's what we should be doing instead," he notes.

Recently, Worldwide Cancer Research has used the combination of television advertising and text messaging to drive new sources of giving. There are "lots of digital channels out there now," says Cumming. "If we come up with an ad, let's see if it works," he adds. "Another good thing about it from a data point of view is it's very, very easy to measure because we've got all these slots booked on the TV, and the text to donate SMS that comes in all links up," he adds. "The first weekend of the TV ad campaign had two big spikes in giving and we were able to see when and where the ads were being successful," Cumming says. "Next time we can pull the stuff that was going on on Monday to Friday and just concentrate on a Saturday, Sunday because that's where all the big spikes were."

Traditionally, TV advertising has been extremely cost prohibitive, but the increased number of digital channels and programs that need commercial slots filled makes it more feasible. Direct response mail has changed to become direct response television (DRTV) and a number of nonprofit organizations are having success in this area. Cumming says, "What we would hope to do with those people is to start to develop a relationship, and then move them into our regular stream somewhere down the line."

This willingness to experiment, test, and change prepared the organization for its biggest change yet. The organization was founded in 1979 as the Association for International Cancer Research (AICR). In 2014, AICR rebranded as Worldwide Cancer Research. "We had seen for a long time that it was getting difficult to recruit people who had never heard of us. We were basically known as AICR, which is just an acronym that didn't mean anything to most people," says Cumming. The nonprofit brought in an outside agency to help them evaluate whether a name change was the right thing to do.

While the scientific and research community knew the organization very well, the general public had little or no awareness of AICR. Market research with existing AICR donors found that many supporters would actually say the names of other UK cancer charities when asked about their giving habits. The organization decided that rebranding was the right change to make. After testing a few different options, they officially changed the name to Worldwide Cancer Research. As Cumming puts it: "We thought, okay, Worldwide Cancer Research does what it says, no explanation needed."

For over 30 years now, Worldwide Cancer Research has funded £173 million ($250.85 million) towards 1,776 research projects in 34 countries. During that time, the organization has seen the rise of direct mail, face-to-face, digital, peer-to-peer, and social media as channels for fundraising. They have built up a culture of change and are willing to try new things. Those risks are calculated using data to drive decisions. In a place like St Andrews, where time often seems like it stands still, the one constant for Worldwide Cancer Research is change.

## ST MUNGO

Sixty-five miles to the southwest of St Andrews is Glasgow, Scotland's largest city. Glasgow's earliest settlement dates back to the sixth century when the Christian missionary Saint Mungo built a church near the Molendinar Burn. Today, Saint Mungo is recognized as both the founder of Glasgow and its patron saint. Glasgow Cathedral stands on the site of that ancient structure and Saint Mungo's remains are buried in the lower crypt.

The city's medieval beginnings have made way for the modern age. Glaswegians, with their distinctive patter, have seen plenty of change in their city over the centuries. A strong reputation for shipbuilding, engineering, and manufacturing has grown to include education, architecture, and culture.

The skyline of Glasgow is a mix of glass, steel, and stone, a reflection of the old and the new converging. Just over two miles from Glasgow Cathedral is a nonprofit organization also in the midst of change: the Scottish Catholic International Aid Fund, better known as SCIAF.

The nonprofit organization is the official aid and development agency of the Roman Catholic Church in Scotland. SCIAF works in 15 different countries across Asia, Africa, and Latin America. SCIAF is also a member of Caritas Internationalis, a worldwide network of 163 Catholic aid agencies.

David Mitchell is the online marketing officer at SCIAF and has been with the organization since 2011. He was the first data analyst ever hired at the charity and now runs SCIAF's online marketing and giving programs. When Mitchell first came to SCIAF, he quickly understood the influence the programmatic work of the organization had on the use of data. "The work we do helping people around the world is strongly driven by metrics and careful monitoring and evaluation. The data we collect ensures our projects are having the best possible outcomes for the communities we're working with, and that we're spending our supporters' donations in the most effective way."

The use of data at SCIAF has largely been driven by the international aid programs that the organization operates. All large funding agencies have standards and policies around monitoring and evaluation that must be followed, and SCIAF always aims to follow international best practices when designing and implementing their projects. These projects are monitored and evaluated on a constant basis. "That has now spread through the whole organization and it generates a constant need for data to be used. Now, the communications team report their progress in a similar way that data is tracked by people who are building wells or teaching communities how to grow crops," Mitchell says.

For most of SCIAF's more than 50-year history, the primary charitable giving source was donations made at the more than 450 parishes across Scotland. According to the 2011 census, Catholics comprise 16% of the overall population in Scotland, which equates to just over 840,000 individuals.[64] But considering that Scotland's Catholic population has fallen by 18% since 1982, the organization realized that it needed to reach a broader set of supporters through more engagement channels.[65] Change in the population, change in donors, and change in the nonprofit sector have driven SCIAF to modernize their engagement and fundraising programs.

Over time, SCIAF has been building a more sustainable fundraising strategy through the use of direct mail, telephone, and online giving programs. There is also a lot of engagement done at the local level across Scotland. "We do a lot of education work and that happens in both Catholic schools and nondenominational schools," says Mitchell. SCIAF is responding to the demographic changes that are impacting faith-based organizations not just in Scotland, but also around the world. Mitchell is quick to point out: "It's definitely true that when we're doing our communications work it's certainly not just Catholics we appeal to. We've got plenty of supporters that are of a different faith or of no faith at all."

SCIAF runs several campaigns during the year that combine the use of multiple fundraising channels. A lot of data segmentation and analysis is used to determine where to focus each campaign. But the most recognizable campaign channel is SCIAF's WEE BOX. (Meaning "little," the word "wee" is common jargon in Scotland.) Simply put, the Wee Box is a small box that supporters put in their home or business and place donations into before eventually sending it back to SCIAF. It was first used during the 1980s and "the initial idea of the Wee Box was that during the 40 days in the run up to Easter, the time Catholics know as Lent, it's traditional to give something up as a form of fasting. Often Catholics give up something like alcohol or chocolate." As Mitchell explains, "Our proposition was that when you give something up, the money you save should go into a SCIAF Wee Box. At the end of Lent, that money is sent to us."

SCIAF mails approximately 25,000 Wee Boxes each year to supporters by direct mail. Another 55,000 are sent to parishes across Scotland and about 16,000 are sent to schools. Today, the Wee Box accounts for 15% to 20% of SCIAF's annual revenue. In 2015 alone, £3.4 million ($4.9 million) was raised from Wee Box donations.[66] In case you're wondering, one Wee Box can hold about £27 ($39.15) in donations. Much like the Salvation Army's red kettles in the United States, the Wee Box has high brand recognition in Scotland.

"It certainly serves as a constant reminder for a lot of people," says Mitchell. "The other place that it's really effective is with school children because, to them, it's very intuitive. Money comes out of their pocket and they see it go into the box. Just getting them used to that and the idea of saving a little bit at a time for SCIAF is really useful," he adds. Increasingly, SCIAF is seeing funds put in the Wee Box donated online instead of sending in the money. Though the organization sees no need to change the recognizable Wee Box, there is an opportunity to modernize the giving experience. Supporters are consciously changing giving channels because it's more convenient to make the donation online. SCIAF sees this trend as a way to remove friction from the giving process. At the same time, the Wee Box continues to have a symbolic presence in donors' homes.

The influence that the Wee Box has on the brand and messaging of SCIAF has also led to more use of data in the organization. Data is analyzed to make sure that donor communication is optimized. "We're messaging people based on their exact relationship to us. For example, if someone has had a direct debit monthly gift to SCIAF for four or five years, then we would reference that and speak to them in a different way than a donor who just started giving monthly," says Mitchell. This approach of tailoring communication based on giving data has also changed how SCIAF engages supporters. "People with a high-value donation rate don't receive a message about how spending £14 can make a great change in someone's life. Instead, we would say that £500 could go towards paying for an entire classroom or a whole year's worth of water for a village." Before Mitchell started working at SCIAF, a lot of these best practices didn't happen. The organization has been willing to change how they communicate with supporters to adapt to a more competitive fundraising environment.

The attention given to getting the right message to the right supporters might seem like a very qualitative decision-making process, but at SCIAF, it is absolutely driven by the data. Over time, SCIAF has continued to test new approaches to engaging with donors. "Really, what we're looking to do is constantly push to find new ways of reaching people. A supporter might not be particularly enamored with direct mail, but they might be willing to buy ethical gifts as they prefer more of a shopping experience," says Mitchell. SCIAF has been successful with their Real Gifts program that allows people to purchase things like goats, chickens, or a bicycle which are then given to family living in poverty in one the countries SCIAF is working. This fundraising approach was pioneered by Heifer International decades ago and many organizations have implemented similar programs. SCIAF tested this approach to see if it would also work with their donors and it has been extremely successful. This reinforces the point that something does not always have to be a new idea. One nonprofit's change is another's established practice.

Embracing digital channels is also an area SCIAF has used data and testing to diversify how they engage supporters. "We were conscious of the fact that if we didn't move quickly on digital, we could be left behind. We have a more traditional and older core supporter and it would be very easy to ignore digital and eventually be left out in the cold," says Mitchell. SCIAF recognized that online and other digital channels were going to change things in ways they could not foresee. Sometimes there are external events that serve as a wakeup call for nonprofits to improve their use of data.

At SCIAF, that event was the 2004 Indian Ocean earthquake and tsunami that struck on December 26, 2004. The massive devastation in Indonesia, Sri Lanka, India, and Thailand led to a tremendous outpouring of disaster relief giving. This was also an event that saw online giving come to the forefront in response to natural disasters. Many of the trends we continue to see with online episodic giving can be traced back to what happened following the 2004 earthquake and resulting tsunami in the Indian Ocean. For example, online giving tends to peak within three to four days after the disaster happens. This trend was seen in 2004 as well as after Hurricane Katrina in 2005, the Haiti earthquake in 2010, the Japanese earthquake and tsunami in 2011, and Hurricane Sandy in 2012. Even 2014's Ice Bucket Challenge saw peak online donations happen over a four-day period of time.

Online giving to SCIAF following the 2004 Indian Ocean earthquake and tsunami stretched their systems from both a website and donor engagement perspective. At the time, SCIAF was using multiple systems for their website, online giving, and donor management. As the tremendous amount of online donations came into the organization, there were performance issues with the website. Additionally, the lack of integration with the back office systems meant there was a big delay in donor communication. Without the right data at the right time in the right place, things can quickly fall apart. "The biggest concern, in addition to the volume, was making sure that supporters had gifts acknowledged correctly and donations were processed smoothly," says Mitchell.

This led to a major change in both the process and technology of online giving and communication at SCIAF. The organization recognized that digital giving was only going to increase and these spikes from international relief emergencies made the current system unsustainable. They replaced several tools for an integrated fundraising system that included the ability to handle both online and offline channels. This also allowed SCIAF to apply the same best practices of direct mail to their email engagement too.

Combining a bit of the old with a bit of the new has helped SCIAF make important changes over time. They are launching an emergency direct debit program to make it easier for episodic donors to give to the organization. Direct debit is one of the primary ways that people in Scotland and the rest of the UK donate regularly to charities. Having this in place with regular donors takes a lot of friction out of the giving process and SCIAF is now extending the practice to donors who give mostly during emergencies. Mitchell says, "We're going to approach them and say, 'We know that's the type of work you want to support through SCIAF, so why not set up a direct debit so your donation is waiting next time a disaster strikes?'"

The use of data to improve donor segmentation can be taken to unmanageable extremes. Mitchell says it wasn't uncommon to do mailing lists with 70 different segments. They are now simplifying the segmentation strategy and using data to help identify the highest performing segments. Just because those segments can be created does not necessarily mean that they should be, especially if there are diminishing returns or no clear value from all that additional work.

This change to diversify fundraising channels and simultaneously improve donor engagement has relied on data to see if it's working or not. "We've undergone a mini-revolution in terms of how orientated towards data we have become. Any major piece of work now is immediately considered in terms of desired goals and how will we define and measure success. Which isn't to say it's become mechanized and impersonal, but that at some level, all the work we do should be moving towards a clear goal or target," says Mitchell.

In many cases, using data to measure a fundraising program or specific activity has helped validated what SCIAF is doing. "With the data, at least now we know we're doing the right things. Whereas before, if someone was to ask you to prove it, you would have no way of knowing," he says. The connection to the program work overseas also helps bring the daily work and the overall mission closer together. Mitchell adds, "When we have a top level goal to help change the quality of life in rural communities in Rwanda, it's important every member of staff is aware of how their work contributes to the end result. It's important the staff have that connection between their daily work in the office and the lives being changed in a village in Africa. They should feel the satisfaction of knowing the two are directly linked."

SCIAF has been building a culture of change through connecting their work in Scotland to the outcomes that work produces in countries around the world. They recognized that change involves using data in new ways, but still preserving the importance of donor relationships. The organization is both maintaining proven traditional methods of donor stewardship and expanding the ways people can support the organization in a modern world. Using data to prove things are working and drive decisions allows SCIAF to move more confidently into the future.

# 10

# TEST

*"The secret to getting ahead is getting started."*

- AGATHA CHRISTIE

## WWF

Support from leadership and a willingness to embrace change at the organization can be important ingredients for a data driven nonprofit. But they are not the only ways the transformation can take place. For decades, testing has been a critical part of the fundraising process for nonprofits with direct marketing programs. It turns out that having a culture of testing is another way that nonprofits can become more data driven.

If you want to know if something will work or not, then you need to test it. There is simply no substitute for testing, in part because the more you test, the better your results over time. This also means that sometimes tests show that something does not work. That is better to find out sooner rather than later, especially at nonprofit organizations where resources can be tight. Some nonprofits say that they can't afford to test, but I would argue that nonprofits can't afford not to test. Let's look at how testing can play an important role in a more data driven nonprofit.

John Schwass began his professional career in business intelligence and data warehousing working for a telecommunications firm. He began to see how the collection of data was becoming an important part of how the company made decisions. "It just seemed really clear to me that marketing was the next area to start to use data in earnest. Finance had already started that and operations, but I thought marketing was going to move in that area," he says. Schwass took a break in his career to get his MBA from Carnegie Mellon University with the goal of using his new skills in a marketing data context.

Following graduate school, Schwass immediately began working for a marketing analytics consulting company. He worked on projects to analyze consumer packaged goods data from resellers but was hoping to do more work on data that had a direct impact on the end consumer. In 2005, an opportunity came up at World Wildlife Fund (WWF) for Schwass to be their new senior marketing analyst. "WWF is the first nonprofit I've ever worked at – the only one I've ever worked at," says Schwass. He had developed some valuable data analysis skills and brought hands-on experience to the organization. Schwass notes that it was an opportunity for him to "move a little bit closer to the consumer…to the person that's really making the decision" based on the analytics.

When Schwass arrived at WWF, he began working on analytics to improve the direct mail program at the organization. "I think there was a large focus on analytics, but it was really more in spreadsheet analysis. It was still largely a meeting of the minds to come up with who we should mail," he says. That observation could be made of countless nonprofit organizations that have turned creating complex spreadsheets into an art form. Some people might just go along with the status quo, but Schwass knew that WWF could take its analytics capabilities to a new level. "Where I saw an opportunity was in being able to bring to bear a lot more of the information we had than could really be put together on a spreadsheet. I do not think that there was a lack of emphasis on analytics, it was just really more about how to best use the information that we have to drive as much value as possible, to be as efficient and as effective as possible," says Schwass.

Not knowing what is possible with analytics and predictive modeling can leave well-intentioned nonprofit professionals with a blind spot. They continue to try and use data within the scope of what they understand, but another level of expertise is often required. Schwass notes, "I just think people really weren't aware of the possibilities that modeling could bring. The concept of modeling wasn't really known and the impact it could have wasn't really known either."

Schwass knew that if he was going to change how WWF used data, then he was going to have to build trust. Just telling others that they needed to start using analytics in a whole new way would be foolhardy. That's generally a recipe for failure when you're trying to move people from the comfort zone to the new normal. Schwass' approach was to slowly begin introducing testing to the direct mail program by introducing a framework for using data modeling. "A model is a framework that you can build on, you can learn from, you can revise. It's not like pulling everything out every time. It allows you to grow with your knowledge," he says. While the models were learning what worked and what didn't, the staff was also able to learn how the models could be used. Small tests over time turned into more trust that model-based analytics could improve results at WWF.

"What we ended up doing was getting involved in direct marketing, using models, and comparing those models to our current approach. We started having great success and we very quickly started to get the models into more and more tests, which came back with very positive results. Usually, we outperformed our current approach by 30% to 40%," says Schwass. A simple yet powerful way of building trust through testing is to always compare the results to the method that the current process suggested. People can see the difference and they loosen their strong ties to how things have always been done. Over time, testing moved the models from being used in a handful of direct mail projects to being used for the entire collection of mailings at WWF.

Previously, meetings to decide the right segments to mail consisted of people bringing their spreadsheets, lists, and confirmation biases. They would often recommend segments that they felt did well before, but they did not necessarily have data to support the decision. One common pitfall in many organizations is having either too large or too small a sample size. A good process applied to a bad sample of data can result in a lot of errors. As Schwass explains, "If it's a low sample size, you literally have 50 to 100 people in a group. If someone didn't give, then the whole group could be removed from the mailing. Yet we knew that one person giving one typical gift for a relatively high dollar group could end up making a big difference. Frankly, where we found success was in making sure that we didn't exclude people because of low sample size problems and that we had a better way of identifying people that we should be mailing." This was a big change from how segmentation decisions were made in the past. "The success that we had was pretty quick and I think everybody started realizing that this was a real opportunity for us to improve our performance and to be more efficient with our mailings," he says.

As segment performance began to improve through testing, the organization began to embrace how analytics could be used. "I think that we've always been a group, and this is a credit to WWF, that is looking to try to do the best we can for the organization. I think people did a very good job of adjusting to change the way mailing is done at WWF in response to the modeling. It's really a credit to the organization that there was little resistance to something that changed things a good bit in terms of shifting the day-to-day work," says Schwass. The old process where people brought their spreadsheets to meetings and spent a lot of time discussing what to do began to fade away. Instead, the meetings focused on what to test or on the results of the latest test.

We know that success breeds more success. The other thing that success in one group leads to is others getting curious about what is happening. Direct mail donors are often a source of planned gifts for nonprofit organizations. The director of gift planning at WWF had heard about some of the success that direct mail was having through testing and wanted to see if the method could also benefit planned gifts. Once again, Schwass and the team built trust through testing. "I thought there was a real opportunity, but they were not really sure what we could accomplish using this technique," he says. He knew that they could not test a predictive model for planned gifts the same way that they would a direct mail segment. Simply put, you can't just wait years for nature to take its course to see if the test worked or not.

Instead, Schwass used an external vendor to make phone calls to direct mail donors that were identified in the model as having a high likelihood to make a planned gift. Donors were asked whether or not they had already included charities, and potentially WWF, in their will. As Schwass explains, "I had developed this model, which I had intended for direct mail, but I hadn't really convinced our director to use it. I said, 'How about this? This is a very small group. This is a lot smaller than the mailings that we typically do. Why don't you let me pick these calls and order it based on the mail model?' The results were very positive. The vendor had obviously done work with a lot of other nonprofit organizations with similar kinds of calls and they told the director of gift planning that they had never experienced this kind of success before."

Within a short period of time, the planned giving group wanted model-based analytics applied to all their direct mail activities. "We started working on business cases so that they could expand their marketing. We helped them provide senior management with a better understanding of the value of this marketing and making sure that people are aware of their gift-giving opportunities," says Schwass. Modeling and predictive analytics help nonprofits understand who to target for certain fundraising programs. At WWF, it also provided fundraisers a way to size the opportunity and ROI for increased marketing spend. Schwass notes, "The model-based approach was really very useful for not only the effectiveness of some of their marketing but also helping them expand their program because, really, there was a lot more value there. There were a lot more opportunities that we weren't taking advantage of because we weren't getting in front of people to let them know about this giving opportunity."

Again, Schwass believed that a few adjustments to the current process of using data for better segmentation could make a big difference in another part of the organization. "Having done their mailings in the past, I knew there was a much better way to do it…Part of that wasn't because there was anything inherently bad about what they had been doing in the past, it just hadn't changed a lot. I think a lot of people were receiving the message over and over again and we weren't expanding it to a group of people who may be more interested in the message, but just had never heard it. Sometimes, it's about variability and bringing in a new group of people," says Schwass.

The positive results of testing began to create a culture that was open to doing more advanced analytics with the data. Other parts of the organization began to take notice and Schwass was able to repeat the same "test, learn, and trust" cycle all over again. Schwass has learned there are certain common questions that fundraisers across traditional and digital channels all want to answer: How can we select people better? How can we get in front of the right people for something? It might be inviting somebody to an event or member travel mailings, or it's planned giving or trying to identify people that might qualify as major donors.

With this model framework in place, different parts of WWF have begun asking next-level questions about what hidden opportunities might be in the data. Schwass says, "Increasingly, we've moved a lot more toward measuring lifetime value and understanding the implications of different kinds of events on lifetime value. What's the meaning if someone gives a second gift to the organization or a third gift or an action? A second advocacy action? What does it mean when somebody RSVPs to an event for the first time, in terms of value?" These are all questions that might never get asked if you're still trying to decide who in the database to focus on. "Understanding the value of those types of interactions helps us prioritize where to put our efforts, prioritize what the value is of encouraging people to make a second gift, a third gift, et cetera," he adds.

None of this strategic thinking would happen if Schwass and the team hadn't achieved some tactical success along the way. People are naturally skeptical about change and our brains are wired to avoid risk. "It would have been a very hard sell before we had been successful at a more tactical level and had produced results in a shorter period of time," he says.

Seeing that a predictive model can outperform what people do in a spreadsheet might make it sound like the human element isn't really needed. But Schwass points out that the experience that his fundraising colleagues brought to the table was still invaluable. "The best way to learn and the best way to do better with your models is to talk to people. All those mail selection meetings that we had were some of the best ways of developing new variables," he says. The key is to focus on the possible variables that could be put into a model, not whether they actually work. Schwass says, "One of the best things to do is to have conversations with people about what they think the motivation is. Some of those discussions are the best things for creating new variables because it helps you understand. Feedback from the donors is very helpful in understanding how do we do a better job of getting to know when they want to give and when they don't want to give." When you remove the burden of having to do all the analysis in your head, people can focus on describing donor behaviors.

Models can also help improve performance because they can weigh the relative importance of all the variables. All data is not equal. You want to not only distinguish the signal from the noise but also pay attention to information that has more value for a particular segment. "People like to talk about demographics and things of that nature, but obviously demographics are minor variables in most cases unless you really don't have a lot of experience with this person. If the person is a new donor to the file, then that piece of information might be a little bit more important to know," he says. But once you have basic demographic data like age, it is not as valuable as other information to predict behavior. This highlights how important the difference between descriptive analytics and predictive analytics is. Schwass notes, "A model can be a little bit more accurate in taking into account how additional information adjusts up or adjusts down our expectations. It's a foundation that you can add to, that you can modify and change." He adds that, independent from the predictions they provide, models can also be helpful in terms of challenging assumptions and helping users understand what is important.

Testing leads to asking more informed questions and it begins to draw out the natural curiosity of many nonprofit professionals. "People will ask questions. They will come up with ideas and ask: Have you thought about that? Have you tried that in the model? How do we improve retention?" says Schwass. The job of the data scientist is then to take those questions and measure the potential value of the answers. That value may be in acquisition, retention, or ways to improve the effectiveness of the organization. Schwass is definitely seeing an increase in data literacy among his colleagues at WWF. "I think there's more understanding that what we're trying to find is additional ways of explaining our understanding of how somebody may behave so that we can be more effective in the way that we're soliciting people or we're communicating with people." He adds, "That's really critically important in the nonprofit world. It's important in the for-profit world as well, but a hefty amount of the way that nonprofits are judged is being effective and efficient in fundraising and making sure that as much money as possible is going to the programs and not to fundraising and operations, et cetera."

Having a culture of testing creates a data driven mindset about looking for the right opportunities. All nonprofits have limited resources and it's simply not possible to try everything. But testing allows you to simulate things on a smaller, faster scale and identify which opportunities appear to be a better choice. It's OK if something does not work, but you want to know that as quickly as possible. Schwass says, "Generally, we've taken the approach of testing incrementally. We might have the opportunity to spend some time on something we think is important and if, as we dig in, we're not getting the traction we thought we would get or the value of that isn't that high, then we'll pull back." There are certainly situations where the use of analytics shows that the organization is already doing a really good job. "We may find after a little bit of analysis and maybe some initial models and some initial approaches that we don't have the data," Schwass says. "We have to be able to implement something that will help, but if we spent several more hours, we would only improve by a couple percent," he adds. All opportunities aren't equal either. If the opportunity is big, then a few percentage points of improvement might mean a lot. On the other hand, small opportunities may not be worth the extra effort.

Does testing always improve a process or a result? Not always, as it turns out, but that does not mean there isn't some value created. "We have colleagues who have seen that we've had some success and so they think that we can do an amazing job. Sometimes, we find that we can't do as amazing a job as they think we can, for a variety of different reasons. It's actually kind of a nice problem to have. A sense from people that you can affect things more than you actually can," says Schwass. It certainly helps the staff to see their activities validated through analysis.

This success has also allowed Schwass to build a larger team and increase the scope of his role at the organization. When he started at WWF in 2005, the small team spent most of its time on ad hoc reporting and testing was practically a side project. The success in model-based analytics and automating a lot of the normal reporting needs has resulted in more resources for testing. In 2008, Schwass was promoted to the role of director of fundraising operations & strategic analysis at WWF. He works with a team of four analysts and they have seen how testing has created a more data driven approach at the organization.

As it turns out, that shift from providing reports to doing more testing and models had an impact in terms of making more data driven decisions. Schwass recognized that reports were often being used to answer questions when analytics should be used instead. The focus shifted to "build, develop, and rebuild models in an attempt to answer important questions by reducing the number of ad hoc requests, especially as it relates to things that really shouldn't be ad hoc," says Schwass. "If you you're going to ask this question again then it shouldn't be ad hoc. If it's a big strategic question, then that's really important," he says. Those big questions are exactly the types of things that you want to move away from reports and to models wherever possible.

There was a recognition at WWF that the analysis work could be made part of the broader decision-making process. Schwass did not want to produce reports that just went stale or were not actionable. "We want to use our tactical understanding in combination with a more strategic value understanding to make better overall decisions. We're trying to understand things as holistically as we can and integrate whatever work that we're doing into a common framework. That continues to be the biggest evolution of the process: How do you bring all this information together in a way that it can be integrated for better decision-making?" explains Schwass.

The use of data to drive decisions is a continuous feedback loop. Every adjustment can create incremental value for the organization. Schwass is not spending time resting on improvements made to old processes either. He says, "It's nice to know that it's better than it was 10 years ago or five years ago, but we're trying to improve over yesterday or over last week. Part of it is trying to focus on better decision-making and also providing an internal view so that people can understand what the impact of these decisions are. It's more than just a black box." Part of that approach is making sure that the leadership at WWF can see the big picture and provide context for the decisions that are being made. Schwass points out, "One thing that's been really great about this evolution is that we work across the organization. I think people value analysis that's viewed as independent." Over time, the work being done with analytics has not only helped improve performance but it has also built up credibility in the minds of senior management.

Schwass is a trained expert in the use of data and analytics, but he would be the first one to tell you that training alone is not enough. "It's not about the data. It's about what you are achieving more effectively with the data…That's really the goal of the organization: how we can get the support that we need to achieve our goals, whether that's conservation or whether that's humanitarian relief," he says. Over the years, he has learned a lot of lessons and has some advice for other nonprofits on this journey.

Schwass believes that if a nonprofit "really wants to understand the whole lifetime value cycle for engaging their supporters, then that means taking a systematic, data driven approach to understanding that value." He adds that "focusing on the overall value and investing energy in the most important questions" will garner the resources and the support that you need to achieve your goals. The success they have had with making data driven decisions at WWF has not only improved the effectiveness of the organization, but has also led to increased investment in key resources.

During the past decade at World Wildlife Fund, Schwass and his team have created a culture of testing that has led to more data driven decision making. Their approach was to start with small projects that built trust through visible improvements in direct mail results. Over time, the old meetings where spreadsheets were examined were transformed into an opportunity for the staff to ask deeper questions. This curiosity spread to other departments, like planned giving, where they wondered if testing could improve their results, too. Schwass and the team were able to shift their focus from ad hoc reporting to using analytics as part of the decision-making process at World Wildlife Fund. Today, the use of data to drive decision making is no longer a new thing; it's now a vital part of how the organization operates.

RNIB

It was a cool and blustery Wednesday night on the Thames River in London back on June 10, 2015. The best minds in British fundraising had gathered together for the Institute of Fundraising's fourth annual Insight in Fundraising Awards gala dinner.[67] The IoF is the professional membership body for fundraising in the United Kingdom; this event brought together charities and their data partners to reward best practice, innovation, and impact in harnessing data insight for great fundraising.

The awards included Most Powerful Use of Insight by a Charity with Fundraising Income Less than £7m, won by Wood Green, The Animals Charity. Alzheimer's Research UK took home the Most Powerful Insight from Digital Analysis award and the Rising Star honors went to Cats Protection. But perhaps the most important award of the night for Team of the Year went to the Royal National Institute for Blind People's Fundraising Insight Unit.[68]

The award for the RNIB Fundraising Insight Unit was the culmination of years of hard work and focus since the group was created in 2009. Mark Langdon manages the unit at RNIB and has been there since the very early days of its existence. "When I joined RNIB, the fundraising insight unit had just been created, but it was more from a theoretical point of view. The director of fundraising at the time had decided that we needed an insight unit and we needed a business intelligence function, so the team was created and people were recruited for this team. There hadn't been that much thought put into exactly what they would be doing, exactly how they would be using data, and where that data would be coming from," says Langdon.

When starting any new initiative, it is often important to be more specific on vision and flexible on the details. That has often been the advice of Amazon's founder and CEO Jeff Bezos, and the leadership at RNIB followed this approach when starting the Fundraising Insight Unit. "The reason that we exist is to help the fundraising teams," says Langdon. There are four different teams across the RNIB fundraising department, each with a different responsibility for raising income at the organization. "They are the individual giving team, which are more the donors that give £10 ($14.50) a month or £5 ($7.25) a year. Then we've got a legacy team who are responsible for making sure that in the future they will have the opportunity to leave legacy gifts.[69] Then there is the community fundraising team, which has just been joined the legacy team because there are similarities between the teams, and then we've also got major donors and corporate. Those teams are served by the Fundraising Insight Unit," he says.

The early days of the team got off to a rough start. "At the beginning, we had a few people leave because it wasn't working so well. The work that we were doing was mostly around basic reporting. Between then and now we've managed to change things so that we're using the data in a far more strategic way," says Langdon. Both the Kübler-Ross Change Curve and Seth Godin's book, *The Dip*, illustrate that the process of change usually means things get worse before they get significantly better.[70] "Most of the work that we do tends to be quantitative rather than qualitative. We don't do that much for maybe major donors and corporate giving, but with individual giving and with the legacy community, there are lots of things that we can do," he says.

The more successful the Fundraising Insight Unit has been at their work, the more areas they have been asked to manage. "I've been asked to look at not just the insights but also the data management and the data governance. That's where we're needing to grow to have the quality and insight that improve results. I tend to think the two key ingredients are in fact good insight analysts and good data governance because the right people can't do anything unless the quality of data is high enough to make recommendations," says Langdon.

He describes a situation in which the team was asked to use data to resolve an internal debate that had gone on for years. "We had a big raffle program where we would phone all of the people that were buying raffle tickets from us and we asked them if they wanted to buy more raffle tickets. The raffle program is huge for us, and we have about 3.5 million people on our database that have come from the raffle program," explains Langdon. "There was an idea that we could go to these people and ask them if they wanted to also make an additional gift," he says. This is a very common scenario where nonprofits are afraid to ask one type of donor to give in another way. For example, asking members at a museum or aquarium to also make an additional donation to the annual fund. I have seen heated arguments about whether activists should be asked to give to a monthly giving program. Staff members protest that it won't work or it will just annoy their constituents.

There is nothing like actually testing to see if asking constituents to support the organization in other ways will work. Testing can help organizations make decisions versus just using opinions or gut instinct. "One of the pieces of work we did for individual giving was to almost act as a referee in the debate as to what we should do with these raffle donors. This was an argument that went on for a number of years actually with no decision really being made," explains Langdon. The Fundraising Insight Unit got involved and "ran a few tests using propensity models to work out who the best people to target were. Langdon says, "We found out that we could ask raffle donors to make a gift without having a very big impact on the raffle program at all." He adds, "What impact there was could be more than outweighed by next year's income that we can get from the recurring giving. We decided to go with that and it's now worth about a £1 million ($1.45 million) to RNIB."

Did the internal opinions cost the organization £1 million a year or did testing find that additional revenue? You be the judge, but this example highlights how good data analysts can use testing to answer important questions. "That's just an example of how the Insight Unit can support the decisions that are being made. Fundraisers will have ideas about what we can do to increase our income, but whether we should do that or not is where having data helps back up the decision," says Langdon. He says they can test to find out whether a decision "means more money now but less money later or less money now but more money later."

Over time, Langdon and the team have also seen how testing leads to better questions from the rest of the organization. He says, "Sometimes... the question that's being asked is not really what we eventually answer. For instance, if someone came to us, they might say to us, 'Tell me how many of our raffle donors are women.' We'll say, 'Well we can do that but why do you want to know?' They'll say, 'Well if we work out that all of our raffle donors are females then we can target asking questions to females.' Then we might say, 'Well it sounds like you're really trying to work out who your raffle donors are or who the best group to target are, and the best way to do that might be to put together a propensity model that might include gender, but it might also include a number of other factors like where they live or how wealthy they are, what their family situation is.' Then we can solve the problem, which isn't necessarily giving them what they first asked for." The Fundraising Insight Unit really enjoys digging deeper into understanding what problems fundraisers are trying to solve and seeing how testing can help drive decisions. Langdon says, "There's certainly a level of knowledge in the team to know what to do and to try to fully support the final objectives as opposed to just giving the internal customers what they need and maybe missing the mark by giving only that."

The team at RNIB has been really trying to improve data quality not only in the fundraising department but also across the entire organization. "In fundraising, because data has been our stock and trade for quite some time, the quality of the data is very good. It's almost grown organically, so if we try to do something that has not worked because the data hasn't been good enough, then we fix the data," says Langdon. "At the moment, we're being asked to do similar things for the rest of the organization outside of fundraising. The quality of the data is far, far behind the quality in fundraising. We've got an organization-wide data governance initiative to fix this, and it includes changing the culture of the organization's data," he says.

Part of the data governance initiative is giving people training around the collection, management, and use of data at RNIB. Data governance is about maximizing the opportunity around data to support the strategic objectives of the business," says Langdon. "For instance, we might get people who are working with our services along the front line, who don't want to ask questions because they see it gets intrusive and they might not take the opportunity to get an email address or a date of birth or something like that," he says. Langdon identifies another common problem at nonprofits in that not everyone understands how having the right data has a significant long-term impact on the organization's mission. In some ways, the good intentions of frontline staff trying not to be intrusive can end up negatively impacting supporters and the services they use down the road. "We've been going around the organization explaining how the collection of data works for our service users, and even though it might feel slightly intrusive, it's for their benefit in the long-term. There's a big training program around that in order to change the culture," says Langdon.

A data and information governance board has also been created at RNIB. "Every month we'll discuss governance policies which are now posted on a wiki that everybody in the organization has access to, so it's clear how people should deal with data," Langdon says. He explains that the top of the policy framework consists of a list of key of statements "around data so that it makes it clear why data is so important to the organization and how it should be used." He adds, "The list includes statements like 'Data is an asset,' and 'Data is secure,' along with 'Data is shared.'"

The Fundraising Insight Unit also works on projects that span multiple groups at the same time. Langdon explains, "One of the projects we've been trying to support with the Insight Unit is looking at how we can support the community fundraisers and what we can do in order to grow their area of the business." He feels it's an area of the business where opportunities haven't been realized to date. He goes on to say, "The community fundraising team might ask people to put on a local event, so somebody might volunteer to put on a local event and raise some money. What we found was that there was a link between the volunteers who helped put on the event and people who would leave a legacy." Unfortunately, there was a policy at the organization that volunteers could not be engaged for any other fundraising activity. It was the raffle ticket problem all over again. Internal policies or opinions not based on data could potentially limit the success of the organization.

The team was once again called in to help resolve the issue through data and testing. "That's the great thing about having data you can't argue with. Until then it's just one person's opinion, and you have somebody else's personal opinion, but with the data you can say, 'Well, for this group of people that we've tested, we've found that there's much higher correlation and people have said that they want to receive more communication around legacies,'" says Langdon. Now that testing has found a high correlation between volunteers in the community fundraising program and legacy donors, both teams can work together on common goals.

A culture of testing and using the results to make data driven decisions has grown since the Fundraising Insight Unit first began. When it first began, the team had six people but quickly lost half the staff members. The shift away from just producing reports and doing more testing was not everyone's cup of tea. But that initial dip turned out to be a blessing in disguise to rebuild a future award winning team. Looking back, Langdon says, "I think just the fact also that we were able to take the data and show how it could be used to inform decisions was quite surprising to others in some cases. That meant that whenever there was a question around long-term strategy, it became important to get the data people involved."

The Fundraising Insight Unit's involvement and the success they have had through testing allowed the team to build up a lot of credibility at RNIB. Langdon believes that "having that credibility within the organization and having a good insight team" has been absolutely critical to building a culture where there are more data driven decisions. So how did they go about building such a great data focused team at the RNIB? "One of the big things for me is just having good quality people. I know charities all over the world have to deliver as much value as possible to the service users and there's pressure to perhaps pay staff a little less. What I find is that if you get people who might command commercial market rates as opposed to charitable market rates, then you'll get much more out of those people and it's worth the extra money," says Langdon.

He also believes that data analysts must not only understand the business but also spend time building relationships with fundraisers and the data management and governance staff. Part of that means recruiting the right people into your data team. Langdon says, "When recruiting for a senior role, for instance, then obviously we'll look to have a proven track record. We'll look for a background in statistics and in being able to take data and move it to support bigger decision. One of the big things in our industry is that we'll get people with great stats skills and great technical understanding, but they aren't very good at the softer skills, like communicating with people. It's really, really important for them to have the ability to communicate and build relationships with other people."

Hiring entry-level data team members has a slightly different profile according to Langdon. "If we're recruiting for a junior role, then I would ideally look for someone with a good degree in economics or maybe mathematics or computing and also with potential to reason and understand business. That's worked quite well for us because these days data experts are quite hard to find, so if we can recruit graduates and then train them up ourselves, then that gives us a chance to mold those people," he says. Langdon adds, "We've been quite lucky here because the team is expanding. Where we've had good people, we've been able to promote them quite quickly, and so giving them growth opportunities is a big part of it." All of these practices have allowed the group to generate results and scale for the organization. "I know a lot of charities…may have one data person trying to do everything. It just doesn't really work. I feel that if they made that extra investment, then they would get a return on it," says Langdon.

Hiring the right people, building credibility through testing, and demonstrating value across the organization all led to the RNIB Fundraising Insight Unit winning the Team of the Year award from their peers. In just a few shorts years, they have grown a culture of testing within an established nonprofit organization and become much more data driven. The success that they have had has now led to the delivery of insights and value beyond just the fundraising department. RNIB has become a data driven nonprofit, and the Fundraising Insight Unit is excited about the future.

# 11

# SHARE

*"The approach to what you do,*
*results in what you get."*

- FREDDY GRUBER

## 1,000,000 DONORS

One phenomenon in the nonprofit sector is the tremendous amount of sharing that takes place. Many nonprofit organizations openly share data, techniques, and information about how they run their operations. This contrasts with the corporate sector, in which a lot of these assets are kept under lock and key.

Some of the most popular sessions at nonprofit conferences are the ones that focus on best practices. Attendees are eager to pick up this tip or that trick that could make all the difference at their nonprofit. The topics range from running an effective advocacy campaign to lessons learned in building a monthly donor program.

One of the challenges with absorbing all of these great ideas is that reality strikes when the conference is over. The emails are piled up, the work from before the conference remains, and implementing just a few of these ideas can become a daunting task. This is exactly the situation Michal Heiplik encountered when he was working at the Houston public broadcasting station KUHT.

"I would go to a conference and learn some benchmarking tidbits that another station was doing better. I would write down 30 or 50 of these great ideas after a week at a conference, get back to my shop, and arrange these things in order of priority," says Heiplik, who started out as the station's database manager before going on to run their entire membership program. He notes, "A year later, I would look at that list and realize that I probably was able to accomplish one thing because of resources, time, and other constraints."

Heiplik recognized very quickly that just having the ideas was not enough, especially at a local level where resources are always constrained. "It was pretty easy to see that I could gather the best idea. That's the easy part and we've been doing that for years as an industry to gather the best ideas and practices. But I really had no way at the local level to actually implement change." As Heiplik talked to people at other PBS stations, it became clear that they were facing the same challenge. No one lacked great ideas, but the issue was operationalizing the best ones at scale.

Over time, Heiplik underwent a transformation from a database manager to a data driven decision maker. There is a bit of irony that the Czech Republic-born Heiplik got so good at using data to make decisions at public broadcasting stations because he knew nothing about American radio or TV programs. "When I took on running the membership program in Houston, it was my first introduction to how data can really transform on-air fundraising. Back then, decisions around programming for pledge drives were largely made by gut feeling. People would look at the available programs and say, 'Hey, Suze Orman or Wayne Dyer! That sounds good. We should put that in the time slot.' There was not a lot of data going into the decision," says Heiplik.

"My problem was I didn't grow up in this country, so I didn't have any of that gut feeling about how programs would perform or how audiences would react," says Heiplik. "We would sit there and watch these previews of concert shows and members of the team would all have some kind of relationship with the content. They would go, 'Oh, that group, that concert was awesome when I went to it in the 80s. The people will love this.' And I would not know who the group was," he recalls. Heiplik says he had to "build [his] own crutch and rely on the data to make these decisions."

Heiplik built up his own reporting and did analysis to drive decisions based on the data, not preconceived notions about what should work. Before too long he had one of the highest-performing membership programs in the entire country. Other stations took notice and wanted to understand what Heiplik was doing differently in Houston. To understand what happened next requires an understanding of the sharing culture among Public Broadcasting System (PBS) organizations over the last 30 years.

During the late 1980s, Sylvia Humphrey was working as the director of research and community projects at PBS station WNET in New York City. Around 1989, she was asked by Larry Lynn, the vice president of development at WNET during this time, to find out why some of the top stations were performing so well. Humphrey began calling around to different stations and started asking them lots of questions about their fundraising data.

Within a short period of time Humphrey was able to assume data from several different stations and their fundraising performance. The stations were happy to share the data because they were also very interested in understanding how well they were doing. But her conundrum was that it was full of apples-to-oranges comparisons. Stations were measuring memberships, renewals, and other metrics in different ways and this made it nearly impossible to benchmark performance.

As luck would have it, Humphrey ran into Roberta McCarthy, the long-time membership program manager at WGBH in Boston at a PBS conference. While catching up on things, Humphrey mentioned the challenge with comparing different stations. McCarthy introduced her to Chuck Longfield, who had previously developed software that WGBH used and was starting a new company to focus on nonprofit data.

In 1991, Longfield and his new company, Target Analysis Group, took on the task of collecting, analyzing, and reporting out on benchmarking trends across the first group of stations. Over time, this would grow into benchmarking nearly every PBS station. In the early days, the stations would review the results on a conference call and eventually meet in person to compare the findings. The benchmarking program would eventually be called donorCentrics™ and it expanded to measure higher education, healthcare, international relief, direct marketing, sustainer, and online giving-focused nonprofits.

The rest is history. Today, Humphrey is the director of development for The Science Initiative at Columbia University, McCarthy retired from WGBH in 2010 after more than 25 years at the organization,[71] and Longfield is now the chief scientist at Blackbaud, after both Target Analysis Group and Target Software were acquired in 2007. The donorCentrics™ program has more than 500 nonprofits that participate in benchmarking across more than 50 different groups in 25 countries and is delivered by Target Analytics, a division of Blackbaud.

This culture of sharing data created a wealth of benchmarking data across PBS stations over nearly 30 years. When senior leaders took a few steps back they also realized that the data was telling them benchmarking alone was not enough for their continued survival. Heiplik indicates that five years ago they "looked back at a decade before and realized that public broadcasting had lost a million donors across the system." He was hit with the reality that he could "build the best program in Houston, but in the end public media as a whole might disappear because of how stations fundraising nationwide." Heiplik says he had the realization: "I'm not really changing our future, and my own future could be gone if we don't do things drastically different."

Several of the larger PBS stations, including Heiplik's Houston station, began to think about what could be done to turn the tide. The 35 largest stations, also referred to as the Major Market Group, represent more than 70% of all the fundraising done by PBS. They have regularly shared data for benchmarking purposes and helped to drive change in the sector. This time, they were discussing how to respond to the alarming trends with donors. Heiplik says, "It was basically an opportunity to really make meaningful and resolute change within the system based on the practices of what I've been already doing at the local market." Making real change would also require some investment, which has always been a limiting factor among nonprofit organizations. But this time, there was a member of the group that knew stemming the tide of donor attrition was just the tip of the iceberg.

Ben Godley, the chief operating officer at Boston's WGBH, could also see that something needed to be done that went beyond just helping their fundraising efforts. In 2015, WGBH had operating revenue over $75 million with donations, bequests, and grants making up nearly half that total. A good portion of the rest came from licensing and distribution fees for the programs WGBH produces.[72] WGBH programs like Frontline and NOVA rely on other PBS stations as a distribution network for that programming. If the smaller stations couldn't survive long-term, then it also put all this programming in jeopardy. That was enough reason for WGBH to fund the new Contributor Development Partnership (CDP) program. A station advisory council was formed to help guide important decisions and support the program across the country.

With that decision, Heiplik packed up his family and made the journey from the hot summers of Houston, Texas to the cold winters of Boston, Massachusetts. The self-confessed "data geek" turned membership director would now lead CDP as its executive director. The first hurdle was taking all the dispersed data systems around the country from independent stations and bringing them together for analysis. The data would form the basis for a national reference file that could be used to uncover what was really happening across the initial 35 stations.

At first glance, this might sound very similar to a normal benchmarking group and certainly resembles the shared data approach that PBS stations had been using for two decades. CDP became an evolutionary step past the traditional benchmarking program by incorporating three key elements:

1. A single goal for the program and stations participating
2. A common set of metrics and regular reporting
3. A support system to help stations implement best practices

Heiplik notes, "CDP essentially has one goal: improve net revenue or donors for stations. Either more donors or more net revenue. That's it. Period." During the early days of CDP, there were many differing opinions about what the program's goals should be. It is not uncommon for any organization to want to have several goals or Key Performance Indicators (KPIs), but coming together and agreeing on a few metrics that determine the success of a program takes a lot of discipline. Heiplik notes, "If you have that as a focus, it becomes really interesting how you make your business decisions to succeed against that goal."

The constraint of just two metrics, increased donors or increased net revenue, actually become very liberating for CDP. "If that's the lens we are measuring everything through, then I don't care how we get to it", says Heiplik. "I either have to convince the local station to improve their practices and actually do it or I have to do it for them, but both ways lead to me succeeding if we set goals that way. Our vehicle donation program is a good example of this. I can call the station to renegotiate the rates with their current vendor or they can switch to my vendor with better rates. Either way, I'm getting the net result that I need," he says.

The next new element in CDP was a core set of metrics that not only benchmarked performance but also showed stations the best revenue or donor opportunities. It took nearly two years to pull all that data together from across 35 different stations, that in many cases were using different underlying technology, to create benchmarks. That seems like a tremendous amount of work, but Heiplik highlights an important reason for all that work: "When we were designing the original metrics, it was important to set metrics that nobody can question. If you don't have trust in those metrics, then the whole thing crumbles."

Self-reported data is always susceptible to problems in any benchmarking effort. This is why CDP made the investment to extract, transform, and load (ETL) raw data from each of the participating stations. It was extremely important that none of the participants could make themselves look better or worse in their own data. The result was something called the Revenue Opportunity and Action Report (ROAR). The initial version of the ROAR was 18 metrics from across all 35 stations where not only performance was compared, but also the revenue and donor growth opportunity for each metric.

Making the ROAR a success also meant applying decades of lessons learned in benchmarking and performance measurement. Every quarter, the ROAR report would show each of the 18 metrics, how the stations performed, how the average station performed, how a good station performed, and what that station could achieve by performing as well as a good station. Notably, the best-performing stations are not used as a benchmark and there is a very important reason for that.

"When we brought out the first report, we essentially started with the best metric. We took the top station and we would try to benchmark everybody to that," recalls Heiplik. After a few discussions with Longfield, they decided that setting the best performers as the benchmark would do more harm than good. "That's not a goal that most people can shoot for and they'll just dismiss it out of hand. Many stations would say, 'I can never reach that goal and I'm just going to try to be average,' and so we decided to give them this middle tier instead," he says.

This is not to dismiss valid concerns about trying to compare lots of non-profits to one really high-performing organization in the group. Outliers in the data set can create unrealistic expectations. Heiplik points to an example of a high-performing station when it came to sustaining monthly donors. The average station had 3% to 7% of their file that were sustainers, but there was one station, Twin Cities Public Television (TPT), in St. Paul, Minnesota that had 20% of their donors giving monthly. "If we would have used their measure, the first thing stations would say is that 'Well, TPT is a different market. St. Paul has a lot more going for them than I do. It's the market. It's not the programs or the practices. I cannot get to that level,' and they would dismiss it because it would be one station," says Heiplik.

Instead, CDP calculated a "good" value that was, statistically speaking, just one standard deviation from the mean. Think of that as one level up from the average; multiple nonprofits will be huddled around that good value. One slight change to the benchmark made a huge difference. "When we made it the top percentile, all of a sudden they couldn't dismiss it because the top 20 stations were doing that. It's not the market, it's the practices," notes Heiplik.

It was also critical to show the value of being average or being good. "We actually calculated the money left on the table of them not achieving that good measure. That's where we came up with the opportunity calculations at average and good value. We do not calculate them as the best value because stations, again, would not trust it," says Heiplik. When a highly contested metric, like corporate matching gifts, was added to the ROAR report there was a need for additional statistical fine-tuning. "People would say it's great that Houston has a great corporate matching program. Of course they do. They have ExxonMobile and Shell in their market. It turns out it has nothing to do with the market. There are a lot more variables involved," he says.

They turned to Longfield and his team to normalize the data, which is the process of adjusting values on different scales to a more common scale. Yes, statistics long ago solved "we're not like those other nonprofits" problem by transforming data to be a better apples-to-apples comparison. For example, normalizing the data allows direct comparison between a large station like Houston PBS and a smaller one like Mountain Lake PBS in Plattsburgh, New York. If one of the stations was truly in an area of the country with under-performing matching gift donations, then the opportunity could be adjusted.

The ROAR has now grown to track 24 metrics that all tie back to either increased donors or increased net revenue. The report works because people trust the data, it fits on a single page, and staff can use its red, yellow, and green traffic lights to help prioritize what they should focus on.

| # | METRIC DESCRIPTION | CURRENT PERIOD | PRIOR PERIOD | % CHANGE FROM PRIOR PERIOD | AVERAGE VALUE | GOOD VALUE | GROSS REVENUE OPPORTUNITY @ GOOD VALUE |
|---|---|---|---|---|---|---|---|
| 1 | Overall Member Retention | 60.09% | 57.76% | 4.0% | 62.3% | 72.1% | $48,142 |
| 2 | Overall Revenue Retention | 72.45% | 63.59% | 13.9% | 68.1% | 81.2% | $63,581 |
| 3 | Overall First Year Member Retention | 45.35% | 42.75% | 6.1% | 39.0% | 48.0% | $27,913 |
| 4 | Overall First Year Revenue Retention | 55.67% | 46.30% | 20.2% | 40.7% | 54.3% | Great job! |
| 5 | First Year Mail Acquired Member Retention | 38.87% | 45.72% | -15.0% | 53.0% | 68.3% | $87,136 |
| 6 | % Revenue From $1000 Cumulative Donors | 28.61% | 25.07% | 14.1% | 18.3% | 28.3% | $13,435 |
| 7 | % Sustainers (of all 12 month donors) | 38.80% | 38.26% | 1.4% | 17.4% | 26.3% | Great job! |

The CDP approach would already be considered a model for other non-profits to follow, but they continued innovating and introduced the third key element of the program. The data and insights revealed in ROAR allowed them to revisit the highest performing organizations to understand what they were doing differently. The CDP team focused on the top three performing stations for each high opportunity metric. They conducted interviews with staff at the individual stations, looked at data, and documented in detail what was happening at the local level.

The result was a series of fundraising checklists that outlined a set of common best practices that came directly from the three top performing organizations in the group. This approach was certainly influenced by Heiplik's experience of going to nonprofit conferences and picking up ideas that were challenging to implement. Instead of just providing a single organization's perspective or anecdotal stories that look good on a slide presentation, they were providing specific guidelines that had been tested and validated to get real results. This development detective work also identified the practices that no one else was doing that made all the difference in achieving higher performance.

The CDP team would also test out ideas that they knew some groups might reject without evidence that the concepts would move the needle in a significant way. The first such experiment was to run a thank-you call program for new donors, but with a new twist — these donors would not be asked to donate as a part of the phone call, just thanked. As one might imagine, the idea of spending money to call a donor and not solicit them for an additional gift was met with some initial skepticism. This idea had been talked about in theory, but never really tested at scale to see whether it worked.

The CDP team quickly tested the thank-you calls with three stations and removed all of the friction for them. "They basically signed a one-page agreement that allowed us to call their donors and that was it," recalls Heiplik. CDP pulled the data, had the calls made, and recorded the results. Stations did not have to do anything else except pay the invoice. Needless to say, the initial test was extremely successful and the program was rolled out to all of the CDP stations.

After more than three years, the thank-you call program has been a tremendous success. Over 300,000 donors have been called, thanked, and tracked as a part of the program. A single thank-you phone call within six months of their first gift has resulted in 56% lift in donor retention and a 72% increase in revenue retention. Over the past few years, I've talked about the thank-you call program in conference presentations and at nonprofit events. There are always a lot of questions from the audience and a few more when people come up to me after the presentation. For all the note taking and interest in the results from this program, very few nonprofits have gone on to implement their own version. CDP's approach of running these services and taking all of the friction out of a practice that is proven to produce positive results has made all the difference for participating nonprofits.

Another underlying reason why running these support services has been so successful is that it allows CDP to create real scale. A smaller station might not be able to get a call center vendor interested in making a few thousand calls, let alone the willingness to do all the data capture and analysis work. But when an organization is making hundreds of thousands of calls, there is leverage that can help drive costs lower and returns higher.

Heiplik points to CDP's vehicle donation program as another example of using a shared services model to create scale and better opportunities for nonprofits. The idea for focusing on vehicle donations came from analysis of the data that showed how one of the PBS stations in Indiana was getting very strong results. "We negotiated a contract with a large national processor of vehicles, pushed down the cost crazy low where instead of getting 65% of the net we are now getting 83% of the net of each car," notes Heiplik. "Now if I'm sitting down with a vendor, I can talk to them about 3 million donors nationwide. That we can bring them an entire market without having to go on 120 to 180 sales calls removes all the cost of sales for each of these vendors. They're eternally grateful and they will cut deals like nobody's business," he says.

Heiplik points out that they "have aggregated the scale so they can negotiate better" and "the data drives it all." The initial effort to extract data from across the stations and to begin to measure a common set of metrics became an engine for growth. Identifying the best revenue or donor growth opportunities allowed stations to prioritize their focus at the local level. The best performing groups helped provide detailed best practices that could be implemented successfully by any nonprofit in the program. The willingness to test new ideas led to innovation and the ability to create real scale across the program using shared services.

Underlying CDP is a culture of sharing among PBS stations that has grown over the years. "Ever since I joined public media, there has always been the sense of sharing. Everybody is very open. You can call up any station and I can say, 'I'm from the WGBH. I'm looking for ways that you guys deal with sustainers.' They'll stop what they're doing and they'll tell you. They'll send you samples. They'll be helpful. That culture of sharing is there," says Heiplik. That is not to say that everyone needs to share or participate.

"We are 100% vested in those that want to improve. Those that want to drive forward, we will move mountains for them. Those that simply do not, we will not drag them along," explains Heiplik. "If we're designing our solutions and our services, we're not designing them to the lowest common denominator. We set up what we believe is the best practice and those that want to join it, they join it. It's not built for everybody. We have always failed in public media in this kind of federated approach. If you design to ensure that it works for everybody, then you are essentially designing a mediocre and low-performing product," he says.

The real test of a program like this is whether or not it is achieving positive results. Between 2012 and 2015, CDP brought stations about $43 million in net revenue directly related to the projects in the program. Over 350,000 donors have been regained across the system. Revenue retention has improved from 65% to 73% by focusing on sustainers, thank-you calls, canvassing, and acquisition direct mail. First-year donor retention went from below 30% to more than 42%. These are all tremendous achievements in a very short period of time.

The stations, the Advisory Council, and the CDP team continue to adjust and improve what they are doing moving forward. Heiplik says, "We're not there 100%. We're getting there pretty quickly. It's only because of that relentless focus on driving your decisions based on data, not on some gut feeling. It's important to have a little bit of a mix of the art and science of fundraising. In the end, it comes down to data."

## 2,500,000,000 DOLLARS

On January 20, 1820, the legislature of the state of Indiana passed legislation to establish the "state seminary" that would go on to become Indiana University. It would be another three years before the first professor, Baynard Rush Hall, was hired to teach the first 12 students for $250.[73] Fast-forward nearly 200 years: IU now provides a range of undergraduate and graduate programs to more than 110,000 students across its eight campuses.[74]

In 2015, the Indiana University Foundation announced a $2.5 billion Bicentennial Campaign to be completed by 2020. IU president Michael A. McRobbie said that "the bold goals of the bicentennial campaign, which are the most ambitious in Indiana University's history and among the largest ever by a public university, will set Indiana University on the course for greatness in its third century."[75] While billion-dollar campaigns may seem to be more commonplace among higher education institutions, the scale and complexity of these undertakings should not be taken lightly.

When the campaign launch festivities were over, it became the responsibility of one person at the IU Foundation to coordinate and manage this significant undertaking. Jeffrey Lindauer is the vice president for advancement services and managing director of capital campaigns at the IU Foundation. Lindauer has been at the foundation for 20 years and worked his way up from the annual fund program to now managing a multibillion-dollar campaign across eight campuses and 50 fundraising units.

The size of the fundraising campaign goal is matched by the size of the institution and the number of moving parts. "We are a pretty large organization in the higher education world. We have 650,000 living alumni, plus any interested friends, and like anyone else, we have limited resources," says Lindauer. "The days where you have 200,000 alumni and you can see the same people over and over just no longer exist. As we're looking to find new prospects and better allocate our limited resources, we need to figure out that if we have ten cents to spend, where are we going to spend it," he says.

This all means that leveraging data to identify the right giving prospects for the right programs is a valuable tool for the institution. Lindauer points out, "We've always been relatively solid when it comes to looking at our data from a standpoint of where we are today. We're pretty good at looking at our performance and all of the key metrics, but I think in the last few years we've gotten better at leveraging that data to make good decisions, particularly in the area of how we're going to solicit and who we're going to solicit."

IU's multi-campus environment also includes top-ranked medical, law, and business schools that have created a diverse ecosystem of interests that need to be served from a fundraising perspective. Lindauer explains, "We have eight campuses and, depending on how you count, well in excess of 50 different fundraising units from the school of business, to the athletic department, to the medical school, to a campus like IU East, which is in Richmond and would be our smallest campus. We're balancing the need to visit the right people with the need to serve some of those units whose very best prospect might not rate highly in this system as a whole. Someone may not seem like our best prospect overall, but if you're a certain school or a certain campus, it might be a fantastic prospect." This balance is important because they "have to be very careful, especially when they're looking at things like predictive modeling and trying to figure out who to see, that they don't let those smaller units fall to the bottom."

Most capital campaigns begin with a feasibility study. This is an evaluation tool used by nonprofit organizations to understand the opportunity, risks, and likelihood of success for a campaign. Often times, external consultants are brought in to help conduct the evaluation and make recommendations to the institution. The IU Foundation took a more modern and data driven approach to their decision to embark on a $2.5 billion campaign. "We did not do a traditional feasibility study where we went around the country and interviewed 200 people and talked to them about what they were thinking for the next campaign," says Lindauer. "We had the luxury of having a lot of data and historical analysis. We were able to look at performance in each of those units and take a pretty good look at the prospects who had committed to those campaigns and those who had not made a commitment or made their commitment recently," he says.

"We parsed that data quite a bit. We looked at each segment. We looked at alumni versus friends versus corporations and foundations. We also had a strong emphasis on our own internal family for faculty and staff. In fact, we put together a matching program for faculty and staff and are making them a key component of this campaign. They're obviously invested already in our institution and many of them have been very, very successful through their work and other endeavors," notes Lindauer. "We did a good job of figuring out where we thought we could land and providing some stretch goals but not coming up with a number that wasn't doable," he says.

This data driven approach was something Lindauer learned and developed during his days running the annual fund at the IU Foundation. "The annual fund has always been data driven. If you look at most universities, the annual funds were doing a better job in this arena than frontline fundraising for a very long time. They have a deadline. It's day to day and they can see the impacts a little more easily by testing their model or various strategies," he says. "It's a little harder when you're dealing with a prospect where it could be 18 months, or in some cases five years, before you realize the benefit of identifying that person," notes Lindauer.

McRobbie became the eighteenth president of IU in 2007. But he did not come from the top job at another university. Instead, McRobbie first joined IU in 1997 as vice president for information technology and chief information officer.[76] He later led the university's research initiatives and was the interim provost and vice president for academic affairs at IU's Bloomington campus before being selected as the next president of the university. You don't get much more support from leadership to be data driven than when the president comes from a computer science and logic background.

"President McRobbie is very interested in data and he loves reports," says Lindauer. "He's willing to look at that data and he is doing a fantastic job of encouraging participation amongst our development officers and our development personnel encouraging them to get the data into the system. That's something as simple as a contact report to utilizing the predictive models when they're out there trying to fill their portfolios with the right people. He's a champion of that and it trickles down. I think that if you have a president who believes in the value of data it helps everyone else either realize the value of data or at least realize the value of saying they believe in the value of data," he adds.

Lindauer believes that the support from leadership has been critical to the foundation's fundraising initiatives. "If we did not have leadership pushing these concepts, especially because we're so large and decentralized, it could be a challenge to get buy-in from a particular school or program or department with its own development staff," he notes. "There has to be both a carrot and a stick to get them to participate in the process and having leadership who believe in the process helps with that," adds Lindauer.

Another key part of the DNA at the IU Foundation is a culture of sharing and transparency that has existed for decades. "We have been pretty consistent in the belief that we are 100% transparent," says Lindauer. "As a development officer, you can look up your own performance. You could look up your neighbor's performance. You could look up anyone's performance. You can see any prospect. All the data that's in the system is transparent. If we know about it, then you can see it and you can measure it," he says.

The culture of data sharing at IU even predates Lindauer's tenure at the foundation. "I've been at the foundation for 20 years and I've never known it any other way. I think we started that way. I think we discussed it at one point, is this the right way to do it? Our board felt very comfortable with it. Data transparency is a mandate and it's not debatable. Believe me, there's not much that's not debatable, but that one is not even brought up anymore," adds Lindauer.

That is not to say that IU doesn't pay an openness tax for the sharing of information across the development groups. A contact report might be missing some details or some information may not always make its way into the system. But over time, the success of the IU Foundation shows that this is a small price to pay to drive a culture of sharing.

I can also speak to how this culture of sharing and openness with data extends to other parts of Indiana University. Early in my career, I worked in the Office of Information Management and Institutional Research on the Indianapolis campus. Many of our projects depended on getting the right data from the right sources to drive better decision making. My past experience with large companies in the corporate world was that getting any data could be a big challenge. To this day, I remember how open the access to data was and how genuinely willing people were to help me find the right information.

The willingness to share data at an organization this large and diverse has several benefits, one of which is the environment it creates for fundraisers and administrators across the organization to compare their performance. Lindauer says, "I don't want us to be competitive, but in a way it does instill a little bit of competition when deans see the productivity of their development officers and compare it perhaps to a similar school somewhere else in the system."

For example, a dean might see in the data a trend that their development officers are making 10 contacts per month compared to 18 or 20 per month by fundraisers in another group. Lindauer also observes that this sharing "allows that development officer to really look at the data, the peer data, and see that they can achieve more. Part of that is competition, but another part of that is also *seeing* that the aspirational goal is possible rather than just being told that it's possible."

The feedback loop can also work the other way around because of a culture of sharing data. It is not uncommon for development officers working with academic units to be asked to help with "other duties as assigned" from time to time. Seeing how others are performing allows them to have a data driven discussion about the best use of their time. "That's a benefit to the development officer who has a dean that's perhaps challenging to work with because they're giving them so much other work that they can't do their core job that they're hired to do," says Lindauer.

It also can't be stressed enough that seeing is believing. At the very least, leadership's ability to see the data elevates their awareness about what is happening in the organization. Lindauer says, "Now that we're able to visualize the data and put it on their desktops more, we have an added benefit of leadership seeing it in a way that they can understand the impact of investments and fundraising." Access to these dashboards allows decision makers to see firsthand the results from investments made in fundraising. "They can see how many prospects are being visited and then they can see how many prospects we don't have enough resources to see. That's helped us gain resources as well," he adds.

Yes, simply making data visible and accessible across the organization makes a tremendous difference in building a data driven culture. In advertising, they say that the human brain needs to be exposed to something seven times for it to make an impression. The monthly group meeting or file attachment isn't enough to make a lasting impression. The use of dashboards and mobile tools provides good face-time for the data and leaders within the organization. Lindauer points out: "I think we can say it as much as we can say it, but actually being able to show it to them makes a big difference."

A culture of data sharing also creates an environment where being more donor-centric is possible. "We have definitely had development officers who entered a contact report on a prospect that has no interest in their particular program, but during the conversation, the prospect is clearly expressing an interest in another program," says Lindauer. In a closed environment or an organization where sharing doesn't happen, that opportunity likely goes nowhere.

"The culture of sharing enables someone to call their development officer peer and say, 'Look, I've had no luck with John, but John really loves athletics or John really has an interest in curing cancer,' and then they hand that prospect over to someone who can pick up the ball and hopefully make that next contact for the right program," says Lindauer.

The level of transparency at the IU Foundation spans the entire organization, especially the work being done by gift officers. This is an area where changes in technology and data open up new opportunities to improve performance. The IU Foundation, like many other nonprofit institutions that depend on a successful major gift program, are increasingly using data to help with performance management. "I would say that's probably our number one focus right now," says Lindauer. "It is critical to us right now to look at the performance metrics and measure the activity of major gift officers or front-line fundraisers," he adds.

Lindauer believes that increasing the emphasis on gift officer performance management creates a better culture for reporting and getting the right information into the system. "The flip side of that is we have to be very careful not to create too many performance metrics so that it's a full-time job figuring out if you're doing a good job, and we don't create analysis paralysis," he stresses.

A recurring theme with the deluge of data in the nonprofit sector is the realization that less is more. "If we could get 100% participation amongst our staff in believing in two or three metrics: (1) how many visits are you making; (2) how many asks are you making; and (3) how successful are those asks, then we would go further, faster than worrying about the eleventh metric," notes Lindauer. The things you choose to measure have to be about moving the needle in meaningful ways, not just trying to look good.

The availability of so much data can also undermine what gift officers do best if you're not careful. "Most of our major gift fundraisers are amazing conversationalists. They're getting paid to build relationships and talk about what interests the donor, but if they go into that first meeting thinking they know it all, they'll just sit there and stare at them," says Lindauer.

There is a cautionary tale here of being too prepared with background information that it takes some of the spontaneity out of a normal conversation with a donor. "We've become so dependent on data that we feel like we need to know everything about a prospect before we meet them. It makes the conversation somewhat tilted because what fun is it to talk to someone you already know everything about?" he adds.

This is especially true when it turns out everything about someone can't be known in advance. The most successful development officers know how to build relationships and at the same time glean valuable information from their interactions. The nuanced details can be missed by bringing on too much information. Lindauer cautions that they sometimes "missed an opportunity to gain data *because* they provided data: too much data."

The IU Foundation has also seen the appetite for data increase the more exposure there is to it across the organization. This can be a double-edged sword and requires some expectation management. "It's my dream that every time someone submits a request for a new metric or a new report or a new dashboard that they would be required to demonstrate how they would change behavior based on the results of that report. If they can't answer that question, then I don't want to waste my time writing that report," Lindauer confesses. "We're trying to keep it as simple as we can, because we still believe that the personal visit goes further than anything else," he says.

Lindauer talks to his peers at other institutions and they all feel increased demands with the same or fewer resources available. There's a concern among advancement services professionals that "instead of making better decisions quicker, what they're really doing is creating more work for people who could be doing other real work," says Lindauer. He admits, "I can only turn out so much data that's meaningful in a format that's readable and understandable. I need to make sure that those resources are being tasked wisely and they're not on a folly creating a report for someone because they were bored this afternoon and just curious."

Lindauer has had the advantage of seeing the use of data mature not only at the IU Foundation but also in the nonprofit sector. He recognizes that organizations of different maturity levels all have their own data growing pains. "I think if you start your career at an organization that believes in data, then you will believe in data. If you start your career in an organization that does not, or maybe you came on board at a time where the data wasn't available, then you are slower to adopt, whether it's a new database or a new predictive model or whatever the new widget is," he says. Lindauer is glad that he's at an institution that chose to believe in data.

The culture of data sharing developed at IU is helping the institution towards its goal of raising $2.5 billion by 2020. The IU Foundation has already achieved 60% of its goal by mid-2016. There is no doubt that it's a team effort to achieve the goal. "We try and preach a concept of one development team. We are all on one development team even if we're on different parts of that team," says Lindauer. A willingness to share data across the organization, combined with support from leadership at IU, has put the organization in a position to succeed.

# 12

# GROWTH

*"Data matures like wine, applications like fish."*

- JAMES GOVERNOR

Some nonprofits have developed a culture where champions have helped lead the way for more use of data in the organization. Others have built trust in using data through testing that improves results. For some organizations, the culture of data sharing is critical to making data driven decisions.

The next important culture type is one in which a growth mindset is adopted to leverage data to maximize results. It builds upon the need for champions, testing, and sharing, but a culture of growth takes being data driven to a new level. Nonprofits with a growth culture understand that using data to drive decisions is a prerequisite for success.

Jann Schultz has been the senior director of integrated fundraising and communications at Project HOPE since 2013. Prior to her arrival at the organization, Schultz spent nearly seven years at Operation Smile, where she was the associate vice president of donor services. Today at Project HOPE, Schultz is responsible for both strategic direction and the implementation of direct marketing, donor services, digital and social media marketing, branding, content marketing, and internal communications programs.

Schultz has honed her craft of using data to improve results and grow fundraising programs over many years now. Implementing a data driven approach successfully at two different organizations has given her a unique perspective. "So many people gravitate to nonprofits because of their compassion and their desire to make a difference, and that certainly was my case. The challenge is that's really not enough. Understanding the use of data is a requirement for working at a nonprofit," says Schultz.

"There is a need for transparency across an organization, and that doesn't include just fundraising, but all programs, no matter what you do," she says. The ability to link program impact to donor communication is just one example of the important role data plays across the organization. "Being data driven is really a skill in demand at all charities, from fundraising to program delivery," says Schultz.

You might think that someone like Schultz, who feels so strongly about the importance of using data, must come from a background in mathematics or statistics – but you'd be wrong. "I actually still have nightmares about flunking third-grade long division," says Schultz. "My roles, both in my for-profit experience and now in charity fundraising, have always demanded understanding and interpreting metrics. It's something that I have to work hard at as it does not come naturally." One secret to her success has been leaning on experts for some of the heavy lifting. "What's important for me is that I collaborate with strong partners on data analytics and then spend the time needed to clearly understand and evaluate my fundraising programs," she says.

The adoption of benchmarking in the nonprofit sector continues to grow as more organizations understand how useful it can be across their programs. In a nonprofit with a culture of growth, the use of benchmarks is simply part of their DNA. There is the old adage: If you and I were being chased by a bear, then I wouldn't try and outrun the bear. I would just try to outrun you. That's benchmarking. Schultz has spent years using benchmarking data to help her grow fundraising programs.

"Benchmarking provides the necessary context from which I can evaluate my fundraising program compared to other NGOs. I'm not really hung up on comparing dollars raised or the number of donors because every program has different investment budgets that they can get from their organizations, but I want to see where my program falls in relation to key metrics like multi-year retention, new donor retention, lifetime value," says Schultz.

Those three Key Performance Indicators (KPIs) may have several underlying metrics that can also be monitored. Schultz notes, "Knowing how my fundraising program is doing on these metrics can influence not just my fundraising initiatives but also the delivery of the donor experience overall. It is about understanding those key metrics and then determining the process improvement and infrastructure enhancements that need to take place to really move the needle on performance."

Schultz has participated in several donorCentrics benchmarking groups facilitated by Target Analytics. Peers at a variety of nonprofit organizations meet together in person over two days to review benchmarking results. "Another benefit of benchmarking is being able to discuss fundraising programs with a broader group of industry peers across many sectors, not just international relief but also environmental, animal welfare, child sponsorship and more. I think what's really great is we are so open about sharing. We regularly get together with just our international relief peers, but then there are also opportunities to look more broadly and to network across many different verticals," she says.

Schultz likes to start by comparing her three KPIs to peer organizations. "I like to know if Project HOPE's first year from new, multi-year retention or lifetime value is comparable to our peers. Are we comparable? Are we in the middle of the pack? Are we exceeding our peers? Benchmarking allows me to see where our program is falling out in relation to other charities on those key metrics, but also to have specific discussions to find out what our peers are doing to impact those numbers," she says. The benchmarking data is used to innovate and grow the fundraising program in a meaningful way.

For more than 55 years, Project HOPE has provided health expertise and medical training, as well as delivered humanitarian assistance programs in more than 35 countries. Their humanitarian assistance programs are often impacted by natural disasters and episodic events throughout the world. The donations that help their programs in times of crisis also require creating a better donor experience to retain those supporters for years to come.

"I think that international relief organizations are coming under greater scrutiny, especially coming out of the recession. As donors continue to refine and make hard choices about where their dollars are going to go, they are taking a deeper look at the organizations they support," says Schultz. Project HOPE understands the importance of retaining episodic donors and what a challenge this can be for many organizations. "In the old days, it was okay to get an annual report and they were satisfied with that. Now, donors live in this world of constant information and the ability to have it at their fingertips. We have to work on providing access to that content all the time. I think our donors do demand that of us," she says.

Schultz notes, "This becomes even more important when a disaster strikes and the donor is choosing the charity they want to support. Reporting back becomes even more vital because that donor, who in the moment of a disaster sees the devastation, the impact on those vulnerable people wherever they may be, has a very emotional response. To truly keep that donor, we have to find a way that demonstrates to them the impact of their gift, the good that's been done with their donation and how continued support will extend that process." Without this type of focus, international relief organizations are highly susceptible to large peaks and troughs in giving. Data shows that these episodic donors are more likely to churn than a typical new donor to a nonprofit.

"We know that some donors are just going to be those one-offs, but my goal is always to retain a portion of those donors and engage them further in the work of Project HOPE," says Schultz. "Something that Project HOPE has always been very proud of has been that any time we respond to a disaster, we actually go in with the intent to stay and provide longer-term global health solutions and programs for beneficiaries. Helping donors who respond to a disaster understand that their gifts are having a long-term impact and reporting back on that impact is a priority." Using the data from the field to support the fundraising programs of the organization is a recurring theme at Project HOPE.

In addition to using benchmarking data, Schultz has learned when to pay attention to the daily flow of data and when to zoom out to look at the big picture. "On a daily basis, I'm looking at number of responses coming into our gift processing center and then turning around to look at our 30, 60, 90-day integrated direct response campaign reports. I get daily telemarketing reports that have data like pledge rates and the cash or credit card percentages associated with them. I can take a look at yesterday's email send and click-through rates and dollars raised. Or the inbound call center conversion rates from a radio broadcast last night at 5:00," she notes.

If you're not careful, it can be easy to slip into the daily data *Twilight Zone*. Schultz says, "I think what happens on a daily basis is you can get sucked into looking at that data on the micro level and not at the macro level. I have to force myself to take a step back. That's really where my use of data has changed over time, because you need to look beyond the short-term reports that can drive you to make some poor decisions based on short-term net revenue." And that's a critical point that nonprofits with a culture of growth understand. They have learned to avoid sacrificing the future on the altar of the immediate.

"I've really spent the past couple of years here at Project HOPE helping to educate senior leadership on the impact of short-term decisions based on annual net revenue," says Schultz. But getting leadership to focus on the key KPIs of multi-year retention, new donor retention, and lifetime value helps to avoid short-term thinking. "What is important for a program's health is taking that step back, taking a look at donor lifecycle data, going back to what influences those key metrics, and focusing on what is really going to drive long-term revenue, improve performance, and move the needle on our fundraising," she says.

Create a culture of growth that embraces the use of data often requires internal promotion of the good results that are happening. Schultz works the metrics into all her meetings and even the office environment at Project HOPE. "When we are having a finance meeting, I make sure to bring other metrics to share before diving into last month's performance. I'm not above promoting the program. Outside the staff break room, I have posters that are highlighting these metrics and why we're focusing on them so that everybody who goes to get a cup of coffee sees the metrics that I'm trying to drive," she says.

This was especially true when Schultz first arrived at Project HOPE and needed to build a growth culture. "When the organization has standard reporting that isn't inclusive of the metrics that you want to drive, then you have to be creative in your approach on how you insert those data points into the conversation," she notes. Earlier in this book, we highlighted the need to not just get buy-in from leadership but also to influence all levels of the organization. "Of course, there's a small group of members at the senior leadership level that I need to influence. But it really comes down to middle management and overall staff having a better understanding of the value and benefits of Project HOPE's direct response program."

Schultz has found that sharing the key KPIs and other metrics across the organization builds confidence and allows others to see the health of the programs. She made it a priority to work her way across the different layers at the organization to get others to understand what was needed in order to grow. "I started working with our finance controller by asking questions on whether there are other ways that we can report, can you help me understand the history, and what else can I bring and share with you about the direct response program. I had conversations at the board level with directors including the board treasurer...helping them to understand the importance of acquisition and different type of metrics that are involved and the revenue impact of donor retention, coverage ratios, and long-term value," says Schultz.

This approach has also extended to staff across Project HOPE. "At the most fundamental level, I've utilized communication initiatives to educate staff on all of the different initiatives that we're trying to implement," says Schultz. "We have shared how we work with our agency partner to win new donors, keep existing donors, and lift the value of donors, what that really means, and defining those initiatives. Those education efforts have come in the form of updates at global town hall meetings, brown bag lunches, posters outside the break room." You name the tactic for getting others on board with a new way of doing things and Schultz has probably done it.

That is not to say that you need to do all the heavy lifting on your own. Over time, Schultz has learned the value of having partners and peers to help. "This is where it is important to utilize your strategic partners and other experts to help educate and inform your organization. You can only do so much yourself. There will always be the perception that you are just promoting your own program," she says. She also recommends using peer benchmark data not just to improve your programs but also to help educate internal stakeholders. "Use benchmarking medians to share how your program compares to peers, bring in an expert that can speak to the state of the industry and how your program is performing compared to those metrics. This is where expertise and data come together to bring understanding to an area of fundraising that requires a long-term approach," adds Schultz.

After generating buy-in to the use of data to drive decisions, the next logical step is to start making some decisions. Schultz has several examples in which using data to drive decisions has resulted in growth in fundraising results. "We've improved response rates by crafting new offers, but it's the testing of them and understanding their performance in both acquisition and cultivation that has really driven significant change for Project HOPE in the last couple of years," she says.

Project HOPE has also invested in predictive modeling, specifically with lapsed donors, to improve their reactivation performance. Schultz also notes that her for-profit experience highlights some interesting opportunities to use data for both prospect and donor survey responses--opportunities many other charities aren't taking. What is commonplace in the corporate data world is still considered exotic in the nonprofit sector. Schultz surveys donors to make sure that messaging is aligned with a prospect's or donor's stated preference.

"We've designed a new monthly giving product and crafted a new sustainer offer based on data from stated preference market research that we conducted with our strategic partners. The online testing included both prospects and our own donors," says Schultz. This type of approach has allowed testing that drives decision-making on a much bigger scale than Project HOPE could have done previously. She explains, "Each participant evaluated 12 different choice sets. That is equivalent to testing over 15,000 packages in the space of about two weeks. I couldn't A/B test my way through 15,000 packages! We tested logos and images along with insert options, including possible premiums. We tested benefit propositions and tangible demonstrations of how their donations would make a difference."

All this high-volume testing is to eliminate the guesswork and gut instinct that can sneak its way into the decision-making process. "We spend so much time worried about the creative aspects--format, logos, image--however, the testing results showed that we need to be focused on clearly defining the reason to give and how much it matters to the donor. Both the Project HOPE donors and the acquisition panel said the same thing in the responses," she says. The testing results were turned into decisions about the organization's positioning. Schultz adds, "Based on the insights we have gained, we have revised our creative both online and offline to reflect the new positioning."

The culture of growth that Schultz is building at Project Hope goes beyond just using data to drive decision-making. She also knows that this growth mindset is necessary to transform the entire donor experience. "This is getting to the heart of the donor experience, gathering feedback on that moment in time where they engaged with Project HOPE. On our website, if somebody goes to a donation form and then moves their cursor to close out before donating, we pop up a light-box and ask for feedback on the experience. We ask what were they looking for and offer an open text box to tell us what they think," she says.

And rather than stopping at just the online channels, they keep the same focus on the donor experience in the analog world too. Schultz says, "If a supporter calls our donor service call center, at the end of the call they are warm transferred into a voice-activated survey and follow-up with an email. Just like if you were to call any commercial call center, they're going to ask 'How did we do?' We're following commercial best practices about sending a survey link and getting supporter feedback on that touch point."

Eventually, all this focus on growth needs to result in actual growth. Schultz's data driven approach has helped her "influence decision-making even at the board level around investment and staying the course in a direct-response program." She also notes, "We've been able to change a long-term downward trend for Project HOPE, and we're starting to see our donor file come back up. Our long-term value has seen significant improvement. Our multi-year retention is seeing incremental gains. We are seeing larger improvements in second year retained and regained donors. It's exciting to watch those metrics start to shift and change."

She also recognizes that you have to balance hard data with the soft skills to get others to buy into a growth mindset. "I'm probably on the soft edge of data versus the hard edge of data. It goes back to flunking third-grade long division. I like to use it in a way that tells stories and engages the organization to better understand what is happening," says Schultz. The organization is seeing growth in a number of key areas and momentum has become a powerful force change at Project HOPE.

Even with this success, Schultz is always looking to improve. Getting better is more important than just being good. For all the ones and zeros in the data, a lot of information is also captured from the contact Project HOPE has with its supporters. Schultz also understands that growing revenue has an exponential effect on the mission. "If we want to be saving lives, preventing disease, promoting health, well, to be able to do that, we've got to shore up and diversify our fundraising," says Schultz. "I want to give our donors an experience that connects them to our cause and lets them know that with their help, we're saving lives and they're making a difference. It comes down to using data to build out the infrastructure needed to acquire compassionate donors, retain those donors, and build their lifetime value," she adds.

The combination of establishing clear KPIs and metrics, leveraging benchmarks to understand performance among peer organizations, looking at the day-to-day data but focusing on the long-term, and getting all levels of the organization to buy into using data has helped create a culture of growth at Project HOPE. This isn't just theory; it's reality and it's working for the organization. "Ultimately, we are responsible to our donors and to our board to deliver on our budget and growth goals. The metrics are the proof points," says Schultz. Those proof points support a growth mindset that is driving Project HOPE in the right direction.

## CAGR

As of April 2016, there were 1.5 million registered nonprofit organizations in the United States. What you might not know is that 31% of those organizations have total annual revenue of less than $500,000. Another 60% of all registered nonprofits don't even report their annual revenue. The more troubling statistic is that these percentages have remained unchanged for the last 20 years despite the growth in the number of nonprofits. In 1996, there were just over 1,000,000 registered nonprofits in the U.S. and 33% of them had less than $500,000 in total annual revenue. The number of nonprofits that did not report their annual revenue remained at 60%. Meanwhile, just 1% of nonprofits have revenue greater than $10 million. That number has been stuck for 20 years, too.

The data reveals that most very small nonprofits do not grow beyond $500,000 in revenue, and yet we know that the causes they support have an abundance of need. The odds of a nonprofit that has been around for nearly 100 years and never grown above $200,000 in revenue being able to transform itself to be part of the nonprofit sector's 1% are almost impossible. But just when you think that you have seen everything in the nonprofit sector, there is an organization that shows you something new. It is indeed possible to build a culture of growth that uses data to achieve remarkable results.

The roots of the Denver Rescue Mission can be traced back to a rescue home for women started by Reverend Joshua Gravett in 1892. Today, the Mission meets the needs of those experiencing poverty and homelessness through emergency services, community outreach, long-term rehabilitation programs, transitional programs, and assistance for permanent housing in six locations in Denver and two more in northern Colorado.

Griff Freyschlag has been the vice president of development at the Mission for the past 14 years. He came to the organization after 23 years in commercial banking, so you might say that he's a numbers kind of guy. The Mission's CEO Brad Meuli knew Freyschlag from his own days in banking and recruited him to join the organization. Meuli had been a board member of the organization for almost a decade when he joined the Mission to eventually become its president and CEO.

"We got into direct mail back in 1987. Up until that point, the Mission had four employees and the overall annual budget was $200,000. We went through the growth spurt years in direct mail from 1987 to 2000. When that started to level off, we were only getting a Compound Annual Growth Rate (CAGR) of 1% to 2% and that was impacting the direct response business," explains Freyschlag.

Meuli had the idea of creating a vibrant major gift program to help grow the organization and he turned to Freyschlag to lead it. "I'm embarrassed to say that I don't think I would have hired me. One of the misnomers in fundraising is that you just need to find a good salesman. I don't think that could be further from the truth. Maybe from a people skills standpoint, maybe there is some crossover, but fundraising is not selling," says Freyschlag. But Freyschlag knew the importance of metrics and he understood that the data contained in them could be used to grow any organization.

At the time, about 80% of the Mission's revenue came from direct response and another 20% came from relational giving. "Just from a business model standpoint, it's not a great place to be with that kind of unbalanced revenue stream," says Freyschlag. As we have seen with other nonprofits discussed in this book, the task of diversifying revenue is not an easy one. But Freyschlag knew that the Mission needed to do exactly that in order to grow.

"We thought that we could go after part of our existing donor base and be able to increase their giving. Most of them gave a traditional acquisition gift of $1.92 or $19.20, which is a function of meals. We never really reached out to anyone. These donors raised their hand by giving larger gifts, and once they gave a gift of $500, then we called it a major gift and they immediately got assigned to a major gift officer," he says. This describes how organizations large and small start out when building a major gift fundraising program. Freyschlag knew that for the Mission to start growing its fundraising revenue, they could no longer operate with business-as-usual.

Creating and growing a real major gifts program was going to take investment, time, and commitment from the organization. "I think that's one of the reasons that rescue missions don't do well in the major gift area. I'm not sure they're really committed to it," he says. "What happens is that they have these unreasonable expectations where they say, 'By golly, we need a major gift program. Go hire somebody and pay them $50,000 a year. Griff says that his major gift officers are raising $1 million. Well, we'll go hire him and then we'll expect him to raise $1 million.' Then they don't, of course, and so they get frustrated and then they decide it doesn't really work. It doesn't make a lot of sense to keep this major gift officer who barely raised their own salary," explains Freyschlag. "That may be true. It may be that way for the first year. Maybe the next year they raise $100,000, but you have to stay committed. You have to start somewhere and begin to develop relationships with these folks, otherwise it doesn't work."

While building up the major giving program, Freyschlag also turned his attention to improving the donor acquisition program without just sending more mail. "The whole business of acquisition, really the last four to five years, has changed quite a bit. You used to go out and find multi-buyers from list brokers and then mail them five times a year," he says. The term "multi-buyer" describes donors that appear in two or more of the rented lists used in a direct mail campaign. In theory, a prospective donor that appears in multiple acquisition lists is more likely to give to your organization than someone that is present in only one list. "We would mail them once in October, three times in November, and five times in December. The average cost per donor would probably be somewhere around $40 or $50. Long-term donor value is probably $250 to $275. Those lists were not producing the same quality as we had seen in the past. We just weren't getting the number of names that we needed," says Freyschlag.

The key to growth was working smarter, not harder, and investing in acquisition lists that contained more nonprofit giving data. Freyschlag explains, "As opposed to just acquiring a name from somebody who bought a lot of stuff from Harry & David during Christmas, these are donors that have given to nonprofits that are like the Denver Mission, that are in the Denver area, and the average gift size is maybe a little bit larger than normal. They give 2.4 gifts a year instead of 1.8 gifts a year." After making this change, the Mission is seeing higher average gift sizes and an increased number of gifts per donor.

The other approach to growth was a willingness to give this thing called the "Internet" a try over a decade ago. "When I first got here, we had a young man on staff who thought he read something about the Internet somewhere. He kind of piecemealed a website together that was baling wire and duct tape, but I think we saw the impact of what a website can do for communication," says Freyschlag. "Every seminar, webinar, conference you went to, everybody is talking about this thing called the web. I guess it's just natural that we saw donations beginning to increase over time. Our online giving still grows by anywhere from 15% to 23% every year," he says.

The Mission uses data and metrics to show how online is helping the organization grow where other channels might be flat. "We acquired 2,600 brand new donors last year on the web, and that's a reasonable measure of new donors that we may never have acquired had they not responded to search engine marketing or any kind of banner ad that goes out there," says Freyschlag. That growth in both new donors and online revenue is a reflection of changing times, and the Mission has been willing to invest in their website, online ads, and Search Engine Optimization (SEO) to boost results.

They also have done a lot of testing to optimize the giving experience for online donors because they know that directly translates to growth. In the past decade, I have seen thousands of online donation forms and have participated in a lot of testing to find out what works and what doesn't. Over the years, one of the most often debated topics is the ask levels on the donation form. We have all seen the $10, $25, $50, $75, and higher ask amounts as if it was mandated law to use those amounts. While there are certainly plenty of best practices that could fill another book, the one thing we know for certain is that any best practice can always benefit from additional testing.

They first thing that I noticed about the online donation forms on the Mission website was that the ask amount starts at $48. Yes, the form is also mobile friendly and it has a very clean design experience for the donor. Those things are extremely important, but the ask amounts on their website move from $48 to $86.40 to $153.60 and on up, including a $1,000 amount and an "other" option. Through testing, the Mission was able to align part of their work with the giving experience. As it turns out, a $48 donation feeds 25 people and a $86.40 donation feeds 45 people. During part of 2016, the

Mission also ran a matching gift challenge campaign that doubled the impact of those online donations.

"Like most direct marketing, we try and try again, which goes back to the use of data. We try to use historical giving data from both the direct mail side and the web side to try and see what sort of average gifts that most people have made. Then try and do the best we can with some A/B testing to say, 'Which dollar handles seem to resonate with donors better than others?' That's really how we got to those particular dollar handles that we're currently using, and that was really just through A/B testing that we did ourselves," says Freyschlag. Testing is always helpful, but there is also no substitute for curiosity.

For many years, there has been a steady increase in the number of significant online gifts. In 2011, 87% of organizations had at least one online gift of $1,000 or more.[77] That trend has only continued to grow with a larger number of donors giving significant online gifts. Out of curiosity, the website manager at the Mission added a $1,000 gift level to the online donation form. "That $1,000 handle, it's amazing how many people have chosen to give exactly that. I'm really curious to see what that $1,000 gift size looks like compared over the year before that. I'd be surprised if it wasn't a 20-30% increase in that dollar amount that's given," says Freyschlag. Even with all the data and metrics, there is some flexibility that allows curiosity to take over and try new things.

The culture of growth in the fundraising programs of the Mission has helped to create a more data-driven organization in other areas. The Mission's senior leadership team is made up of the CEO and the leaders of the development, programs, operations, and finance and administration departments. "Our culture has become much more data driven than ever before. Every conversation we have is based off of data and research," says Freyschlag. He shared examples of how the organization uses data to make other decisions. "Every two years we do a pretty extensive industry salary survey to make sure that we're in line with what we need to pay people. On the operations side, we track insurance incidents that happen. In order to reduce our insurance costs, we research safety data and we have all kinds of training programs in place. After a year, we showed that injury incidents dropped by 25%, and that saved us about 20% on our overall insurance costs," he says.

While all of this has been going on, Freyschlag has also been growing the rest of the fundraising program at the Mission. Remember that back in 1987, the Mission had annual revenue of $200,000 and a staff of four people. In 2015, the Mission had total revenue of $32 million. $20 million of that is from fundraising, another $11 million in gift-in-kind along with an additional $1 million in earned program revenue. The development department is made up of 24 full-time staff members, including five major gift officers, one mid-level donor officer, a full-time planned gift officer, and a full-time prospect researcher.

Direct mail was once 80% of fundraising revenue and had flat growth. Today, it's only 50% of giving and the overall program is growing at 6-12% annually. A major gift used to be considered $500 and donors had to go out of their way to get noticed by the Mission. "Now, our level for a major gift is $5,000. We have a full-time prospect researcher and anytime somebody makes a $1,000 gift, then they go through our researcher. Those donors over a certain giving capacity get assigned to someone to thank them, begin to steward that gift, and then begin to develop a relationship with the donor," says Freyschlag.

Diversifying giving at the Mission led to a growth culture to eliminate financial risk and create a more sustainable organization. Along the way, data became a key element to get staff members to focus on growth. "Data is very important to us in all areas of the Mission. On the program side, we developed our own software to track program outcomes. Not only is this important in measuring the success of the program but it's also critical as we seek funding from foundations asking for this kind of accountability. On the finance side, we run CAGRs on all our areas, especially in fundraising. We even still measure daily donations that come in through the mail. It's a throwback to the days when the Mission didn't know if it had enough money to pay the bills," says Freyschlag.

The investment in major giving, mid-level donors, planned gifts, and even online giving has helped grow revenue and reduce dependence on direct mail revenue. While some in the fundraising world foresee the death of direct mail, the Mission knows it can actually help drive future revenue in ways that major giving will not. "We have a full-time planned giving person on staff and she's grown the membership in what we call the Good Heart Society from 100 people to 255 people in about four years. If you just look at the future value of that based on average bequest size and some age parameters, then that's about a $11 million or $12 million annuity of future giving amount down the road," says Freyschlag.

The biggest source of these planned donors is the direct mail program. Donors who have made smaller annual contributions to an organization have a high likelihood of making a planned gift. "Because of our aging database, I would anticipate that that number will continue to grow substantially. I think 10 years from now we're going to see planned giving probably provide somewhere in the neighborhood of $2 million to $3 million a year," he says. That compares to the current annual revenue from planned giving in the $750,000 to $1 million range. "The profile of our typical planned giver has numerous gifts and an average gift size of $100. They're retired school teachers, they have a home and an IRA, and when they pass away they give a third to their church, a third to the Denver Dumb Friends League, and a third to the Denver Rescue Mission. Average planned gift size is about $43,000. We know a lot about the profile of these donors, and yet about 80% of the gifts that come in on the estate side we don't even know about," says Freyschlag.[78] He notes that their dedicated planned giving staff member can hardly keep up with the number of people that respond to direct mail campaigns focused on bequests. "It's crazy. It's just unbelievable. I'm excited to see where that's going to go," he says.

Every time Freyschlag talks about the future of the Mission, he always focuses on the growth potential of the organization. "I would anticipate in the next five years we'll be raising $7 million to $8 million in the major gift area. We'll probably have two more major gift officers, maybe one more planned giving officer," he says. That banker-turned-fundraiser couldn't imagine doing anything else. Few would believe a story about 125-year-old nonprofit that was able to grow so significantly in a short period of time, but don't tell Freyschlag that. He believes the truly significant growth at the Denver Rescue Mission still lies ahead.

# 13

# AGILE

*"If the statistics are boring, you've got the wrong numbers."*

- EDWARD TUFTE

## MANIFESTO

Any technology that evolves over time can eventually become overweight with structure and overly burdened by process. This is exactly what happened during the mid-1990s after decades of software development methodologies become too slow, restrictive, and failed to meet the needs of users.

The traditional waterfall method used to develop software involved long cycles of planning, development, and testing where the end product could take months or years to actually deliver. The increasing pace of change, customer needs, and competition meant that by the time the project was finished, the deliverables could be insufficient or obsolete.

All of this left software developers, end users, and everyone in between frustrated. The tipping point came when 17 software developers met for a few days in February 2001 at The Lodge at Snowbird, a ski resort in the Wasatch mountains of Utah. They developed what is now known as the Agile Manifesto:

"We are uncovering better ways of developing software by doing it and helping others do it. Through this work we have come to value:

**Individuals and interactions** over processes and tools
**Working software** over comprehensive documentation
**Customer collaboration** over contract negotiation
**Responding to change** over following a plan

That is, while there is value in the items on the right, we value the items on the left more."[79]

The similarities between building software and a strategic plan or a communication strategy are probably apparent. The words about software could easily be replaced with the fundraising or programmatic lingo of a nonprofit. Ultimately, agile is about constantly trying to improve a process or end product through iteration. Moving quickly, making decisions as you go, shortening the feedback loop, and then repeating the process all over again every few weeks is essential.

Agile development also involves a series of daily rituals along with work done in short sprints that are reviewed upon completion: a daily stand-up meeting to review the team's progress; projects that last no more than a few weeks; retrospective meetings at the end of a project to share lessons learned. What is sacrificed in long-term visibility is made up for in short-term certainty.

This all sounds like the clockwork of a software company using the agile development process. But it also describes the regular pace of activity inside the marketing communications department at The Humane Society of the United States. The marketing communications department includes digital, direct marketing, events, membership, advertising, corporate relations, major gifts, celebrity relations, and publications. All of these groups report to the chief development officer at the organization. Over the past seven years, several groups within the organization have been adopting and adapting agile approaches to their daily work.

There is a daily 10-minute meeting in which all the channel communication leaders meet to discuss what was completed yesterday, what they are working on today, and any blocking issues that all the teams should know about. Everyone quickly talks about what is going out that day to make sure any major conflicts or dependencies can be addressed. This simple, repetitive, and time-boxed meeting has significantly improved communication across the department and eliminated lots of potential cross-channel communication mistakes.

There is another meeting at 10:00 a.m. every day to triage all the intake requests from across the organization for communication support. This centralizes all the incoming requests and helps to eliminate "drive-by" requests that interrupt staff. Anything that needs more information or looks like a larger project request gets moved to a weekly meeting to be reviewed in more detail. This process allows the teams to not only prioritize requests, but also have the ability to pivot when an important opportunity is brought to the group.

Anyone familiar with the agile methodology would quickly recognize the daily stand-up meetings, triage meetings for new requests, and backlog grooming session every few weeks to size and prioritize work. For the marketing communications teams at HSUS, it's just how they get things done. What started out as an experiment with elements of the agile process is now woven into the habits of staff members.

Carie Lewis Carlson is the director of social marketing at The Human Society of the United States and has spent more than 10 years at the organization. She works within the digital marketing arm of the marketing communications department that includes web, social, and email. Carlson has seen firsthand how the shift to an agile approach has enabled HSUS to achieve remarkable results. Along the way, she has become a respected expert in the use of social media across the nonprofit sector.

Carlson notes, "The first thing the organization did was to develop a group of project managers, which we never had before. Now we have project managers for each major project that we're working on, which is so helpful." The project managers help bring the teams together, schedule additional meetings when they are necessary, and keep the project on track. "They help clear up mistakes like leaving people out, not having the right people in the meeting, whatever it may be. It really makes us more efficient," she says.

As this agile culture developed at HSUS, so too did the importance of using data to measure results. This is especially true for the digital channels that are constantly emitting lots of data. "The challenge with digital data is that there's just so much of it and you've really got to dig through all of it to see what matters. It's also not just about what data is important to you, but also to the stakeholders that you're reporting to and the executive team," says Carlson. She notes, "When we first decided that we were going to try and become more data driven, instead of more internally focused and going with our gut or whoever's opinion, it was a real challenge."

The deluge of data was overwhelming initially for the digital team. "At first, we started utilizing all these different data sources to develop reports that were pages and pages long. We just wanted to show the executive team that we were making progress, but if you give them a 13 page report, they have no idea where to find or make sense of it all, and rightfully so," says Carlson.

Using the data to make decisions and measure progress was an everyday activity, but the team found that how they communicated the findings was equally important. In some cases, this meant developing different versions of information depending on the audience. "I think the lesson that we learned is that you really have to pare it down. Address your specific goals and always have an executive summary," she says.

Carlson shares an example of this approach that involved their year-end social media campaign results: "For me and my team, that report is about 20 pages long. The version that my other coworkers in digital marketing see is just one page. We're figuring out what matters to our stakeholders and not just trying to force them to make sense of all of the data at once," she says. Knowing the audience and setting the right context is absolutely critical when using data to communication and drive decision-making.

This was something that Carlson and her team members learned how to do while adapting to a more agile cadence. "Instead of just giving a spreadsheet of hundreds of thousands of records and saying, 'Here's what we did this month,' we began translating them into charts and graphs and methods that are more digestible. That's something that we never really did before, but now we're doing. We're communicating to people the data that they want and can easily understand," she adds.

Digital media like websites, email, and online advocacy have required nonprofits to move quickly and social media has only quickened the pace. As Carlson notes, "It's stressful. It's nonstop. Social media is not a 9-to-5 job." Those daily stand-up and intake meetings have helped all of the marketing communications teams know what is going on. The real-time nature of social media offers a unique challenge because it's always on. "We use social for direct response fundraising and advocacy efforts, but there's also the customer service angle that in the past couple of years I've really been paying attention to. Now, I'm pushing to integrate more with our call center and our other feedback channels such as phone and email," she says.

Carlson admits that being an agile organization is not easy, especially when the marketing communications department at HSUS consists of more than 100 people. "But we've worked really hard to operate this way because one thing that both our CEO and COO have said from the beginning is that we want to be an opportunistic organization," she says. "That means that if something is happening in the world where we can insert our messaging and make progress for animals, then whatever you're doing — you need to stop doing it and you need to jump on that opportunity," adds Carlson.

One such example was the tremendous public reaction to the killing of Cecil, a Southwest African lion that was allegedly lured outside of his protected nature sanctuary and killed by an American trophy hunter in July 2015. Cecil had been tracked and researched by scientists since 1999 and became a very popular animal in the Hwange National Park in Zimbabwe.[80] Pictures of the lion along with the news that he had been illegally killed began appearing on social media.[81]

Carlson saw that the story began trending on Facebook and Twitter within a day of the initial news reports. She says, "With Cecil, although we weren't the only organization to engage on the issue, there was an opportunity for us to make a difference." The ability to look at trends in the data and be agile enough to respond quickly was extremely important. "We were able to activate quickly and were successful inserting our message into the situation. We literally stopped everything we were doing at the time. We had a vehicle donation email scheduled to go out right before all of that happened, and we had to make the decision that that even though that is a crucial program for us, and it raises a significant amount of money, this was an opportunity that we had to jump on. While it's not perfect, everyone understands that is what we are expected to do," says Carlson.

The response to campaigns by HSUS and other animal welfare organizations was overwhelming. Within a month of Cecil's killing, over 40 major airlines banned the transport of exotic animal trophies on their flights. The power of social media was evident as these airlines, including Delta Air Lines, American Airlines, and Air Canada, used Twitter and Facebook to announce the new restrictions. Carlson notes that these situations always create an opportunity for the organization to learn and improve their responsiveness.

A common aspect of agile organizations is to have a retrospective meeting after a significant amount of work is completed. The marketing communications department at HSUS holds that type of meeting about a month after every single large campaign. "We have a format where we talk about what we did, what we learned, and what we'll do differently next time. That meeting format has really helped us in discussing these important takeaways without fear of blame of failure or anything like that. It also gives us a chance to celebrate our successes," says Carlson.

Using the data to make decisions can also help to overcome confirmation bias or that gut feeling that something will or won't happen without any data to support it. "When I first took on the social media role, I didn't want to use social media for fundraising, because all I had heard is that it's impossible and no one's doing it. You would hear that people on social media don't want to donate, they just want to talk and complain," says Carlson. A lot of people would stop right here and give in to what they think they know.

But Carlson was willing to take the risk and do some testing to determine if what everyone else was saying was actually true. "Through time and testing we were able to make it work and I realized what my boss has been saying all along: if we are putting time and money into an online platform, it needs to tie to our goals. This is how the HSUS digital strategy became so successful, and social media is no different," she says.

This also meant measuring how social helped contribute to the organization's goals. "Our goals are advocacy and fundraising, not eyeballs on content," says Carlson. "I still have to report how many fans and followers we have on a monthly basis, but now we are reporting on a regular basis about our fundraising and advocacy efforts" that are driven by social media campaigns, she says.

Looking ahead, Carlson sees other ways that social media and measuring its impact on constituents can improve a nonprofit's performance. "I believe that more and more people are going to be taking advantage of social media as a customer service tool," she says. She adds that some companies are even making "reduction in call center traffic" one of their key performance indicators. HSUS is already seeing an increased volume in the use of social media for a variety of donor relations activities ranging from changing an address to renewing their membership. She notes, "We've got to integrate and address how social media is affecting us from a customer service standpoint."

Carlson believes that digital and social media will continue to have a profound impact on the nonprofit sector its constituents. The importance of being agile, using data, making decisions, and acting quickly is unlikely to diminish in the future. "We're at the tip of the iceberg right now. We are moving towards being a completely data driven organization, and moving away from making decisions based on opinions, egos, and politics — all of those internally focused situations that I think a lot of nonprofits still make their decisions based on," she says.

Change is indeed coming and nonprofits with an agile culture have an advantage over those that stick to the status quo. Carlson firmly believes that "organizations need to think about this, prepare for it, and they need to put processes in place that will make sure that this change can happen." She says, "I don't think nonprofits or businesses or anybody are going to have a choice eventually. Change is really, really hard, especially in a large organization, but I think we can make it easier by addressing it head-on."

Being agile is more of a mindset than any one set of processes. The original manifesto reminds us that individuals and interactions are more important than the processes or the tools, that collaboration trumps negotiation, and that responding to change is important even when there is a plan in place. The daily, weekly, and monthly activities of the agile process are simply a way to form good habits and increase the pace of change in an organization. HSUS embodies these qualities and its teams are committed to using data to both guide their work and drive decisions to have a positive impact on the world.

## MOSAIC

The explosive growth of agile development processes in the 1990s was fueled by the equally frenetic growth in Internet use. Come on, you remember those early days on the Web with a 14.4 modem that had a whopping 2400 baud rate on dial-up. Yes, dial-up. That thing before Wi-Fi and before broadband and before ADSL and before ISDN. You had to remember to disable call-waiting or it would kill your connection. Back when most people still had a stationary telephone in their homes. And no one under the age of 30 will recognize any of these completely obsolete technologies.

This was the golden age of AOL, CompuServe, Prodigy, and random bulletin board systems (BBS). Everything was slow, pixelated, difficult to use, and full of amazing possibilities. It wasn't perfect but it was the only thing we had. My parents used to tell me about watching black-and-white television, but I never quite grasped what that must have been like. My children are digital natives and they are sure to laugh at how archaically simple the early days of the Web were compared to today.

Back in 1995, I wrote my first lines of HTML code and built websites as an undergraduate at Indiana University. The path that I was on to law school quickly took a detour towards this new and unknown digital territory. I recall sitting in a computer lab at the Indiana Memorial Union on campus and an email from a friend told me to go to something called a URL on another unknown thing called Mosaic. I turned to the person next to me and asked if she knew what this Mosaic thing was.

Mosaic was one of the earliest web browsers. It had very few features and even less visual appeal. Imagine a black-and-white TV for a web browser and that pretty much sums up the experience. Within moments, I was browsing several websites and was completely fascinated by what people had built. Within hours, I was starting to hack together my own code to see how to build something myself. Within days, I had designed and built a website that immediately started getting traffic. It would have been built sooner if not for those classes getting in the way.

What followed were several years of website projects, each one bigger and more complicated than the last. Corporate clients, e-commerce websites, nonprofit organizations, news and content sites, and just about everything in between. Over time there was a transition from designing and coding websites to hiring people with more talent than I possessed. But both the understanding and appreciation for the underlying technology have never left me.

Those were the early days of the web before Google or the eventual dot-com bubble burst. Both existing and brand new nonprofits would soon be using the web too. The initial brochureware websites made way for more advanced capabilities. The first online donations happened in the late 1990s and other ways for people to engage with nonprofits began to transform the digital landscape.

Greg Baldwin has been at VolunteerMatch, an online community that brings good people and good causes together, since the very beginning back in 1998. He joined the nonprofit startup after several years in advertising as VolunteerMatch's chief imagination officer. Today, Baldwin is the president of the organization and has witnessed firsthand the emergence of the online space as a thriving ecosystem for the nonprofit sector. He says he's amazed not only by how over-hyped the web sounded in 2000, but also by "how most of what has happened in the last 15 years has wildly exceeded all of that hype." Baldwin adds, "I mean we're surrounded by technology, data, and information in a way that was completely unimaginable to me in 1998."

From the very beginning, using data to understand what was happening and to drive decision-making was part of VolunteerMatch's DNA. "The very first VolunteerMatch website we built in 1998 had the number of connections made right on the homepage as a ticker. That was our first metric to help us keep track of…whether or not anybody was using this new contraption that we had built" to make it easier to find local volunteer opportunities, says Baldwin. He notes that they've been tracking this same number for 18 years as the fundamental metric measuring the success and health of the work that they do. "Our mission is to make it easier for good people and good causes to connect. This is our number one metric," he adds.

Those early days of VolunteerMatch established a set of habits and attitudes about measurement and using data that has only matured over time. Baldwin remembers, "We spent what seemed like a hundred meetings talking about what we should be measuring. We measure a bunch of other things in the background, like how many opportunities are in the system, how many nonprofits have registered with the system, the delta between new opportunities in any given day, opportunities that have expired. We keep track of page views, unique visitors, repeat visitors." But he says those are secondary to their "connection metric, which only happens when all of the other ingredients are really working well."

Distilling all this data down to the one metric that matters the most to VolunteerMatch's mission allows the organization to see outcomes, not just outputs. The secondary metrics act as a way to see how website visits turn into connections over time. "You have to have lots of opportunities in the system, and you have to have enough users coming into the system looking for those opportunities. It really is a byproduct of a lot of other variables coming together to create the circumstances or the environment in which somebody can actually find something that touches and inspires them," says Baldwin. "For someone to actually come in and find something that appeals to them, given how personal volunteering can be, is the highest measure of success," he adds.

The danger with anything that leverages the internet is the sheer volume of data that can be produced. That constant real-time stream of bits and bytes can be completely overwhelming. Baldwin notes that "raw data is a recipe for complete overload" and he says, "Data is only useful when you really connect it to your goals, your activities, and your targets." He adds, "Data doesn't help you choose where you want to go. It's a tool for helping get where you want to go more effectively."

Staring into the abyss of data can paralyze people from making decisions. Baldwin has seen firsthand how other organizations get caught up in analysis paralysis. "I do feel like there's a lot of people who stare at the data as if it will tell them the answer to where they should go. A lot of people get stuck there.

They look and look and look and look and it never tells them the answer. Then they just get overwhelmed," he says.

Over time, VolunteerMatch has turned data into useful information about what is happening. "I think that what is powerful with something like VolunteerMatch is that we are awash with data, but we use data as a tool to help us make it easier for good people and good causes to connect. That's our goal. That goal doesn't just come out of the data. We use the data to advance that goal," Baldwin notes.

Another challenge when making the leap from collecting data to actually using it to measure progress is the tendency to focus on the metrics more than the mission. It is often said that what gets measured gets managed, and that can lead people to lose sight of the big picture. A metric is not a replacement for a strategy supported by strong underlying organizational values.

Baldwin notes that VolunteerMatch has had to address this issue over time. "We spent a lot of time talking about operationalizing our values. You get all these metrics and yardsticks, but you can never confuse your measures for your values," he says. That is a powerful statement and a reminder that success takes leadership and a culture that understands what really matters to the organization. Baldwin notes, "Culturally, operationally, and strategically there's very little enthusiasm for doing anything that we don't think is directly connected to one of these metrics. Preferably, to the connection metric. Almost everybody at the organization has some direct responsibility for organizing activities."

Sometimes the organization needs to make sure the metrics are measuring the right things. Baldwin vividly recalls a time when they were debating the cleanup of some old and duplicate records in the system. "There was a manager whose annual goals included having that number grow by 5,000 organizations. If we cleaned up the database, she'd lose 1,500 organizations. That would set her behind her goals. Those are the great moments where you're like, 'Can you be bigger than your metrics?' It's clear that you should clean it up," he says.

For Baldwin, it all comes back to understanding his organization's values and aligning them with the metrics that matter. "Our underlying value is we want to be an amazing service for nonprofits to recruit great volunteers and amazing service for volunteers to find great nonprofit organizations. We count the number of nonprofit organizations, but having two of the same organization in there, that's not helping at all. Those are the moments when your values need to be stronger than the metrics you're using to operationalize those values," says Baldwin.

Another test of values versus metrics was a decision to change one of the fundamental features on the website. In the early days of VolunteerMatch, users did not need to be registered before they could make a connection. The team did not want to create too high a barrier for someone to start their engagement with a nonprofit volunteer opportunity. The result was that they "were getting people that were coming in and sending out 1,500 requests to nonprofits. It was basically just spammers." Baldwin acknowledges that this made the numbers look great, but they knew that in reality it was pushing them in the wrong direction.

The team made a change that required registrations before a connection could be created. The result was a 30% drop in the connection rate that year. Baldwin recalls that people would ask "What happened there? You guys were doing so well." He had to correct them, saying "No, that's what's right! That is measuring a healthier system." This is also a sign of how an agile culture responds to both positive and negative feedback. The VolunteerMatch team constantly iterates on ideas and looks for opportunities to improve the user's experience.

"For about four years now we've been doing agile development work. That has made a huge difference in creating short enough cycles so that you're able to create a feedback loop for the engineering teams even when it's not fully connected to every top metric," says Baldwin. He is the first one to admit he can't take credit for bringing agile to the organization. "I was supportive of it, but it was really a product manager who we were lucky enough to get. We had kind of been dabbling with it, but kind of our own version of agile for two or three years. Now this thing has great rhythm when it comes to building stuff and getting the feedback and building more stuff. I think it all added up to a culture that is very feedback and data driven," he says.

Baldwin also believes that the introduction of agile among the project and engineering teams has spread throughout the rest of organization. "VolunteerMatch has been extraordinarily lucky in ongoing business revenues and having resources from foundations, but as the market continues to transform you get new opportunities. You need a culture that's willing to experiment with new things. Agile creates a framework where there's much less resistance to trying something new in the organization. People are exploring new revenue streams and exploring new ways to communicate our value to nonprofits. That's very different than it was before we had agile in the culture," he says.

When an agile mindset takes root across the organization, it can change attitudes and perspectives. "Before we had agile at the organization, there were times where it felt like you were just staring at the scoreboard. Kind of waiting for it to go up. It wasn't quite clear what we needed to do right now to get the next success. Agile really improved our willingness and ability as a culture to try new things," says Baldwin.

The culture of using data combined with an agile mindset across VolunteerMatch was critical three years ago when they completely rebuilt their website. Baldwin says that one of the rebuild's goals "was to increase the connection rate and to build better interfaces that increased the likelihood that someone would find an opportunity that really touched and inspired them" to get involved. The project also allowed the teams to test some new ideas and leverage lessons learned from successful online sites.

"The hypothesis that we were working on was that personalization based on an issue area and skills would increase the likelihood that you'd be able to help someone find something that was really relevant for them," says Baldwin. This was a shift away from their earlier approach of offering a "volunteer opportunity buffet" that required the user to wade through the 100,000 items on the website. Adding just a few questions for the user to answer allowed a more prescriptive set of opportunities to be highlighted.

"We built a lightweight recommendation engine that takes those variables, overlays it with your geography, and it recommends opportunities that fit your profile," he says. The team also began curating additional volunteer opportunities and emailing them to registered users. Every few weeks, a set of hand-picked opportunities arrived in the users' inboxes to not only inform them, but keep them engaged too. Baldwin says, "Those two changes to the public website over the last three years have double our connection rate."

The connection rate continues to grow after these new changes to the website, resulting in a 21% growth rate in the last year alone. "We knew what success would look like and had a hypothesis in place about what we could do differently. We rolled it out and we can see whether it worked, which is awesome when you get that kind of feedback loop," says Baldwin.

Showing what success looks like is also at the heart of VolunteerMatch's culture. Not only does the website provide a number of key metrics for website visitors, but anyone in the San Francisco offices can see them too. The moment anyone walks off the office elevator, there is a giant flat panel display showing a live view of the last few hours of connection activity on the VolunteerMatch network. The display is the first thing staff see in the morning and it's impossible for guests to miss.

"We certainly go out of our way to be enthusiastic about being a tech social enterprise where we can demonstrate what we're doing so visually. I think it's both reassuring and creates a shared appreciation for what success looks like," says Baldwin. This is also the new normal for most companies in the Bay Area, even if not every nonprofit is quite ready to replace their logo in the reception area with a display of real-time metrics.

VolunteerMatch's location certainly allows for a lot of exposure to how tech companies of all shapes and sizes prioritize the utilization and visualization of data in the work environment. Baldwin says this puts them in a different position from other organizations. Other nonprofits might not have this level of measurement and visibility into their activities, but it "would be hard to operate in Silicon Valley and San Francisco without something like this," he says.

Inside the offices, two other displays help the staff understand what is happening with the website and the current projects under development. Vital statistics about the website are shown so that people get a highly visible picture of the VolunteerMatch network's health. They installed another display to show the status and progress on engineering projects. Now staff that depend on the new website capabilities can see firsthand what is happening without having to be at every stand-up meeting or sprint review.

VolunteerMatch has continued to evolve over the past 18 years right along with the rest of the internet. Both before Google and with Google. Both before Facebook, Twitter, and LinkedIn, and with an ever-increasing number of social media sites. The adoption of both an agile mindset and a focus on being data driven has allowed them to succeed over time. These are also the key elements to their continued growth and adaptation in the future.

# 14

# DATA

*"If you're offered a seat on a rocket ship, don't ask what seat! Just get on."*

- SHERYL SANDBERG

## FSU

There are two types of highly data driven cultures: Nonprofits that have been data driven from the very beginning, and those organizations that made a significant change at some point in their evolution. While some organizations are born data driven, others have to reboot their system in order to successfully make the transition. Both situations have their own opportunities and challenges. Let's begin with the journey of an established nonprofit striving to build a data driven culture.

It starts with one system in one department and a completely different system in another. It spreads to rogue spreadsheets and hidden stockpiles of contacts. Then every species of report, dashboard, and data warehouse begins to grow in all manner of places. Organizational silos become insular and isolated from each other. They collect their own data, measure their own metrics, and reinforce a culture that others should mind their own business. Duplication of cost, effort, and data begins to spiral out of control. The more you struggle, the faster you sink into the data abyss.

After several years, the amount of data debt built up can seem overwhelming. It usually takes a data intervention--or simply admitting there's a major problem--to get support to hit the reset button. What follows is the story of a nonprofit institution that forced itself to become data driven because the costs and challenges of living with so many data silos would not allow it to grow enough to meets its goals.

Jeanne Pecha is the vice president of advancement services at the Florida State University Foundation. She is responsible for leading and overseeing advancement operations activities in concert with the other fundraising organizations at the university. This means not only the FSU Foundation but also the Alumni Association, the Seminole Boosters, and the Ringling Museum. This complex, multifaceted environment is a perfect example to show that building a highly data driven culture is possible.

The data produced by these groups and systems had continued to grow over time. It wasn't just the multiple departments and data sources that had grown, but the sheer volume and variety were increasing at an ever-accelerating pace. "We're not only dealing with constituents that have an interest in the university or that have given to any number of organizations, but we're also dealing with that data for alumni, faculty, staff, parents, currently enrolled students, and everything in between," says Pecha. Within any one constituent type, there was also "biographical, demographic, educational relationships, giving histories, memberships, event attendance, call center information, communication preferences, and even athletics ticketing data."

In 2008, the FSU Foundation began an ambitious project that eventually became branded as oneFSU to bring all this data into a consolidated system. This meant that various departments and academic units needed to dismantle their data silos and begin working more in unison. Many nonprofit organizations talk about bringing together all their data into a single system, but it is no small undertaking. This is the story of how FSU did it and, in doing so, created a more data driven culture.

The impetus for the project came out of the success of the 2005 FSU CONNECT capital campaign that raised $630 million for the university.[82] While the campaign was a tremendous success, it also highlighted the challenges and pain points of attempting to manage so many different systems and processes and so much disparate data over the years. Pecha recalls that "getting information during the campaign literally meant calling around to people in different groups." For more detailed data requests, the response was often that someone would need to call back later with an answer.

This archaic approach resulted in three major challenges for fundraising across the university: First, only high-level summary information was being shared. That limited the capacity for any deeper, meaningful analysis. Second, getting answers to important questions took days or weeks. Third, the quality of the data across each department varied widely, from very good to very bad. Other than that, it was great.

At the same time, several of the fundraising units were making budget requests to replace their aging systems that had been in use prior to and during the campaign. Other groups wanted to stay in their own separate systems. T.K. Wetherell, president of FSU at the time, set the tone for the consolidated systems project: If the university was going to pay for all these systems, then all the direct support groups needed to use the same one. There would be no more data silos, which meant the end of different tools being used by different groups. They could use any system they wanted to as long as it was the same one.

Under the oneFSU project, multiple fundraising systems would be replaced with a single system to be used by all the major fundraising units. Data from across the legacy systems would be cleaned up, converted, and maintained by the advancement services group. All reporting and ad hoc requests were also centralized to ensure that all information could be compared apples to apples.

The project's other major aspect was to consolidate multiple online websites, email, and donation tools into a single platform. FSU wanted to ensure that they were future-proofing their digital data to allow them to improve online engagement and fundraising efforts. Different groups could still have a unique design and online experience, but the underlying system would manage data the same way for everyone.

Pecha and her key stakeholders believed that being able to provide a higher level of data quality, management, and activation would outweigh any perceived loss of control by individual groups all managing their own data. The advancement services group would not only become stewards of the data but also a high performing service bureau for the other departments.

"As with any large institution, when we first started bringing these data sets into a consolidated system, there was some reluctance on behalf of the academic units to share their information," says Pecha. She knew that part of the key to getting buy-in from various groups was to make sure that the consolidated system would provide a higher level of quality information delivery than any individual group would be able to do on its own.

"We've worked really hard in the advancement area to bring in that data, maintain that data, and invest in the tools and expertise to monitor the data on an ongoing basis. They wanted to get into our consolidated system because we have the expertise and skills to maintain it and provide it back to them in a timely fashion," she says.

In many ways, Pecha was transforming her team from a traditional back-office operation to a modern data service agency that served the needs of groups all across the university. Pecha notes, "It's taken time, but I feel like the staff and the foundation and advancement area have proven themselves good stewards of the data and really worked for the greater good of the organization to provide services that are meaningful and timely for as many areas as we possibly can across campus."

This may sound counterintuitive, but FSU found that the easiest way to serve the widest set of academic units and fundraisers on the far reaches of the university was to centralize as much of the data as possible. "No one system is perfect, but the effort has been consistent day in, day out, week by week, month by month, year by year tending to that data. Being able to leverage the information and [have] a way to deliver it back has really won the academic units over. We make it easy for them to pass that information to us in the central area, and then we monitor our turnaround times to make sure it's updated in the system in a timely fashion," says Pecha

This approach has allowed the FSU Foundation to both achieve economies of scale with their data quality investments and raise the bar across the board for data integrity. "We've invested in an annual data hygiene initiative.

We're trying to be strategic when we do certain data scrubs," she says. The data quality spans everything from regular National Change of Address (NCOA) updates, email address clean-up, appending phone and demographic data, as well as working to locate lost constituents. "All of that is timed and strategized so that we can leverage when we're pulling large data sets, either for screenings or for large direct mail pieces that are going out on behalf of the university."

One decision that came out of the consolidated system project was to create a data integrity committee to handle the ongoing governance needs of all the stakeholders. Since 2008, the data integrity committee meets weekly and includes representatives from across various departments along with the advancement services team. They meet to discuss data projects at a detailed level and keep everyone updated on outbound campaigns so that everyone knows what each group is doing.

"When we need a change to the data or something new we want to report on, then we go through an approval process with the data integrity committee. It's like a data governance process where we can keep track of what each group is doing," says Pecha. She notes, "Data is a living, breathing organism. It's going to grow and change, so we need to stay on top of that, especially down-stream from a reporting perspective." The data integrity committee helps to maintain the accuracy of the information that is produced and also acts to help the different groups understand new ways that they want to use the data.

Any organization that claims to be donor-centric must also have data at the heart of what it does. Jeanne points to an example of tracking and manag-ing communication preferences that benefitted from having the data integrity committee involved from the start. "We track all of the communication pref-erences of all the different academic units in our colleges. It was important to become more granular in the communication preferences tracking so that if the person wants to hear from the college where they graduated from but they don't want to hear from another group, that can be managed," she says. The weekly meetings allowed for progress to be made quickly in this area.

A consolidated view of the data combined with governance has allowed FSU to be nimbler and donor-centric at the same time. The data integrity committee has also helped bring groups together to see what's possible with data management. The Seminole Boosters group now tracks constituents' interests in non-fundraising-related activities like ticket purchasing, specific sports, and other areas. "We can analyze whether people are being invited to events, sent direct mail, opening our email and newsletters, and responding to solicitations because we're very transparent and we are in one system that allows people to see what they need to improve their engagement or fundraising results," says Pecha.

The leaders across FSU aren't the only ones taking notice of all these data driven improvements; supporters are noticing, too. Pecha says, "Our constituents, donors, and alumni, they just want to see one institution interacting with them in a concerted way, not siloed like we had been previously." While she acknowledges that the different groups have varying resources and skill sets, Pecha sees progress. "We're in this system and it forces us to talk to one another and help each other out. It definitely fosters an environment to utilize the data and the tool sets cohesively," she says.

The oneFSU project was an ambitious move from lots of data silos, tools, and costs to a consolidated system. Today, data quality across the fundraising groups at FSU has never been better, and they're able to negotiate better pricing because of the volume of data handled. "We're in one system, and when you take a look at efforts like data hygiene or wealth screening, we don't have to do it multiple times. We're doing it one system and we do it across the board so that the information returned can be leveraged by any of the fundraisers across the organization," says Pecha. She adds there are "definitely economies of scale" in terms of how they handle and maintain their data.

The next big step after getting all of the data assets consolidated was to create self-service reporting that could scale to meet the university's needs. "When I first got here, everything was almost all ad hoc reporting. We're still a work in progress, but we've come a long way. We've been able to create a reporting environment that is a lot more self-service," says Pecha. This has freed up the advancement services staff to spend more time on data analysis and less time on responding to requests.

"As you can imagine, when you're in a large institution, not everyone is going to ask the same question over and over and over. There's always a different flavor of the requests that come through, which requires us to alter the way we provide that information," says Pecha. Finding the right balance between self-service access to data and knowing when to provide additional assistance is very important.

One thing that Pecha has found very advantageous is to have report developers that understand fundraising. "They understand the business of what their data consumers are doing and they can help safeguard that person." It allows them to meet the end user halfway to help them determine exactly what information they need. "They're listening, but it's a two-way interaction that takes place because a lot of times the end user doesn't know how to articulate what they need," she says. It is certainly true that someone can have great technical knowledge about managing data and creating reports, but if they don't understand the definition of lifetime giving or soft credits, then the answers they provide can be wrong.

Those subject matter experts have also proven useful elsewhere in advancement services. Pecha says, "Having a really good partnership between your information services area, your functional areas, and your subject matter experts is critical for a successful data driven nonprofit." This is especially true when senior leaders have asked the group to help them get the right information. "I'm really lucky that we have people who understand the subject matter and can translate what the executive leadership wants into the right information," she says. These subject matter experts help remove a lot of the friction from the process and understand the difference between managing data and using it to measure results.

The FSU Foundation's data maturity has continued to grow as they've automated more of the day-to-day activities. "We're moving toward looking at patterns, trends, and then trying to predict what we need to be doing next," she says. This has meant using external data and modeling to help drive results. Pecha notes, "We use a partner to bring in major gift predictive modeling and planned giving predictive modeling data. Then our own internal resources leverage that data to make a strategic decision." The scoring is used for a range of activities from prospect management, portfolio assignments, and even who is sent invitations to special events.

Pecha is also careful to point out that there is always more that can be done, but it has to be something that can be executed consistently. "Being able to bring data in and layer it so we can consume it in an efficient manner is key," she says. "You and I both know there are other external datasets out there, like social media data, but for me, it's how you get to better identity management. When you really think about what information that is out there that could help me identify the behavior of our constituents, it's just over-whelming to think about. But if I can't tap into it and bring it back to leverage it, then it's a lost opportunity."

The temptation to take on one-off data projects would be a step backward for the work that has been done at the FSU Foundation. There are often requests to look at LinkedIn or Instagram or exotic-data-source-of-the-day. Pecha admits, "I want to keep an open mind to new possibilities and what is possible from a pure technical perspective, but it's not always actionable infor-mation. I have to pick and choose what is valuable and not just adding to the noise that I'm already working with."

It has been more than a decade now since FSU recognized that playing the telephone game to answer key questions was no longer sustainable. The oneFSU project set out to solve three major problems and it has been a suc-cess by any measure. High-level summary information has been turned into more granular data that can be used for meaningful analysis. Response times for information have dramatically improved thanks to consolidated systems and a growing set of self-service reporting capabilities. Finally, data quality has a single owner in the organization and a governance structure that allows for meeting the growing needs of stakeholders.

Pecha has been instrumental in building a data driven culture at the FSU Foundation.[83] "I'm a big believer in a centralized area that is responsible for the data integrity and data management. You've got to start there, and it's an ongoing effort. You've got to dedicate resources to make sure the data at the lowest level is as accurate as it can be. In my opinion, that's the first step of a data driven nonprofit," she says. In her case, that opinion is a very informed one, spoken from first-hand experience.

## GPS

There are moments in history when completely unrelated events occur around the same time, and when they converge it has a powerful impact that few people would ever predict. This exact scenario happened over a decade ago and the world is no longer the same as it was before.

It's 2004 and Scott Harrison is on board the *SS Anastasia* for its journey to Benin in West Africa, a stark contrast from the glamor of New York City, where Harrison spent a decade as a nightclub promoter.[84] Harrison says, "I traded my spacious midtown loft for a 150-square-foot cabin with bunk beds, roommates, and cockroaches. Fancy restaurants were replaced by a mess hall feeding 400+ army-style. A prince in New York, now I was living in close community with 350 others."[85] He gave up his late-night lifestyle, sold most of what he owned, and asked friends to help support him when he decided to volunteer to work for Mercy Ships, a nonprofit that operates a fleet of hospital boats to provide medical care in the development world.

Harrison spent the first four months in Benin as a photographer for the organization and another four months in Liberia. In Liberia, he saw first-hand the connection between quality of water and quality of life. Back in New York for the first time in many months, someone bought him a $16 margarita at a club. "I had just returned from Africa and I thought, 'How dare they?' But then I relented and saw an opportunity: If my friends have $16 to spend on a drink, wait until they hear what they can do with that money in Africa," said Harrison in an interview with *Wired*. Earlier in 2004, a Harvard College student named Mark Zuckerberg created a social network for other students to engage with each other.

While Harrison was spending another year volunteering with Mercy Ships, another piece of the puzzle clicked into place. The growth of Global Positioning System (GPS) data got a big boost when Google Maps launched in February 2005. Very quickly, there was an explosion in both the accessibility and use of mapping data by consumers. Google Maps has since gone on to become one of the largest providers of mapping data around the world. There were others before Google Maps, but the decision to allow maps to be embedded on third-party websites and as a part of mobile phone applications changed everything.

Now it's the night of September 7, 2006, and Scott Harrison is celebrating his 31st birthday at a party in Manhattan's Meatpacking District. The $20 cover charge was actually a donation to raise money to drill wells in Africa. By the end of the night, Harrison had raised $15,000. It was enough to fund three wells and repair another three broken ones in northern Uganda, bringing clean water to 31,638 people. Harrison then sent the GPS coordinates and photos of the wells to the people who attended his birthday party. "This was a big deal. Some people didn't even remember the party. Seriously, people could not believe that a charity would bother to report to them on a $20 gift. And that something actually happened with the money that they could see, that they could connect with. And we said, 'Let's just keep doing this. Let's keep closing the loop until this problem is solved.'"[86] This was the beginning of charity: water.

A year later, Harrison asked people to stay home instead of attending his birthday party, and he also asked them to donate $32 to fund a well. But this time, the well could help supply clean water to a hospital in Athinai, in the region of Nakuru in Kenya. charity: water used a compelling campaign on their website that featured powerful imagery and a video. They raised $124,000, which was enough for a well at two hospitals and a school.[87] They had visibly and powerfully closed the loop for their donors. A few months earlier, Apple launched the first iPhone on June 29, 2007. Many of those birthday donors saw the videos of charity: water's work for the first time on their mobile device.

Fast forward 10 years and several seemingly unrelated events have converged and changed the world we live in. Facebook now has more than 1.6 billion monthly active users. Nearly 2 billion people have smartphones. Google Maps is the most popular app for smartphones, with over 54% of global smartphone owners using it once.[88] charity: water has funded over 20,000 water projects in 24 countries in coordination with 25 local partners, providing clean water to more than 6,300,000 people.

"Data was there from the very beginning," says Christoph Gorder, chief water officer at charity: water. He joined the nonprofit in 2012 after 15 years at AmeriCares, the largest privately-funded relief organization in the United States, in senior global program roles. At charity: water, Gorder leads the programs and day-to-day operations of the organization. "When Scott started charity: water, it was just him. He did a fundraiser, raised a bunch of money, and that money was just to build six water projects in Uganda. He emailed everybody back to say thank you afterward and sent them links to GPS coordinates on Google Maps, which was this new product out there," says Gorder.

The idea of keeping track of the GPS coordinates of a project out in the field might seem obvious today, but it was a completely novel idea in 2006. Gorder says, "People were blown away by the fact that he came back and said, 'Your money actually did something,' and they had this sense of the impact because they could see it on Google Maps. The level of accountability and transparency within that very first project is why they have stayed with us and just grown and grown on a personal level around us."

The culture of data was indeed there at charity: water from the very beginning. "We track and require GPS coordinates, photographs, and a whole range of data at every single water project that's out there," says Gorder. "We publish all that on our website. It creates an enormous amount of programmatic accountability because I have data sets for 100% of the projects that have been completed," he says. Think about that for a moment. charity: water has tangible, visible, and measurable data for every single project that the organization has ever completed. That has profound effects not only on donors but also on partners and the entire social good supply chain. One set of coordinates on a map can be traced back to the people impacted, to the drillers, to quality control, to local partners, and ultimately to the donors that funded the project.

The charity: water model is simple: they use 100% of all public donations to directly fund water projects and they prove each one using GPS coordinates on Google Maps. All of the administrative costs of staff salaries to light bulbs and technology are funded entirely by private donors, foundations, and sponsors. This approach divides many in the nonprofit sector. Some established organizations claim that, at best, it isn't fair and, at worst, it sets the wrong donor expectations. Other nonprofits view it as an innovative approach to dealing with the "overhead problem" and see it as a viable model for other organizations to follow. For me, the charity: water exemplifies what I call MacLaughlin's Maxim: The nonprofit that creates the shortest distance between a donor's gift and the expected outcome or impact wins.[89]

Yes, the model looks simple until you realize how hard the organization focuses on making it work. Over the past decade, charity: water has evolved its use of data and how it handles that data going forward. Gorder notes, "One of our key questions, having completed these projects, is, 'How are they performing over time?' It's been a big push for us over the past few years to go back and visit these sorts of projects and see how they're doing. First of all, we're able to do that because we have tracked 100% of our projects since day one, which is a luxury of having been an organization that was created in the digital age."

Showing the impact of the donation from the very beginning and being able to demonstrate what happened is a game changer. It is also important because the reality is that sometimes projects fail. "We had to truly understand what went wrong and then do something about it. We're able to go back because we have data from years ago to see the ones that are working and the ones that aren't and draw a whole bunch of conclusions from that. It's very powerful for us," says Gorder. This is an agile mindset being applied to programmatic thinking.

As we have seen with other nonprofit organizations, it is not enough to collect the data. There must be some validation of the data, which often does not happen until it is put into practical use. Gorder explains, "When we collected GPS coordinates, we collect them so, in theory, we can go back, but in practical reality, you only go back to a small number. What we found going back now is a certain amount of data was collected erroneously. A certain amount was transcribed wrong so when you go back to it, you get a GPS coordinate and, 'Where is that water point? I'm in the wrong place.' You realize all these data entry errors tend to happen in the normal course of business. The reason those exist was because no one was actually using the data. It didn't yet have a practical utility." Over time, the data driven mindset has changed at charity: water to ensure any collected data also has utility. "Now our data collection is so rigorous, in part because I feel really strongly that if we're collecting data, we have to use it and we have to validate it," he says.

Gorder tells the story of how a data collection project launched over a year and a half ago illustrates just some of the challenges there can be with data collection: "We launched a set of household surveys to collect data in some project locations before they got a water point and after," he says. They surveyed heads of households in the field and asked what their walking times were before and after the water project was put in place. "We got a whole lot of data that was really encouraging. Walking times have been reduced by more than 50%, et cetera," explains Gorder.

Then Gorder had an opportunity to validate some of the data in the field. "The last time I was in Ethiopia, I pulled out my mobile device and I looked up the surveys and I went and spot checked. I went to just a random village that had been surveyed and then to the actual GPS coordinates for the households that were chosen. I went and actually walked the distance myself. One household that was in the survey said it was 30 minutes to walk. The other household, which was right next to it, said it's 15 minutes to walk. I walked to both of those households and now I'll be able to actually correct it. Otherwise, I would've told you that the average walking time was 22 minutes and I would've been wrong. The average walking time was actually 16 minutes", he explains. Gorder stresses the point that "it costs so much money to collect data and manage data." He adds, "We really focus on doing the best that we can with data that can actually be validated to make decisions."

charity: water collects GPS coordinates, photos, and a lot of other information from the field. The photos, in particular, aren't just for marketing or donor communication purposes. They act as that critical confirmation from thousands of miles away that water is indeed flowing at the project site. "We require from our local partners the photographs of every single water point. We're really specific about the photographs and sometimes it drives people crazy, but there has to be water flowing out of the system," says Gorder. "It seems like the dumbest thing, but that rule came up because we were finding instances where the partner would say, 'Oh yeah. We built everything. Everything is all set. We did all the training, but we're waiting for the local government to bring the electricity in.' Well, what am I supposed to do with that? That's not helping anybody," he says. Having the photograph of every single water point with water coming out of it is another valuable piece of data charity: water uses across the organization. Gorder adds, "The accountability that's created downstream is great because I don't have projects out there not helping anybody."

A moment ago this all looked so simple. Collect donations. Fund projects. Deliver projects. Repeat. But making something look simple is really, really difficult. "Good data, it's really hard to do. Your staff members have to be well-trained. They have to be well-supervised. The data has to be cleaned. You can tell when you look at the data whether it's used or not, like right away. If somebody's using this data, there's no way data isn't normalized," says Gorder. "We see a lot of effort in the industry around data collection, around measurement and evaluation. Honestly, it doesn't really matter if it's not able to close the loop for all the data that's out there," he says.

Having a culture of data in the office is one thing. Getting a culture of data to work in all the projects across the globe is something charity: water is constantly working on to improve. Gorder understands first-hand that this is both a complex challenge and an extremely powerful tool once it is in place. He points to another example of how the value of data has to be present in every part of the programmatic supply chain: "In Ethiopia, there are a number of mobile mechanics, guys on motorbikes who are paid for by the local partner from charity: water. They cover about 3,500 villages, serving about 800,000 people, and help them keep their water points working," he explains. "Every time they arrive at a village, they're supposed to fill in a survey on their mobile phone. That survey gets uploaded and we get to see it. We can track the activity level of every single one of these mechanics every week. We have a conversation with the supervisor out there and say, 'Wow, your numbers really dropped off over the last week. What's going on out there?' It turns out the guys claim that they're making the visits, but they haven't been doing the surveys. Well, a big part of this program is to collect the data so that we understand what the intervention should look like in the future. The collection problem gets corrected in a week," he says. Gorder goes on, noting, "In the old world, we would have never known that. Today, it's real time. We are sitting here in New York looking at the data, talking to the team in Ethiopia."

They're making management decisions, which is ultimately converted into better service and more accountability at the beneficiary level, at the village level, which is what we care about."

The world is mobile. The world is social. The world is real-time constant stream of data. That is the new normal. It is also part of the culture at charity: water. "There's a very strong culture of data…There are dashboards all over the office that are displaying all sorts of data: marketing data, hits to the website, and a lot of project data. Visually in the office, it's there," says Gorder. In addition to the visual importance of data in the office, the organization's operations are centered on being data driven. "Then in our regular meetings, there's a culture of data. Meetings often begin with a metrics session, where we've agreed on a set of metrics that we're looking at on a weekly basis or a monthly basis," he says.

When data is omnipresent and part of how everyone does their job, it becomes part of the daily ebb and flow of the organization. At the same time, you have to be careful not to overcomplicate things. "We don't overthink it. It's not about having a Rolls Royce for a tool. It's about, 'What's the information? What does it actually mean? And how do you disseminate it to the right people?'" says Gorder. Over time, charity: water has used a variety of metrics to measure outcomes and impact. Gorder says, "I'm on the side of fewer metrics. I'm always trying to distill stuff down so I can look at what is happening in our programs. Last year, there were nine Key Performance Indicators (KPIs) for the program portfolio of which three were really, really important: Are the grants finishing on time? Are we getting the output we paid for? Are they coming in on budget?" Other people across the organization will need more detailed information and metrics, but getting people to focus on the most important things that drive results is very powerful.

Keeping the metrics simple and understandable also aids in people being able to communicate what the data is saying. "I think you should be able to explain almost everything to people in simple terms. I believe if you really understand what you're talking about, you should be able to use the numbers around it. When you're really able to get the essence of things, you understand what's important and what is secondary," says Gorder." That does not mean that secondary metrics are not important, but they are not necessarily equal to the most important metrics.

Gorder explains how this thinking directly applies to the work that charity: water does: "The work that we fund is very complex. It's not just water. It's water, sanitation, and hygiene. It's extremely diverse across many countries. The interventions are very diverse. For example, in Rwanda, we built $500,000 pipe systems where the Rwandan government is a co-financier, putting in 45% of the cash budget, and there are private utilities operating the systems. On the other extreme of the portfolio in Cambodia, there are $65 biosand filters that are in people's houses that they build themselves. Out of all these projects, the metric has been, 'How many people are getting access to clean water?' Then the second one would be, 'How many projects are we actually executing?'" he says. When you only have a few seconds or minutes to communicate what your organization is doing, simpler is better. Gorder understands that this does not diminish all the other things going on and the complexities involved. "Of course, there's a ton of other stuff happening in the process. We care deeply about it and we have a lot of money invested in it and we understand it very well, but when we talk about it, the easiest way to explain it to somebody is how many people got access to clean water," he says.

It would be easy to be completely overwhelmed by the deluge of data at charity: water, but the culture has allowed the organization to absorb a lot of it. "Everything we do, from our fundraising to our marketing teams, is very, very data-driven. It's very much part of the culture. There's a lot of numbers floating around here, and yet it's also a very creative and artistic culture, which is interesting. There's a real love for specificity," says Gorder. This culture of data thrives on curiosity, but it also gets channeled to produce measurable results. "We're constantly trying to push the boundaries and asking the hard questions: How do we get more effective? How do we help more people? How do we move faster? How do we do it cheaper? There's a ton of curiosity and optimism to really try things in a different way here. We believe that there are simple technological tools and simple uses for data and information that can really help save people's lives. It has an urgency, an immediacy to it, and it gets people up in the morning," he says.

One of those people is Carlos Medina, the data scientist at charity: water. Medina has a strong background in mathematics and physics and worked at DonorsChoose.org as part of their data science team before joining charity: water. "My role at charity: water covers different areas since I collaborate with different teams. I look for patterns and hidden dynamics inside, and between, our different products based on our users' behavior," says Medina.

Medina learned some valuable lessons at DonorsChoose.org, including that "in order for an organization to grow, the growth has to be integral. No team can be left behind in any matter whatsoever." He says, "In particular, when it came to the access to information in a timely and effective manner, democratization of information was one of the priorities." Part of this meant implementing an organization-wide tool that allowed staff members to become their own data analysts. Today, charity: water uses a similar set of tools to have what Medina calls "a single, integrated data ecosystem."

We already know a lot about how charity: water uses data on the programs side, but the culture of data has permeated the rest of the organization as well. This is especially true on the fundraising and revenue side, where Medina helps to analyze different kinds of data. The charity: water team has a bi-weekly meeting to look at specific trends with their monthly donors, called subscribers. "We will openly discuss what each member in the meeting has discovered, and what they have explored. Then, if any ideas are suggested, we consider how an A/B test would look, or other kinds of analyses, and how can we learn the most from it. The test would be implemented, and then we could reconvene at a follow-up meeting," says Medina.

An example of this ongoing testing and analysis is how the team focuses on learning from what is working or not. "We are trying to evaluate the impact of a group of actionable insights. Is that idea actually improving revenue? What happened when we did something different a couple of years ago?" says Medina. This is both a combination of a testing, agile, and data mindset that involves taking the time to measure whether something is getting the desired results. He notes that "most typical projects will involve an element of past data and present data and a contrast between the two and, if necessary, a further analysis of the consequences based on data models."

charity: water is taking advantage of the culture of data and constantly trying to improve both access and use of the information. Medina says, "Not all data is information, so my number one task is to derive information from that data and make recommendations based on my analyses. Then people can make better decisions based on that information." This is the vital role that a data scientist can play at a nonprofit organization. They have the right skills to make sense of all the data, but it doesn't stop there. He notes, "I try to democratize information as much as I can." All this leads to empowering people with information they can use to make better decisions.

Over time, charity: water has focused Medina on using his data science skills with three types of projects. The first one is answering questions made by someone in the organization. "Since different departments track different things and report on different numbers, sometimes it is my job to analyze the data provided by them and then look at the question itself to see if it makes sense under the new light or not. That is, to see if it's something actually happening. If the problem is there, some detective work allows us to retrace the cause so that we can solve it," says Medina.

The other type of project is analyzing an entire part of the business or a revenue area from end to end. "You can think of this as me trying to 'discover the equations that govern the behavior of the organization,' in the same way as in physics one would try to discover the equations of a certain system," he says. This is detective work on a much higher level. Data science can be used to look at all aspects of the monthly donor acquisition and retention lifecycle. These types of projects look for leapfrog changes in process or performance versus smaller incremental changes.

Medina describes the last type of project as trying to answer "questions no one else is asking." This is the type of project that people often think data scientists spend most of their time on. In reality, they are kept very busy answering day-to-day questions and analyzing existing parts of the organization. But when Medina is able to do more exploration, he can focus on questions about the future of the organization. "I try to come up with the questions that are not relevant to the organization as of today, but that I know will be required eventually," he says. This involves a variety of different scenarios that might mean apply different data science techniques or trying to see if a model for one group of data can be applied to another one. Medina adds, "Obviously, the first type of project is the one that takes most of my time, but the last two are the ones that I've always found provide the best surprises."

This exploration of the data led to one big surprise that had a tremendous impact on the organization. Medina explains, "At one point, our organization believed that our average campaign raised $1,000. When I started looking at the data, this number turned out to be true only if one considered all of our campaigns to belong to the same category." He did some exploratory data analysis using machine learning tools to find out what was really happening. "I found that there were actually at least four different 'clusters' of campaigns, and that our main cluster was actually raising only around $300," he says. This was a significant difference than what was previously known and data exploration helped to see what was really happening. Medina notes, "This had a huge impact on our forecasting models, and the way we viewed our business. It also allowed us to know what parts of the business could be properly forecasted and which parts couldn't, allowing everyone to make better decisions regarding how to channel resources and time."

The culture of data at charity: water continues to evolve. Medina sees lots of opportunities to look at how the program data also ties back to donor behavior. Gorder already sees first-hand how fundraisers at charity: water don't really think about it as using data. Gorder says, "They're not thinking of this as like, 'Oh, I have all this data on my laptop.' They're thinking about this as, 'This is the business. This is what I do.'" The more data is a fundamental part of doing your job, the less it becomes a strange or unknown substance.

"Data is not a foreign object. Data is just part of what you do. It's part of the day-to-day fabric of the organization. The more you're able to harness it, the more effective you're going to be," says Gorder. He goes on, "I feel like the world is changing so quickly and so much data is becoming so readily and cheaply available that if you're not putting money behind it, you're just going to get left behind." His work with program delivery around the world and the convergence of both data and technology has shown Gorder first-hand how this changes everything. "For $100, we can put a smartphone in somebody's hands on the other side of the world and see live data from the field. You could never do this before and it's only going to change exponentially," he says.

charity: water is also moving into the future and embracing what has come to be known as "The Internet of Things." That is the network of devices, sensors, buildings, cars, and other physical objects that have been embedded with the ability to collect and exchange data with one another. If you think we live in a world with a lot of data now, just wait until the Internet of Things becomes part of everyday life. charity: water is already living in the realm of the Internet of Things through the use of remote sensors.

In the past year, charity: water has placed over 1,000 remote sensors on water points across Ethiopia. 700 of them are in cell phone coverage range, which means there is a constant flow of data. "All of a sudden, I have live data coming in. It's just a massive data dump right now," says Gorder. "It's abso-lutely incredible...We see if the wells break and there's no water flowing. We see when the water comes back on. We see what time of day they're pumping water. We're really breaking new ground now, and it's a fascinating process. It just opens up all sorts of possibilities and questions and challenges that we hadn't wrestled with before. I think it's going to be really revolutionary," he adds.

Ten years after it first sprang to life, charity: water has funded over 20,000 water projects and helped provide water to more than 6,300,000 people around the world. As Gorder says, data was there from the very beginning with that first set of GPS coordinates and photos from the water project in Uganda.

## 2.5791667 Latitude.
## 32.3539333 Longitude.

In 2006, this was the site of the largest Internally Displaced Persons, or refu-gee, camp in the Gulu province of Uganda--a town called Bobi. That first water well was in a refugee camp. When the fighting ended, the people there were able to leave. The water point had served its purpose and was no longer needed. But those coordinates established a key part of charity: water's culture of data from the very beginning. Today, you can visit the charity: water website and see the projects, view them on a map, know who funded the work, understand the partners involved, and see that photo of water flowing. This is what being data driven looks and feels like in a remarkable way.

## SMS

Some established nonprofits hit the reset button and make a conscious decision to build a culture of data. Other brand new nonprofits decide from the very beginning to make data a central part of their organization. This is the story of a nonprofit that began because of 64-bytes of data.

DoSomething.org was founded in 1993. Since then, the nonprofit has become one of the largest organizations in the United States centered on young people and social change. DoSomething.org runs a variety of campaigns that engage young people in programs that make social change.

Teens for Jeans is an example of a DoSomething.org program that was started back in 2008. People are encouraged to bring their gently worn jeans to Aéropostale retail stores and donate them. The program's research found that the number one thing young people in homeless shelters ask for is jeans. It's a way for them to feel part of the social fabric of teenage life, especially in their schools.

A major component of DoSomething.org's communication strategy with young people is the use of text messaging. According to Pew Research, 73% of teens have a smartphone and text messaging is one of the most used communication methods.[90] DoSomething.org engaged millions of young people a week with volunteering opportunities sent via text messages. Then the organization began to see what they called "out of flow" messages. Young people were texting back with messages about being bullied, experiencing eating disorders, or struggling with coming out as gay.

Then, in August of 2011, an out of flow text message was read by a staff member at DoSomething.org's offices in New York City. The first two texts read:[91]

*He won't stop raping me.*
*He told me not to tell anyone.*

A short time later another text message was sent to DoSomething.org:

*R u there?*

The staff member responded to the individual, but did not get a response until the following day:

*It's my dad*

It was then that the staff member texted back information for the Rape, Abuse & Incest National Network (RAINN), but the texter indicated that they were too scared to call. She encouraged the texter with an additional message, but there were no replies after that. The staff member then shared the text messages with Nancy Lublin, then the CEO at DoSomething.org.

"I'll never forget the day. It was like I'd been punched in the stomach," says Lublin. She knew that these few text messages were just a bigger part of what was happening in the lives of young people.

Lublin knew right then and there that there was a need to help with crisis intervention on a number of issues including suicide, bullying, abuse, depression, family issues, school problems, self-harm, LGBTQ issues, substance abuse, and more.

Lublin was no stranger to starting something from the ground up. In 1997, with the help of a $5,000 inheritance, she founded Dress for Success, a global nonprofit organization that provides professional attire to low-income women to help support their job search and interview process. Today, Dress for Success has expanded to almost 145 cities in 20 countries and has helped more than 850,000 women work towards self-sufficiency.[92]

Between that text message in 2011 and the next two years, Lublin would go about raising the $4 million needed to launch what would become Crisis Text Line. This was no easy task, and Lublin admits that "raising funds for not-for-profit startups is hard. Nobody wants to fund new things."

The new element, of course, was the use of text messaging as the channel of interaction with people in crisis. "Texting turns out to be incredibly effective for counseling in a crisis. It cuts right to the chase. You don't get hyperventilating and crying. You just get facts. By the third message, they're spilling their guts," says Lublin.[93]

Lublin explains that in 2013, they "launched Crisis Text Line, very quietly, in Chicago and El Paso — just a few thousand people in each market." She says, "In four months, we were in all 295 area codes in America. Just to put that into perspective, that's zero marketing and faster growth than when Facebook first launched."[94] Someone in crisis can text 741741 in the United States at any time and a live, trained counselor receives the text message and responds quickly. The Crisis Counselor helps the texter move from a hot moment to a cool calm to stay safe and healthy by using effective active listening and suggested referrals, all through text messages using Crisis Text Line's secure platform.

From the very beginning, part of the Crisis Text Line DNA was the idea that the data itself could save lives. In one of her TED Talks, Lublin notes, "We have the data to know what makes a great counselor. We know that if you text the words 'numbs' and 'sleeve,' there's a 99% match for cutting. We know that if you text in the words 'mg' and 'rubber band,' there's a 99% match for substance abuse. Now, that's interesting information that a counselor could figure out, but that algorithm in our hands means that an automatic pop-up says, '99% match for cutting — try asking one of these questions' to prompt the counselor. Or, '99% match for substance abuse, here are three drug clinics near the texter.' It makes us more accurate."

The first two people Lublin hired at Crisis Text Line were a chief technology officer and a chief data scientist. "We are a tech company that happens to do mental health, not a mental health organization that happens to be very tech savvy," says Lublin. Bob Filbin came over from DoSomething.org to be the chief data scientist at Crisis Text Line. Filbin holds a Master of Arts degree in quantitative methods in the social sciences from Columbia University. He says, "I've always been a scientist. My undergrad degree was in biology. I got into data science because I realized it was a universal skill that could be applied to any social change problem."

You might think that the first thing Filbin would have done at Crisis Text Line was to start with the data, but all the underlying technology still needed to be built out. Instead, he spent the first six months on the job visiting 11 different crisis centers and talking to over 100 Crisis Counselors. Filbin was able to learn some important insights from this time spent on the road. "I learned that our primary user for the technology we build is our Crisis Counselor, not our texter. The texters are on their phones. Their experiences of Crisis Text Line are almost entirely mediated through our Crisis Counselors. Our Crisis Counselors log into our private, secure online system to exchange messages with texters. The role that our technology can play is to help Crisis Counselors increase the efficiency and accuracy of their care," says Filbin.

This meant that the technology Crisis Text Line was developing needed to meet the needs of counselors extremely well. This went beyond the functionality and got down to the look and feel of the interface. "I noticed that Crisis Counselors' eyes were drawn toward our red logo; it was distracting. We realized that creating our online crisis counseling platform in our brand's strong red and black color scheme was counterproductive to counseling. Instead, Crisis Counselors would benefit from seeing calming colors. We re-skinned the platform in slate blue, a color recommended by a psychiatrist on our advisory board as the most calming color," says Filbin.

Filbin's first-hand experience with what Crisis Counselors do on a daily basis also shaped how the tools were developed. "We originally had a welcome screen. Multiple counselors said to me, 'Why are you showing this to me? I want to get straight to crisis counseling.' Part of what we can do with our technology is reduce barriers to Crisis Counselors doing what they do best: converse with texters. This philosophy impacts our conversation reporting, too, and led us to create a branching survey report for Crisis Counselors to fill out after each conversation. At other centers, Crisis Counselors would fill out reports after each conversation that could often be over 100 questions. Most questions weren't relevant in any given conversation. I saw some counselors take 15 minutes to complete a report. Our report has, for most conversations, five questions. It takes one to two minutes. Additional questions pop up only when relevant," explains Filbin.

This feedback directly from Crisis Counselors helped shape the resources that Crisis Text Line provided and also influenced how data was used to drive decision-making. Filbin notes, "Crisis Text Line has a dual purpose. Primarily, we help texters move from a hot moment to a cool calm. Secondarily, the data in itself saves lives." The simple fact that every text message has a timestamp and can be tagged with additional information can suddenly help identify trends in the data. "Crisis Counselors tag each conversation with the crisis issues that the texter experiences; every conversation has between three and five issues. Our top issues right now are depression, suicidal ideation, anxiety, family issues, and romantic relationships. These issues interrelate; we can see correlations in how they both fluctuate over time," says Filbin.

"The great thing is that we set up our data collection systems early, so now the data is flowing," says Filbin. The very nature of Crisis Text Line's work emits a constant stream of data. At the same time, the amount of data can be completely overwhelming if not handled properly. "Collection is one of data's greatest challenges. Can you collect data that's useful and can you structure it in a way that's usable? When I see not-for-profits starting to collect data, the vast majority of time is spent figuring out how to automate collection. Then, for existing data sets you need to restructure it to make it usable. We tackled these major hurdles early on. Now, we can spend much more time analyzing the data, pulling insights that create a better service," he adds.

The deluge of data gets collected at Crisis Text Line and is funneled into a set of metrics that let staff know how the organization is performing. Crisis Text Line uses a set of Key Performance Indicators (KPIs) to measure overall health and performance of the organization. "We think about these as the heartbeat of the organization. Just like if you were going to measure somebody's health, the most important thing you want to look at is their heart rate. It's not the only metric you should look at, but it's the first one. Our KPIs serve the same function for the health of our organization. If our KPIs are healthy, then we are healthy as an organization," says Filbin.

Just as too much information can be overwhelming, too many metrics can cause problems in an organization. The Crisis Text Line team decided that they would use no more than five KPIs to measure organizational health. "We chose five because we wanted everybody on staff to be able to rattle these off; not only what metrics they are, but also how we're doing on each one," he says. It's not uncommon for KPIs to come up in conversation, and this has reinforced the importance of a data driven culture. "In a given month, we're usually focused on one of these at a time. That means we choose this as the primary business problem and therefore we build products and policies around improving our numbers on that particular KPI," says Filbin.

Today, Crisis Text Line uses four KPIs to measure organizational health to understand demand, capacity, and quality. The KPIs are:

1. Number of Texters
2. Number of Active Crisis Counselors
3. Conversation Quality
4. Texter Wait Time

The KPIs have changed over time, but they are almost always trying to measure the same trends. Measuring the number of texters allows Crisis Text Line to measure demand at any point in time and over. A texter is considered a unique phone number that is contacting the service. As Filbin explained, "If the same phone number has five conversations with us in a day, that counts as one texter." The number of active Crisis Counselors is a measure of capacity for the service. "That is defined as a Crisis Counselor who has taken their first conversation. Crisis Counselors who we have but aren't taking conversations are not counted because they're not providing actual capacity at this time," he says. Measuring both demand and capacity allows Crisis Text Line to understand usage of the system and plan for spikes.

Conversation quality is a KPI based on responses from texters at the end of each conversation. They are asked, "Did you find this conversation helpful? Y/N," and a percentage helpful score is calculated and measured. Finally, wait time is measured by how long a texter waits for a response from the moment they text into Crisis Text Line. Filbin says, "Those are our four KPIs; our staff knows them by heart. We show the last 24 hours and last 28 days rolling" to show both how they did yesterday and how they are trending over time," says Filbin.

Filbin has found that providing this trend data in a simple and accessible way gets the best results. You won't find complex visualizations or fancy charts in use at Crisis Text Line. That was something that Filbin learned through trial and error over time. "I used to think that data science should try to provide people with the ability to find their own insights. Now I believe that what's most useful is sharing data that allows people to ask the right questions," he says.

Using data to get people to ask the right questions has allowed Crisis Text Line to improve data literacy across the organization. "Showing what happened in the last 24 hours each morning allows staff to ask things like, 'Why did the number of texters jump by 200 yesterday? Why did number of Crisis Counselors fall by 20?' It allows staff to ask questions that are critical for organizational health. The data science team can then dive into the data to find answers," says Filbin. Nonprofits can spend a lot of time and resources developing ways for staff to analyze the data, but there's also the potential for wasted effort.

Filbin notes, "I realized that creating interactive visualizations for staff still doesn't give them the context around the data necessary to interpret it. Staff are good at asking the right business questions; data science teams are good at finding answers."

The use of data and the importance of KPIs to drive decision-making have been part of Crisis Text Line from the very beginning. In many ways, the organization began with and continues to have a data driven culture. Filbin explains, "Everything we do on the data team depends on our culture of data. We started our culture by developing a shared understanding of organizational health: our KPIs. The KPIs show us on a daily basis where we need to focus staff energy to drive growth and quality." The teams then make sure that any product improvements or policy briefs that need to be done can be tied back to that KPI of focus. "Products and policies are held accountable to KPIs. Our organizational agenda stems from our KPIs," adds Filbin.

"Some nonprofits that I've talked to have over 100 KPIs. It leads to a lot of confusion about what is an organizational priority. Some people I've talked to don't believe you can boil down organizational health to four or five KPIs. You do lose some fidelity, but you gain so much in focus that I think it's worth it," he says.

During the early days of Crisis Text Line, Filbin spent several weeks on the road to learn from real users. In 2015, Lublin took Filbin and other members of the team on a road trip to the West Coast. Filbin explains, "We went and visited some of the biggest tech companies in Silicon Valley, like Facebook, Twitter, Uber, and Coursera. We wanted to see how the best tech companies were running product and data." The small group spent time with 16 different startups in five days. They wanted to see how the best startups use data and they knew that many of these practices would not be found among other nonprofits.

"We see ourselves as a tech nonprofit, in some ways more like a tech company than a traditional nonprofit. I think that mindset's been critical for us in terms of constantly iterating our product and creating a better service. That mindset has allowed us to improve our service more quickly," says Filbin. That mindset sums up the new normal in the nonprofit sector. Many nonprofits started in the last few years, and the ones that will be founded in the near future may choose this mindset as well. It combines the elements of an agile culture with data use from the very beginning to get results in a shorter period of time.

After this latest road trip, Filbin came back to the organization with some other ideas about improving how data could be used at Crisis Text Line. "One concrete change we made in terms of thinking like a tech company is we think of data in terms of iteration, not evaluation. Most nonprofits, when they collect data, use it to provide impact evaluation data to funders. You roll out a product or program and then two years later, you see how effective it was. Our data collection moves much faster. Within two weeks of rolling out a product, we look at the data to see is having the intended impact. If so, we can leave it alone. If not, we can iterate on the product design," says Filbin. This approach has allowed Crisis Text Line to make incremental improvements over a short period of time versus waiting years to measure success.

An interesting thing happens when you start moving and measuring at a faster rate: failure becomes more accepted. When organizations invest in something for two years and it turns out to be a failure, they become more risk averse. When you focus your resources on something for two weeks and it doesn't work, you adjust and move on. This is exactly what Crisis Text Line has experienced. "I think the organization is just as excited about failures as successes. Knowing that we failed or knowing that we succeeded are equally valuable because both inform our product development," says Filbin.

Filbin describes a situation when they built something that they thought would help users, but it was doing more harm than good. All of the Crisis Counselors are volunteers and they have scheduled shifts for four hours per week. The Crisis Text Line team thought that it would be a good idea to send them a reminder 30 minutes before their shift was scheduled to begin. "We thought it's only once per week, what if you forget your shift is upcoming? Let's create shift reminders and then send them to people's phones. Our hypothesis was that this would drive up our active Crisis Counselor KPI," he says. The team also had the new feature instrumented to see usage data.

Two weeks after the shift reminder feature was rolled out they were able to measure that there was no significant difference in the active Crisis Counselor KPI. "From talking to Crisis Counselors, we discovered that many of them found the feature annoying. Crisis Counselors said, 'I know when my shift is,'" adds Filbin. They continued to measure the impact of the feature for another two weeks; once again, no significant benefit was found. "It didn't work, so we turned it off," he says.

All this talk of data, KPIs, and an agile approach to using them might suggest that the mission of the organization is completely removed from the process. But at Crisis Text Line, the value placed on data is absolutely linked to the mission. "It's amazing how much the value of data is strictly a cultural component of the organization and not about technology or data warehousing," notes Filbin. "The fundamental way for us to understand the value of our data is the KPIs, because the KPIs come from our organizational goals. We have two main goals: One is to move texters we serve from a hot to a cool moment, so moving them out of crisis as well as providing them coping skills to stay safe in the future. The second one is using our data and technology to improve the crisis space as a whole," he says. "I think any organization can articulate the change they want to see through a set of three to five KPIs. Any theory of change allows for the creation of KPIs."

Once again, we see that the problem contains the solution. The data and KPIs allow a nonprofit to truly see the mission in action. Filbin notes, "Data collection comes after choosing KPIs. First, define your organizational goals. Then choose KPIs that will allow you to monitor your progress toward those goals. Finally, start collecting data. Data collection that isn't tied to organizational priorities is simply building a bigger haystack to sift through."

Another valuable lesson that Filbin has learned is that anyone who works with data must also be a good storyteller. "About half of my job is storytelling. Half of my time is analysis and setting up our data systems, but the other half is thinking through how data insights can drive organizational change," he says. "I think that data storytelling not only leads to organizational change, but it also reinforces and reinvigorates that underlying data culture." Over time, Filbin has refined what it takes to turn data into a good story. "Any good data story starts with how it relates to organizational health, either by finding a new problem or opportunity related to a KPI or evaluating a solution that was meant to impact a KPI," he says.

To illustrate the point, Filbin tells a story of a recent time when they found a new need. Wait times for testers were 12% longer during the last 15 minutes of a Crisis Counselor's shift. Here is how he broke down the elements of that data story:

1. Choose a KPI: wait time
2. Define a business problem related to the KPI (which usually takes the form of a predictable anomaly): 12% longer than expected during 15 minutes of every two-hour block
3. Frame the business problem within a human context: Last 15 minutes of a Crisis Counselor's shift

Filbin goes on to note, "Usually, there is a user problem associated with the business problem. In this story, something is happening within the last 15 minutes of Crisis Counselor's shifts. This data story led the team to explore why that user problem was occurring." There is also another important point to make about data stories: "Data stories rarely include a solution. Data is good at identifying problems. It's not good at coming up with solutions," says Filbin. But he is a believer that creativity comes from constraints. "The tighter data can define a problem, the better the data enables staff to come up with creative solutions that will solve that problem," he says.

The data does not replace the human element or the need for creative problem solving. Filbin has witnessed first-hand how people often react initially to using data as a part of the decision-making process. "I think some organizations believe if they allow data to drive decisions, it constrains creativity. But good data simply holds creativity accountable to an end goal. Data says that anything that we do creatively should drive a better result. If it doesn't, then it wasn't the right creative solution," he says.

Building a data driven culture is not easy and, even for the best nonprofits, it is a constant challenge that requires vigilance. "People can be resistant to data. I don't think that goes away completely. What we try to do is make sure that every project, policy, or program starts with the question of, 'What does the data say?'" says Filbin. He adds, "You need the CEO's buy-in to be able to move forward with culture of data, and luckily Nancy's been on board from the very beginning."

Lublin has valued data from the very beginning, but she also understands the key role of the human element. "We have a human-first policy here. We think sentiment analysis is not good enough to mimic human empathy and the entire point of reaching out to Crisis Text Line is to connect with another human, to be heard, to be valued. We take that responsibility very seriously," says Lublin.

Since 2013, Crisis Text Line has processed over 17 million text messages. On any given day, as many as 50,000 messages might be processed by the organization. Filbin notes, "We have the largest corpus on crisis in the country. The closest thing is the Centers for Disease Control and Prevention." The CDC has an annual survey that attempts to capture data on mental health across the youth population. But it should be noted that surveys can have biased data and the results have a significant time delay from the moment of crisis. Filbin stresses that the Crisis Text Line data has a lot more immediate potential to help people. "It's people in crisis in the moment. Our data leads to unique insights on how people behave in a moment of crisis," he says.

Crisis Text Line was a data driven nonprofit from the very beginning. Lublin's call to action came in the form of text messages that were just 64-bytes of data. In just a few short years, the team at Crisis Text Line has been able to move people out of crisis and prove that data can save lives. Referring to 2015, Filbin notes, "0.7% of our conversations were active rescues, where we send out emergency services to intervene in an active suicide attempt. Being able to help more texters in crisis directly translates into lives saved."

But the work isn't done yet, and the organization knows that more lives can be saved by using their data. In 2016, Crisis Text Line announced they will be making their data available to approved researchers, who must meet stringent requirements, including that research will help more people in crisis.[95] "From day one, this was the goal: to help people one-on-one and leverage the data for smart system change on a broad scale. I'm pretty darn excited that we're making it happen," says Lublin. The announcement was met with praise from a broad range of people and groups, including the president of Yale University and the White House.

Later in June 2016, Crisis Text Line announced that it had raised $23.8 million in funding. The funding round was led by LinkedIn founder Reid Hoffman, followed by Melinda Gates, The Ballmer Group, and Omidyar Network. Additional funds were granted by the John S. and James L. Knight Foundation, the founder of craigslist and craigconnects, Craig Newmark, Mark and Alison Pincus, Anne Devereux-Mills, Joe and Suzy Edelman, Amy and Rob Stavis, and an anonymous donor. Lublin notes, "There is no equity; no possibility of a liquidity moment. Crisis Text Line is a tech startup, so it makes sense for us to fundraise like one. The amount raised and the caliber of the people we attracted underscore the quality of what we're doing."[96] The funding will be used for organizational expansion and development of more technologies to reach teens. Lublin was quoted as saying that she expects to reach 4,000 Crisis Counselors in the next two years.[97] Crisis Text Line not only shows other nonprofits what is possible, but also serves as a window into the future of the entire nonprofit sector.

# 15

# FUTURE

*"In a world where I feel so small, I can't stop thinking big."*

- NEIL PEART

PAST

A t the same time that Charles Ward and Lyman Pierce were perfecting the art of fundraising in the early 1900s, a man by the name of Abraham Flexner was about to transform the science of medical education. By the early 1900s, there were over 150 medical schools in the United States and Canada. Medical education in North America was essentially a for-profit business that produced a lot of poorly trained doctors. There was very little standardization of admissions requirements, training, curriculum, and graduation requirements.

By 1908, the Council on Medical Education commissioned the Carnegie Foundation for the Advancement of Teaching to conduct a survey of medical education across North America. The Carnegie Foundation chose an unlikely person, Flexner, to conduct the assessment. Flexner was not a doctor, medical educator, or even a scientist. He founded a college preparatory school in Louisville that broke from the rigid traditional methods of most schools and garnered a lot of attention. The president of the Carnegie Foundation, Henry Pritchett, took notice of Flexner and his critique of the higher education system in a 1908 book, *The American College.*

Over the next two years, Flexner visited nearly every medical school in North America and presented his findings and recommendations. Officially titled "Medical Education in the United States and Canada," the result is widely referred to as the Flexner Report.[98] The groundbreaking report sums up the need for change within the first few pages:

*"The requirements of medical education have enormously increased. The fundamental sciences upon which medicine depends have been greatly extended. The laboratory has come to furnish alike to the physician and to the surgeon a new means of diagnosing and combating disease. The education of the medical practitioner user those changed conditions makes entirely different demands in respect to both preliminary and professional training."*

The Flexner Report defines the very standards for medical education and recommends several changes including:[99]

1. Establish and enforce entrance requirements to medical schools
2. Train physicians to use the scientific method in their practice of medicine
3. Students must receive significant hands-on experience in the lab and clinic
4. Most of the current schools should be either closed or consolidated
5. All surviving schools should be university schools committed to medical research and academic excellence

The recommendations resulted in sweeping changes in medical education. Within 10 years of the report's publishing, 92% of medical schools in the United States required at least two or more years of university education in order to be admitted. More than half of all American medical schools merged or closed by 1935. This transformation was also fueled by significant funding from both the Rockefeller Foundation and the Carnegie Foundation. Flexner went on to work on the Rockefeller Foundation's General Education Board. Later in his career, he led the Institute for Advanced Study, which during the 1930s became a refuge for scientists fleeing Nazi Germany, including one Albert Einstein.

Today's modern medical education structure continues to reflect Flexner's recommendations. Over the past 100 years, tremendous progress has been made in the medical profession and its direct benefits to society. Most professions like medicine, law, accounting, engineering, science, and education have established education and training programs. One hundred years after Ward and Pierce revolutionized the art of fundraising, a similar structure does not exist in the nonprofit sector. Yes, there is the Certified Fund Raising Executive program facilitated by the Association of Fundraising Professionals. There are similar programs like the Certificate in Fundraising from the Institute of Fundraising in the United Kingdom and other countries around the world. But these programs are not prerequisites and requirements to be a professional fundraiser.

The future of the nonprofit sector must also be a more professionally trained and developed group of individuals. Not only would this improve the sector's impact but it would also help nonprofit professionals who want to create meaningful change in the world. We need a modern-day Flexner Report that includes recommendations around data literacy and data informed decision-making. And just as the Carnegie Foundation and the Rockefeller Foundation helped fund the implementation of Flexner's recommendations, this transformation will require funding from institutions with a vested interest in the growth of the nonprofit sector.

We need to think big about what the future looks like for those who work in and with the nonprofit sector over the next 20 years. What changes do we want to see in the world and how might we best achieve them? Futurists said that by now we should be driving flying cars and living on the moon. Perhaps that is why we should be cautious about future predictions in any industry. But it would be hard to argue that the use of data, information, and insights will not be a big part of the future of the nonprofit sector.

## PRESENT

We live in an age in which the analog and digital are in convergence. A time when technology accelerates change. There is indeed a shift happening in the nonprofit sector: A shift from direct mail to digital. A shift from tribal knowledge to data driven insights. A shift from the old guard to the new ideas. History shows us that patterns repeat in the past and the present. Perhaps that is why it is important to look at places where the past and present are converging to give a sense of what might happen next.

Henry Timms is the executive director of the 92nd Street Y in New York City and co-founder of GivingTuesday. He both understands what it takes to run an organization founded in 1874 and has first-hand experience with starting an entirely new movement. GivingTuesday is a worldwide movement dedicated to giving back that first began in 2012 and now includes more than 40,000 partners in 71 countries.

Timms has a unique perspective on both the nonprofit sector and how social movements are shaping our society. "The nonprofit sector typically beats itself over the head for being a late adopter, but the world at large is struggling a lot with all these shifts. The largest challenge is people are obsessed with technology without thinking about the human change happening alongside. The deepest shift here is not about how technology is changing, but about how people are changing and power is shifting," says Timms. For all the attention spent on the latest gadget or tool, the impact it has on people can often be overlooked.

Managing the human element of change is perhaps the biggest challenge faced by nonprofit leaders. "We're getting to a point where even the most Luddite nonprofit leader recognizes that technology needs to play some bigger role in their world. The organizations who are really going to crack it will not be those organizations who understand the technological shift, but who understand the human shift which is underneath it," says Timms. "I think we're right at the beginning. I think there's a huge amount of opportunity ahead and I think the most important conversation isn't about technology," he adds.

Timms strongly believes that we are seeing a shift from old power to new power in the world. "The old power mindset says, 'We control everything, we centralize everything, we own everything, and that's how we think of our work and our status.' The new power world thinks, 'We are engaged because we share, because we understand how to convene, because we understand how we mobilize, and success for us isn't how much we can contain, but how much we can create," says Timms. He is careful to point out that this is more about mindset than simply age. "We shouldn't oversimplify this idea as young people versus old people. One of the dangerous arguments is currently that this is 23-year-olds against 73-year-olds and I don't actually think that's what is happening," he says. "There are a lot of people who have very agile minds as leaders who are shifting their institutions in this direction. They are not digital natives in any way, but they are people who understand where the wind is blowing and how they need to get there."

Even the most change-averse organizations are recognizing this shift in power, although some nonprofits can't always quantify the short-term benefits. Timms says, "One of the traps ahead is to not make this shift because there is no obvious immediate incentive, but in five years' time, you will have fallen too far behind." By then, many nonprofits will simply be making reactive decisions rather than choosing to be proactive today. "The easiest way for people to do anything is if they're under some kind of crisis, and that's probably the worst way to make these kinds of decisions," he says.

These shifts are not all instantaneous, but instead a gradual transition of changing mindsets, cultures, and values around data. "I can't imagine one Thursday in November we will suddenly decide to all become more data driven. I actually suspect it's more incremental than that," says Timms. For some, this will not be an overnight or easy transition. "I think it's easy to get overwhelmed. We went from a kind of data drought to data deluge pretty quickly. I think the people are struggling in general with that shift," he says. "Lots of people are going to hold out because they're basically data-phobic. If you spent 40 years of your career succeeding at the highest level and you're suddenly being asked to do all these new things that you don't truly understand, then it's not an attractive proposition," adds Timms.

Getting more comfortable with using data to make decisions is not finished when you have the data. "Simply the existence of more data doesn't make the world better. It depends on what the information says and how it's presented. If we all received on a weekly basis confusing information that was faulty and wasn't helpful in our daily lives, that wouldn't improve outcomes.

What needs to happen is that data needs to be structured for participation so it actually becomes both useful and engaging," says Timms. Data is not a thing to be controlled or used to force through an agenda. "Data isn't a hammer you hit people over the head with. That's not the way to do it," he adds.

The ability to understand and filter information without being overwhelmed is an absolutely critical skill for nonprofit leaders and staff. Timms says, "We have a lot more good information about our world than we used to. The question is how you filter that in ways that become useful. That's the frame for institutions…You're more efficiently working out what this data really means and not being overwhelmed by it." Filtering out the signal from the noise might also be sharpened by the multi-screen environment in which we now live. Right now, someone is probably doing research to see if our filtering skills get better over time because of simultaneous multichannel engagement.

Throughout this book, the discussion of art versus science in nonprofit organizations has come up. Timms clearly believes both are important, but for different reasons. "We're always balancing our need for the data driven efficiencies versus our need to let hearts soar and let joy be freed," says Timms. We have seen how successful organizations have been able to find this balance of art and science. "There's a danger in the data driven nonprofit being the least interesting person at a party. They answer you right and correct but they're really not joyful in any way. There is a point at which not everything can be turned into a machine. There is a point at which things retain their human characteristics to best understand them, but I do think all of this data is a huge net positive for our sector," says Timms.

Balance is the key for the times we're living in. While the primary focus of this book has been on what can be done using data, it should never be overlooked that the goal is to use that information to drive impact and change in the world. Timms says, "I think impact should be driving us. Changing lives should be driving us. Better data will improve that outcome. We want to be fully enabled by data, but not letting data be the new mission statement. The new mission statement is not to create reams of data. The new mission statement is to do the things you're supposed to be doing, but to do it in a way that is more empirical, more effective, and you learn more."

As we move from the present into the future, the importance of data informed decisions to drive change cannot be overstated. The consequences of remaining too tied to the old power ways of the world will limit the potential of the entire nonprofit sector. If we focus on building the right data driven behaviors, there is a tremendous opportunity to increase the velocity of change in the world.

## FUTURE

In the later years of his career, Lyman Pierce wrote a book called *How to Raise Money*, published in 1932. It was a compendium of the knowledge and wisdom he gained over the years in the nonprofit sector. In the book he notes that "these major factors, which determine to a considerable extent in advance the potentialities of a campaign, are as follows:"[100]

    I. An appealing case
    II. Competent agency management
    III. A reasonable objective
    IV. A friendly, well-informed constituency
    V. Timeliness
    VI. Numerous points of contact
    VII. Unhurried period of preparation
    VIII. An adequate scale of giving
    IX. Substantial preliminary gifts
    X. Tested methods
    XI. Competent direction

Fast-forward more than 80 years and those factors still hold true. The question for the future of the nonprofit sector is how organizations can grow and thrive to meet the demands of the twenty-first century. Those demands come not only from current donors, but also from prospects, volunteers, members, beneficiaries, advocates, staff, and board members. The challenge is to increase the impact of an organization's mission at a sustainable scale. In a world in which resources are constrained and the demand to show more progress is increasing, nonprofits must be able to create scale.

The scale needed to drive greater impact is unlikely to come from doing more of the same. Nonprofits are unlikely to improve donor acquisition or retention efforts simply by trying harder. The future demands an evolution of attitudes, behaviors, habits, and culture. For all the talk about the wonders of technology, there is no substitute for having the right culture to drive meaningful change. Data driven nonprofits have evolved to develop certain cultural traits that are allowing them to elevate from the norm.

We have seen how champions in all levels of the organization can act as change agents. The willingness to take calculated risks and embrace change is another cultural trait that enables change. Testing new ideas and approaches and being willing to fail in the short-term to succeed in the long-term helps build a more data driven culture. Having a sharing mindset when it comes to data and information allows organizations to learn from one another and promotes behaviors that drive better performance. A growth mindset supported by goals and meaningful metrics can truly achieve remarkable results and serve as a lighthouse for others. Adapting an agile approach to meet the demands of a nonprofit organization can allow for greater speed-to-value in a changing world. Believing in the opportunity and power of data to change minds and save lives can bring about so many positive benefits to society.

When I started this book project nearly two years ago, it was not clear what I would find along the way. Would people in and around the nonprofit sector choose to cling to the old ways or would they embrace new possibilities? Would the evolution necessary to make more data informed decisions be too much for leaders and organizations to make? Would the future of the nonprofit sector move closer to the brink of crisis or were there signs that a pivot was possible?

Having come all this way, engaging with so many people across many different kinds of organizations, it is clear to me not only that the nonprofit sector is ready to be more data driven but also that there are plenty of successful examples to follow. These are examples that nonprofits can look to for guidance and reassurance that change can lead to success. We only need to be willing to take that first step.

The poet, playwright, and social critic Thomas Stearns Eliot, better known by his pen name, T.S. Eliot, clearly saw the future coming when he wrote these lines in *The Rock* in 1934:[101]

*"Where is the Life we have lost in living?*
*Where is the wisdom we have lost in knowledge?*
*Where is the knowledge we have lost in information?"*

We can choose to be overwhelmed by the data or we can choose to turn it into treasure. We can choose to rely on tribal knowledge or we can be enlightened by information and insights. We can choose to believe that our culture is set in stone or that it evolves and adapts to its environment over time. We can choose to accept low donor retention rates or we can ignite a growth mindset that drives performance. We can choose to treat data as a foreign object or we can put humanity in the data. We can get lost or tell the skeptics to get lost. As Neil Peart once wrote, "If you choose not to decide, you still have made a choice."

Data driven nonprofits accelerate change in the world by using data to influence strategy and inform decisions to produce value and impact. Data is their raw material, and they convert it into information and insights that create value. Data driven nonprofits learn from the past, understand the present, and move into the future with confidence. This is an exciting time to live and work in the nonprofit sector. We need leaders without titles or corner offices to stand up and take the first steps toward the future. We need people who believe that an informed decision is a better decision. We need to unleash a lot good in society and we need to do it with purpose and passion. The nonprofit sector needs it. The world needs it. Let's get started!

# THANK YOU

First, let me thank you, the reader. If you have made it this far, then you have made a conscious decision to invest your time in improving yourself and the nonprofit sector. You are being a change agent. Let me know who you are by taking a photo of yourself and the book, then send it to steve@datadriven-nonprofits.com or on Twitter at @smaclaughlin.

I need to thank my wife Lynsey for giving me the encouragement, support, and the kick in gear to write this book. I had considered the idea of potentially possibly maybe writing another book and she said that I either needed to do it or move on. The prospect of devoting a year-and-a-half of your life to writing a book is no easy undertaking. It gets even harder when you have a very busy work schedule and two young children too. If this book helps people in some way, then part of the credit goes to Lynsey for being my partner during the writing, editing, and publishing process.

All the credit for the book cover design and the graphics go to Veronica Volborth. She is an extremely talented person who was able to take rough ideas and design a book that looks amazing. Lots of thanks and appreciation go out to Erin Duff for editing the book. She helped at a critical time to take the book to the next level. The process of bringing a book to life is not an easy one. I was very fortunate to have had a team of all-stars like Veronica and Erin working on this project. I want to acknowledge Sandi Schroeder from Schroeder Indexing Services for helping to put the final section of the book together. My thanks to Courtney Sakre, Becca Curtis, and Jack Meyer at CreateSpace for helping me navigate the process of printing this book.

Thank you to my colleagues at Blackbaud, Target Analytics, and the support of the company's leadership throughout this project. Catherine LaCour, Rachel Hutchisson, and Mike Gianoni at Blackbaud were extremely supportive of this project. Many thanks to Richard Becker, Carrie Cobb, Page Bullington, Rob Harris, and Alan Dix at Target Analytics for the wealth of data they were willing to share. Thank you as well to Nicole McGougan and Ashley Thompson for their feedback throughout the writing process. Both Chuck Longfield and Jim O'Shaughnessy deserve a lot of special thanks for their help, patience, and expertise over the years too.

Thanks to the people who agreed to be interviewed and participate in this book project. Thank you Roger Craver, Michal Heiplik, Carie Lewis Carlson, Jann Schultz, Beth Kanter, Nancy Lublin, Bob Filbin, Greg Baldwin, Margaret Williams, John Schwass, Henry Timms, Jeanne Pecha, Jeffrey Lindauer, John Sall, Chuck Longfield, Kate Chamberlin, Mark Langdon, Jack Cumming, Griff Freyschlag, David Mitchell, Christoph Gorder, and Carlos Medina.

Thank you to these companies and nonprofits for giving me access to your talented teams. Thank you Blackbaud, The Agitator, SAS, WGBH, Contributor Development Partnership, The Humane Society of the United States, Project HOPE, Crisis Text Line, VolunteerMatch, University of South Dakota Foundation, World Wildlife Fund, 92nd Street Y, GivingTuesday, Florida State University Foundation, Indiana University Foundation, Worldwide Cancer Research, Memorial Sloan Kettering Cancer Center, RNIB, Denver Rescue Mission, SCIAF, and charity: water.

Thank you to the nonprofit professionals that I have had the great fortune to have worked with over the years. Thank you for wanting to make the world a better place. This book has been brought to you by the letter M.

# NOTES

1.  "1905 Washington, DC Daily Weather." WeatherDB. https://history. weatherdb.com/d/a/Washington,-DC/1905.

2.  "MONEY IS BEST TALKER." *The Washington Post*. April 5, 1905.

3.  Cutlip, Scott. *Fund Raising in the United States: Its Role in American Philanthropy*. Transaction Publishers, 1990.

4.  Wooster, Martin Morse. "The Birth of Big Time Fundraising." The Philanthropy Roundtable. http://www.philanthropyroundtable.org/ topic/excellence_in_philanthropy/the_birth_of_big_time_fundraising.

5.  *Voluntary Giving in a Free Land: A History of Ward, Dreshman & Reinhardt And Its Influence On Fundraising In The United States*. Ward, Dreshman & Reinhardt, 1955.

6.  Full Disclosure: Blackbaud has been my employer since May 2004. While the company was supportive of this book project and provided access to information, they did not have any editorial control over its content.

7.  Weiner, Robert. "Donor Databases and CRMs." Social Source Commons. https://socialsourcecommons.org/toolbox/show/1661.

8. Cox, Michael, and David Ellsworth. "Application-Controlled Demand Paging for Out-of-Core Visualization." *Proceedings of the 8th Conference on Visualization '97*, October 1997, 235-44.

9. Hays, Constance. "What Wal-Mart Knows About Customers' Habits." *The New York Times*, November 4, 2004. http://www.nytimes.com/2004/11/14/business/yourmoney/what-walmart-knows-about-customers-habits.html.

10. Facebook. "Three and a half degrees of separation." https://research.facebook.com/blog/three-and-a-half-degrees-of-separation/.

11. The Giving Foundation. "Giving USA 2016: Annual report on philanthropy for the year 2015." The Giving Institute.

12. Bureau of Economic Analysis. "Gross-Domestic-Product-(GDP)-by-Industry Data." http://www.bea.gov/industry/gdpbyind_data.htm

13. Bureau of Labor Statistics, U.S. Department of Labor. "The Economics Daily." http://www.bls.gov/opub/ted/2015/household-spending-increased-for-most-categories-in-2014.htm

14. Internal Revenue Service. "Exempt Organizations Select Check." https:// www.irs.gov/charities-non-profits/exempt-organizations-select-check.

15. Daniels, Alex. "Fewer Groups Got Charity Status in 2015, but Numbers Still High." *The Chronicle of Philanthropy*, March 30, 2016. https://philanthropy.com/article/Fewer-Groups-Got-Charity/235904/.

16. Target Analytics. "donorCentrics Index of Direct Marketing Fundraising." Q4 2015. https://www.blackbaud.com/files/resources/target-index-results-summary-q4-2015.pdf.

17.   Wikipedia. "Atmosphere of Earth." https://en.wikipedia.org/wiki/Atmosphere_of_Earth

18.   Marr, Bernard. *Big Data in Practice: How 45 Successful Companies Used Big Data Analytics to Deliver Extraordinary Results.* Wiley, 2016.

19.   Kayyali, Basel, David Knott, and Steve Van Kuiken. "The big-data revolution in US health care: Accelerating value and innovation." McKinsey & Company. http://www.mckinsey.com/industries/health-care-systems-and-services/our-insights/the-big-data-revolution-in-us-health-care

20.   Dragland, Åse. "Big Data - for Better or Worse." SINTEF. http://www.sintef.no/en/corporate-news/big-data--for-better-or-worse/.

21.   Ranj, Brandt. "15 Things that Happen on the Internet Every Minute." http://www.businessinsider.com/15-things-that-happen-on-the-internet-every-minute-2016-2.

22.   Intel. "What Happens in an Internet Minute." http://www.intel.com/content/www/us/en/communications/internet-minute-infographic.html.

23.   James, Josh. "Data Never Sleeps 3.0." Dom. https://www.domo.com/blog/2015/08/data-never-sleeps-3-0/.

24.   UN Water. "Facts and Figures." http://www.unwater.org/water-cooperation-2013/water-cooperation/facts-and-figures/en/.

25.   Anderson, Monica. "Technology Device Ownership: 2015." Pew Research Center. http://www.pewinternet.org/2015/10/29/technology-device-ownership-2015/

26.  Granger, Brandon. "Mobile Donations Up 45% in 2015 Giving Season." npENGAGE. http://npengage.com/nonprofit-fundraising/mobile-donations-up-45-in-2015-giving-season-infographic/

27.  Poe, Edgar Allan. "The Purloined Letter." In The Gift: A Christmas, New Year, and Birthday Present. Philadelphia: Cary & Hart, 1844. http://xroads.virginia.edu/~hyper/poe/purloine.html

28.  United States Census Bureau. "U.S. Mover Rate Remains Stable at About 12 Percent Since 2008, Census Bureau Reports." https://www.census.gov/newsroom/press-releases/2015/cb15-47.html

29.  Miniño AM, Murphy SL. "Death in the United States, 2010." NCHS data brief, no 99. Hyattsville, MD: National Center for Health Statistics. 2012. http://www.cdc.gov/nchs/products/databriefs/db99.htm

30.  For the purposes of this book a major gift is defined as 4 and 5-figure donations. A principal gift is defined as 6 and 7-figure donations.

31.  Ackoff, R.L. "From data to wisdom." Journal of Applied Systems Analysis. 15: 3-9. 1989.

32.  "Leadership Bio." SAS. http://www.sas.com/content/dam/SAS/en_us/doc/other1/bio-john-sall.pdf

33.  Davenport, Thomas H, D.J. Patel. "Data Scientist: The Sexiest Job of the 21st Century," *Harvard Business Review*. https://hbr.org/2012/10/data-scientist-the-sexiest-job-of-the-21st-century/

34.  The political scientist Raymond Wolfinger is often misquoted as the source of this observation. Instead, what he actually said was that "the plural of anecdote is data." I understand and appreciate Wolfinger's context for his original remark, but respectfully disagree.

35. David Preston and Twin Cities Public Broadcasting have been participants in a special benchmarking program called the Contributor Development Project. This program is examined in more detail in Chapter 11 of this book.

36. "Frequently Asked Questions About Genetic and Genomic Science." National Human Genome Research Institute. https://www.genome.gov/19016904/faq-about-genetic-and-genomic-science/

37. Pareto, Vilfredo; Page, Alfred N. (1971), *Translation of Manuale di economia politica* ("Manual of political economy"), A.M. Kelley.

38. donorCentrics Index of Direct Marketing Fundraising Performance." Target Analytics. https://www.blackbaud.com/nonprofit-resources/national-fundraising-performance-index

39. Bernardo, Richie. "2015's Most and Least Charitable States." WalletHub. https://wallethub.com/edu/most-and-least-charitable-states/8555/.

    Gajanan, Mahita. "Utah residents ranked most-charitable as Rhode Islanders give the least." *The Guardian*. http://www.theguardian.com/us-news/2015/dec/09/us-ranks-high-world-giving-index-donate-charities.

    Motif Investing, Inc. "Who Gives the Most to Charity and Where Does It Go?" https://www.motifinvesting.com/blog/who-gives-the-most-charity.

    American Baptist Home Mission Societies. "Online Donations." https://secure.nationalministries.org/give-today/online/.

    The Alfano Group. "We Love Giving: All about charity and philanthropy in the U.S.A." http://thealfanogroup.blogspot.com/2015/03/giving-nation.html.

Compassion International. "Charitable Giving Facts." http://www.compassion.com/poverty/charitable-giving.htm.

Williams, Sean. "America's 7 Most Charitable States." The Motley Fool. http://www.fool.com/personal-finance/taxes/2014/12/14/americas-7-most-charitable-states.aspx.

40. U.S. Trust and the Lilly Family School of Philanthropy. "The 2014 U.S. Trust Study of High Net Worth Philanthropy." http://newsroom.bankofamerica.com/files/press_kit/additional/2014_US_Trust_Study_of_High_Net_Worth_Philanthropy.pdf.

41. Bank of America and The Center on Philanthropy at Indiana University. "The 2012 Bank of America Study of High Net Worth Philanthropy." ttps://philanthropy.iupui.edu/files/research/2012_bank_of_america_study_of_high_net_worth_philanthropy.pdf.

42. University of Michigan. "Panel Study of Income Dynamics." https://psidonline.isr.umich.edu/.

43. MacLaughlin, Steve. "450 Email Subject Lines from End of Year Fundraising." *The Huffington Post.* http://www.huffingtonpost.com/steve-maclaughlin/450-email-subject-lines-from-end-of-year-fundraising_b_8902980.html.

44. Bernardo, Richie. "2015's Most and Least Charitable States." WalletHub. https://wallethub.com/edu/most-and-least-charitable-states/8555/.

45. Philanthropy News Digest. "Utah 'Most Generous State,' Analysis Finds." http://philanthropynewsdigest.org/news/utah-most-generous-state-analysis-finds.

46.  Network for Good. "The Network for Good Digital Giving Index." http://www.networkforgood.com/digitalgivingindex/.

47.  Network for Good. "2015 Online Giving Trends." http://www.network-forgood.com/digitalgivingindex/2015-online-giving-trends/.

48.  Myers, Ben, Eden Stiffman, and Ariana Giorgi. "Online Giving Through Network for Good Exceeds $215 Million in the Past Year." *The Chronicle of Philanthropy.* https://philanthropy.com/interactives/online-giving-dashboard.
     NOTE: Network for Good confirmed in an email exchange that the most popular causes data was not weighted and that the online giving by region data was not normalized.

49.  Manyika, James, et al. "Big Data: The next frontier for innovation, competition, and productivity." McKinsey & Company. http://www.mckinsey.com/business-functions/business-technology/our-insights/big-data-the-next-frontier-for-innovation

50.  Carlson, J., Fosmire, M., Miller, C. C., & Nelson, M. S. (2011). Determining data information literacy needs: A study of students and research faculty. Portal: Libraries and the Academy, 11(2), 629-657.

51.  Wheelan, Charles J. *Naked Statistics: Stripping the Dread from the Data.* W. W. Norton & Company, 2013.

52.  Tufte, Edward R. *The Visual Display of Quantitative Information.* Graphics Press, 1983.

53.  Tufts, Edward. "PowerPoint is Evil." *Wired.* http://www.wired.com/2003/09/ppt2/

54. Agarwal, Amit. "Choose the Right Chart Type for your Data." http://www.labnol.org/software/find-right-chart-type-for-your-data/6523/

55. Few, Stephen. *Now You See It.* Analytics Press, 2009.

56. Carol Dweck, Carol. "What is Mindset." http://mindsetonline.com/whatisit/about/index.html.

57. Beckhard, Richard, and Reuben T. Harris. *Organizational transitions: Managing complex change.* Reading, MA: Addison-Wesley, 1977.

58. Dannemiller, K. D., & Jacobs, R. W. "Changing the way organizations change: A revolution of common sense." *The Journal of Applied Behavioral Science*, 28(4), 480–498. 1992.

59. Memorial Sloan Kettering Cancer Center. "About SKI." https://www.mskcc.org/research-areas/programs-centers/ski/about.

60. Memorial Sloan Kettering Cancer Center. "History & Milestones." https://www.mskcc.org/history-milestones.

61. "Memorial Sloan Kettering Cancer Center." *U.S. News & World Report.* http://health.usnews.com/best-hospitals/area/ny/memorial-sloan-kettering-cancer-center-6213060/rankings.

62. Schellenberg, Lisa. "Congratulations to the 2015 APRA Award Winners." Association of Professional Researchers for Advancement. http://www.aprahome.org/p/bl/et/blogaid=523.

63. At the time of the publishing of this book the currency conversion for £1 GBP was equal to $1.45 USD. This is the conversion rate used throughout the book.

64. The Scottish Government. "Summary: Religious Group Demographics." http://www.gov.scot/Topics/People/Equality/Equalities/DataGrid/Religion/RelPopMig.

65. Alderson, Reevel. "Strength of the Catholic Church in Scotland." *BBC Scotland.* http://www.bbc.com/news/uk-scotland-11301579.

66. "Charity SCIAF Calls on Scots to back Wee Box appeal." *Herald Scotland.* http://www.heraldscotland.com/news/14267500.Charity_Sciaf_calls_on_Scots_to_back_Wee_Box_appeal/.

67. "Winners Announced - IoF Insight in Fundraising Awards 2015." Institute of Fundraising. ttp://www.institute-of-fundraising.org.uk/about-us/news/winners-announced-iof-insight-in-fundraising-awards-2015/.

68. Straker, Katie. "And the winners are…" Institute of Fundraising Insight Special Interest Group. http://insightsig.org/winners-are.

69. Planned gifts or bequests are referred to as legacy gifts in the UK.

70. The Kübler-Ross Change Curve is also known as the stages of grief model. Seth Godin's book *The Dip* is an excellent read and will help you understand how to get through the dip that occurs with almost anything worth doing.

71. "Human Capital: People on the move, Feb. 17." *Boston Business Journal.* http://www.bizjournals.com/boston/news/2011/02/17/human-capital-people-on-the-move.html.

72. "WGBH Educational Foundation and Subsidiaries Consolidated Financial Statements with Supplemental Consolidating Information Years Ended June 30, 2015 and 2014." WGBH Educational Foundation.

http://www.wgbh.org/UserFiles/File/WGBH_FY15_Consolidated_Financial_Statements.pdf.

73. "Chronology of Indiana University History." Indiana University. http://www.indiana.edu/~libarch/iuchron/iuchron.html.

74. "Fast facts about Indiana University for media covering the College World Series." Indiana University. http://newsinfo.iu.edu/news-archive/24325.html.

75. "IU launches historic $2.5B bicentennial campaign, announces $20M gift from David H. Jacobs." Indiana University. http://news.iu.edu/releases/iu/2015/09/bicentennial-campaign-indiana-university%20.shtml.

76. "Office of the President – Biography." Indiana University. http://president.iu.edu/about/biography.shtml.

77. MacLaughlin, Steve, Jim O'Shaughnessy, and Allison Van Diest. "2011 Online Giving Report." Blackbaud. https://www.blackbaud.com/files/resources/downloads/WhitePaper_2011OnlineGivingReport.pdf.

78. Yes, the Denver Dumb Friends League is a real organization. I had to double-check just to make sure that Griff wasn't kidding. The DDFL was founded in 1910 and was named after an animal welfare group called "Our Dumb Friends League" in London. In those days, the term "dumb" was widely used to refer to animals because they lacked the power of human speech. Today, the Denver Dumb Friends League is the largest community-based animal welfare organization in the Rocky Mountain region.

79. "Manifesto for Agile Software Development." http://www.agilemanifesto.org.

80. "Cecil the lion killed in Africa." CBS News. http://www.cbsnews.com/pictures/cecil-the-lion-killed-by-hunter.

81. Miceli, Max. "Cecil the Lion's Death Prompts Social Media Outcry." *U.S. News & World Report.* http://www.usnews.com/news/articles/2015/07/29/cecil-the-lions-death-prompts-social-media-outcry.

82. Elish, Jill. "FSU names new Foundation president." Florida State University. ttps://www.fsu.edu/news/2006/08/17/foundation.pres.

83. Shortly before the publishing of this book, Jeanne Pecha became the Associate Vice President of Advancement Services for the University of Miami.

84. Baker, David. "Charity startup: Scott Harrison's mission to solve Africa's water problem." *Wired.* http://www.wired.co.uk/magazine/archive/2012/12/features/charitystartup.

85. "Meet the Founder." charity: water. http://www.charitywater.org/about/scotts_story.php.

86. Duarte, Nancy, and Patti Sanchez. *Illuminate: Ignite Change through Speeches, Stories, Ceremonies, and Symbols.* Portfolio, 2016.

87. "September 2007." charity: water. http://www.charitywater.org/september07/.

88. Cooper, Smith. "Google+ Is The Fourth Most-Used Smartphone App." *Business Insider.* http://www.businessinsider.com/google-smartphone-app-popularity-2013-9.

89. Yes, I really did just refer to myself in the third person and attempted to create a philosophical maxim. If you have made it this far into the book, then I hope that you will be able to both forgive me and indulge me on this point.

90. Anderson, Monica. "How having smartphones (or not) shapes the way teens communicate." Pew Research Center. http://www.pewresearch.org/fact-tank/2015/08/20/how-having-smartphones-or-not-shapes-the-way-teens-communicate/.

91. Gregory, Alice. "R U There?" The New Yorker. http://www.newyorker.com/magazine/2015/02/09/r-u.

92. "About Us." Dress for Success. https://www.dressforsuccess.org/about-us/.

93. Morris, Alex. "How Crisis Text Line Founder Nancy Lublin Is Saving Lives, Text by Text." *Glamour.* http://www.glamour.com/story/crisis-text-line-founder-nancy-lublin.

94. Lublin, Nancy. "How data from a crisis text line is saving lives." TED. https://www.ted.com/talks/nancy_lublin_the_heartbreaking_text_that_inspired_a_crisis_help_line/transcript?language=en.

95. "Crisis Text Line Opens Nation's Largest Set of Crisis Data for Limited Research." Crisis Text Line. http://www.crisistextline.org/enclave-press-release/.

96. "Crisis Text Line Raises 23.8 Million." Crisis Text Line. http://www.crisistextline.org/media/crisis-text-line-raises-23-8-million/

97. Rao, Leena. "Melinda Gates, Steve Ballmer, Reid Hoffman Back Text-Based Counseling Service." *Fortune.* http://fortune.com/2016/06/15/melinda-gates-steve-ballmer-reid-hoffman-counseling-service/

98.  Flexner, A. "Medical Education in the United States and Canada: A Report to the Carnegie Foundation for the Advancement of Teaching." http://archive.carnegiefoundation.org/pdfs/elibrary/Carnegie_Flexner_Report.pdf.

99.  Ludmerer, Kenneth M., MD. "Commentary: Understanding the Flexner Report." *Academic Medicine.* 2010; 85: 193-196.

100. Pierce, Lyman. "How to Raise Money." Harper & Brothers. 1932.

101. Eliot, T.S. "The Rock." Faber & Faber. 1934.

# INDEX